# MODERN
# THOMISTIC PHILOSOPHY

## AN EXPLANATION FOR STUDENTS

BY

## R. P. PHILLIPS, D.D., M.A.,

*Professor of Philosophy, S. John's Seminary, Wonersh*

IN TWO VOLUMES

Vol. I.

## THE PHILOSOPHY OF NATURE

" Vidit scalam stantem super terram
et cacumen illius tangens caelum."
(Gen. c. 28, v. 12.)

LONDON
## BURNS OATES & WASHBOURNE LTD.
PUBLISHERS TO THE HOLY SEE

*First printed* . 1934
*New edition* . 1939

*Printed by offset in Great Britain by
Billing and Sons Ltd., Guildford and Esher*

# NOTE AS TO THE METHOD OF QUOTING ARISTOTLE AND S. THOMAS

The references to Aristotle's works are, in accordance with the usual practice, numbered according to the pagination of the edition of Bekker (*Aristotelis Opera*. Berlin, 1831–1870. 5 Vols.). Since the Greek text in this edition has a consecutive pagination throughout, it is a simple matter to find any passage referred to. Thus, the first number given refers to the page, the letter *a* or *b* to the first or second column of that page, and the final number to the line of the column in which the quotation is to be found. So, e.g. 952$^a$26 refers to a passage beginning on the twenty-sixth line of the first column of page nine hundred and fifty-two. The same numeration is followed by the Oxford translation of Aristotle. (*The Works of Aristotle*, translated into English. Ed. J. A. Smith and W. D. Ross. 11 Vols. Clarendon Press, Oxford.)

With regard to S. Thomas, the method of reference is as follows : The references to the *Summa Theologica* give first the part of the Summa from which the quotation comes, i.e. I., the first part ; I. II., the first part of the second part; II. II., the second part of the second part ; and III., the third part. Then follows the number of the question, after which is given that of the article referred to ; and finally, if necessary, the number of the objection or its answer, to which reference is made. Thus : I. II.,77,5, ad 3 would mean that the passage is to be found in the answer to the third objection to the fifth article of the seventy-seventh question of the first part of the second part. The disputed questions are referred to by name, e.g. *De Veritate*, followed by the number of the question and article. So, *De Veritate* 3,2, ad 6 refers to the answer to the sixth objection to the second article of the third question of that work. The *Summa contra Gentiles* is referred to by the number of the book and chapter. So, II.*C.G.* 12 refers to the twelfth chapter of the second book. In the commentaries on Aristotle the number of the lecture in which the reference occurs is given.

# PREFACE

THE purpose of this book is to present a simple explanation of the philosophy usually taught to Catholic students. No attempt has been made to introduce novel doctrines, but merely to set out, as clearly as possible, the meaning of those which are commonly received. Since such teaching at the present day is predominantly on the lines of the system originated by S. Thomas Aquinas, it is this system, as developed by modern Thomists, which it is the object of this book to explain. It is clear that in a single work it would be impossible to give a full account, and absurd to try to vindicate the truth, of the various philosophical systems which are included under the generic name of Scholasticism ; so that no systematic exposition is attempted of even the chief of the non-Thomistic systems, those of Scotus and Suarez. The divergencies of their doctrines from those of S. Thomas frequently throw light on the precise meaning of the Thomist contentions ; so that to make some mention of them is not foreign to our purpose. Similar considerations will apply to our treatment of those other philosophical systems which diverge still more widely from the Thomistic plan, such as those of Spinoza or of Hegel. It appears to be as unreasonable to expect, in an exposition of Thomism, a full account and refutation of Hegelianism, for example, as it would be to look for such an account of Thomism in Hegel's *Logic*. Consequently, all that seems necessary to be done in this direction is to notice the principal divergencies of modern philosophies from the Thomistic, so bringing into higher relief its positive teaching ; and, as far as space allows, to meet the more urgent of the reasons that have been advanced against its truth.

The questions which were most prominent in S. Thomas' day are not so much to the fore at present, while many of those most debated now, were, in the Middle Ages, hardly discussed. The emphasis and accent, therefore, of a modern presentation of Thomism must be different from those of the expositions of a John of S. Thomas or a Goudin ; though the basic principles may remain the same. These principles contain a view of the universe ; and no decision can be reached as to the truth or falsity of this view, by considering merely the arguments which may be advanced in support of particular doctrines, but only from a consideration of it as a whole. Just as in circumstantial evidence for a crime each item taken separately may be insufficient to make certain the identity of the criminal, yet if a large number of facts of different kinds all point in a particular direction, the conclusion is almost irresistible ; so, in judging of the validity of a philosophical system, conviction is reached when it is seen that, from all sides, our consideration of the various elements of the universe converge to establish it. For the philosopher is, as Plato says, a ' synoptical man,' taking a unified view of all knowledge. The world-view of S. Thomas is essentially such a unity, and must, therefore, be judged as a whole. Consequently, an attempt has been made, in the following pages, to keep the main principles of it in the foreground, and to show that from every side the roads of thought lead up to them. To do this at all adequately a discussion of moral philosophy ought to be added, but this would have necessitated making the book impracticably long. Fortunately, Fr. Cronin has already given us all that can be desired in this way ; while an account of the Cosmological and Metaphysical sections of Thomistic philosophy is not available in English in a handy form. The only single work of this kind is the translation of the *Manual of Modern Scholastic Philosophy*, compiled by professors of Louvain University, but this includes, in addition to these subjects, Logic, Ethics, and the history of Philosophy, so reducing considerably the amount of space available for those which we are to deal with.

It is hoped, therefore, that a somewhat more detailed explanation in English, of Natural and Metaphysical philosophy, contained in a single book, may be found useful by those who are professedly making a study of Scholastic philosophy ; and possibly also by others who have not the time or opportunity for reading the several volumes of the Stonyhurst series, or the very full expositions by Dr. Coffey of some of the subjects here dealt with, but who, at the same time, would like to know something of this philosophy as a whole.

# CONTENTS

# CONTENTS

# CONTENTS

# MODERN THOMISTIC PHILOSOPHY

## I. INTRODUCTORY

### SECTION I

#### THE DEFINITION OF PHILOSOPHY

To be Looked for in Philosophy as an Existing Fact—In Its History—Thales and the Ionic School—The Pythagoreans— The Eleatics—Heracleitus—The Atomists—Anaxagoras—Socrates and Plato—Aristotle—Conclusion.

MOST people have the vaguest ideas, if any, of what philosophy is, or of what the word philosophy means. It is commonly used only in such expressions as : ' he took the affair philosophically,' in which, no doubt, it is implied that philosophy helps a man to bear up against misfortune, and that philosophers are calm and unexcitable people ; though why they should be so does not appear. Consequently, we are not much nearer any knowledge of what philosophy is in itself. It is, however, essential for the student to have, at the start, some notion of the nature of the subject which he is about to study ; though it is evident that it can only be a rough and provisional one. He will have to determine for himself at the end of his study (if that ever comes) whether it is finally satisfactory. The definitions which the text-books of Scholastic philosophy put on their opening pages are often hurled at the reader's head without much proof that they are correct, so that they have to be taken on faith, on the authority of the author. They thus fail to satisfy the mind or arouse the interest. It seems desirable, therefore, that a man should be led to discover for himself what philosophy is in fact. Now, everyone will agree, that if we want to discover the nature of a thing the right way to do so is to examine it. To do this in the case of philosophy, we must see what subjects are discussed by it, i.e., examine it in the course of its history. It will not, however, be necessary to review its entire history, but it will be sufficient if we see what its character was during the period of its formation, which is that of the Greek philosophers till the time of Aristotle.

Though it may well be that further precision might be imported into our definition by continuing our enquiry down to the present day, nevertheless, if it be granted that the thought of Aristotle and his predecessors is philosophy in process of formation, we shall, by examining it, be able to discover what the essential character of philosophy is. Just as the child is the father of the man, and retains the same nature throughout his life, so Greek philosophy is the father of modern, and thus in its nature the same. By following this *a posteriori* method we shall avoid the danger of making philosophy out to be what we think it ought to be ; and at the same time the glimpse which will thus be caught of the beginnings of philosophy will be a help and a guide in the subsequent study of it.

The reason of our choice of Greek philosophy for our enquiry is, that it was in Greece that philosophy first appeared as an autonomous science, distinct from religion, so that it can be examined there in a more or less pure state.

*Thales.*

According to Aristotle, whose opinion on this point is generally accepted, Greek philosophy begins with Thales of Miletus (*c.* 624–550 B.C.). He and his immediate successors were engaged on the problem of discovering the nature of the visible world ; and this is natural, for as soon as a man begins to think, that which first attracts his attention is the world as presented to him in sensation, as being the most obvious aspect of it. The opinions of Thales, as far as we know them from tradition, since he left no writings, are summarised in two propositions : first, that water is the principle of all things ; and secondly, that the earth is a flat disc floating on water. Strange and crude as these statements sound, they have a considerable importance for our purpose, since they show that what Thales tried to do was to explain the material constitution of the universe by the aid of reason alone, without appealing to religious myths, or the intervention of the gods ; whose action was then normally invoked to account for anything whose origin was obscure. He and his successors were seeking what was later called the material cause of the universe. All the pre-Socratic philosophers followed the line suggested by Thales, viz., that under the multiplicity of phenomena, of the world as perceived by sense, there must be some one permanent principle. Just as Thales asserted that this principle is water, so his successors advanced other theories as to its nature. For Anaximander it is indefinite matter, for Anaximenes air, for the Pythagoreans number, for the Eleatics being, for Heracleitus fire, for Empedocles the four elements, and for Democritus atoms.

*The Ionic School.*

Thales was the founder of what is known as the Ionic School, from the fact that its three principal representatives, Thales himself, Anaximander and Anaximenes, were all men of Ionia. They have been called materialists, though they were not so in the modern sense of denying the existence of anything but matter : they were simply concerned to discover what the material world was made of. Just as a child might pull a toy to pieces to find out what it is made of, so these philosophers tried to pull the world to pieces with their wits, and having discovered the answer, as they thought, asked no further questions about it.

*The Pythagoreans.*

The next attempt to discover the primary constituent of the material word which calls for notice is that made by the Pythagoreans.

B

Pythagoras was born at Samos at some time between 580 and 570 B.C. ; and in middle age settled at Crotona in Italy, where he founded the Pythagorean Society, which was primarily a religious and moral order, not a philosophic school.  It was closely connected with the Orphic Sect, from which it took the doctrine of Metempsychosis, which would be better named Metasomatosis, since it is the theory that souls pass from one body to another.  The philosophy of the Pythagoreans is the philosophy of number, for they held that number is the stuff of which the world is made.  They were probably inclined to this strange opinion by their mathematical researches, for which Pythagoras himself was remarkable.  It is thought that the first book of Euclid is substantially attributable to him, and he is said to have sacrificed an ox in honour of his discovery of the 47th proposition.  Observing the world about them the Pythagoreans remarked that we recognise objects by means of their qualities.  The various classes of things have, however, different qualities, and it seems at first sight that there is none which is common to all.  Further examination shows us, nevertheless, that there is one characteristic which is possessed by everything, that of quantity or number.  All things are numerable, and can be counted.  We are reminded of the saying of Galileo : ' Philosophy is written in the great book which ever lies before our eyes—I mean the universe —but we cannot understand it if we do not first learn the language in which it is written.  This book is written in the mathematical language ' ;[1] though the ideas of the Pythagoreans were much more primitive, and enveloped in an atmosphere of mysticism.  They concluded, indeed, from the universal character of number and from the order and harmony of the universe, not merely that number is a most important element in it, but that it is its very essence, that the universe is made of number, just as Thales had said it is made of water.  Number is the ultimate, the only reality.  Further, from the opposition of the determined and the indeterminate or infinite, are derived all the fundamental

---

[1] *Galileo Opere*, Vol. IV, p. 171, quoted by Burtt.  *Metaphysical Foundations of Modern Science*, p. 64.

contrarieties : equal and unequal, one and multiple, left and right, male and female, rest and movement, light and darkness, good and evil. These dominate the nature and activity of things, so that every essence has its number, and every essence is a number. This doctrine, fantastic as it is—though it has marked affinities with the way in which the universe is regarded by modern mathematical physics—is nevertheless some advance on the teaching of the Ionians, since it declares that the ultimate material of the universe is something more abstract and so more universal than was allowed by them. It belongs, however, to the same type of enquiry as that of the Ionic School—the enquiry, namely, as to the stuff of which the material universe is, in the last resort, constructed. Consequently, it is on sense knowledge that all these thinkers rely, for it is by the senses that we are made acquainted with material things ; so that the first stage in philosophy is similar to the first stage in the development of the individual mind, when the child is filled with curiosity as to the things around him, trying to find out what they are made of by sucking them, sticking his fingers in them, and pulling them to pieces ; but hardly asking the reason of them or using his intellect about them. This will be the next stage in his mental life, and so it was also in the growth of philosophy ; for the group of thinkers who now claim our attention try to investigate the reason of things, and not merely the stuff of which they are made. They ask not merely *what* things are made of, but *why* they are as they are. In this way they are of importance for our present purpose since they add a new feature to the conception of philosophy.

### The Eleatics.

These philosophers are known as the Eleatics, since their school was situated at Elea in Southern Italy. The founder of this famous school is said to have been Xenophanes, a kind of troubadour, but its chief representative is Parmenides, who was born about 514 B.C. His reflections take their rise from the observation of the changing character of things. Since everything about us is constantly changing, it seemed to him that no knowledge of it was possible. Just as in sense knowledge, it is impossible, when looking at a rapidly revolving wheel, to have knowledge of the spokes, since they have passed on before they can be seen, so knowledge in general demands that its object should be momentarily, at least, at rest, in order that it may be seized. If, then, there is to be knowledge at all, there must be some unchanging reality underlying this shifting surface of the world. This reality cannot be known by the senses which tell us only of this superficial aspect of the world. If it is to be known at all then, it must be by the intellect, which penetrates beneath the surface, and what this sees everywhere in things is that they are, is their being. This, then, must be the reality of things, and all that is not being is unreal. Being is (i.e. is reality)—not-being is not : the first formulation of the principle of identity, the supreme law of thought. As he considered further this underlying reality of pure being, which is wholly unmixed with not-being or becoming, Parmenides saw that it must be perfectly one and completely immutable : it has no beginning or becoming ; for if it has, it must come either from being or not-being. If from being, it does not come to be, since it already is : and from not-being or nothing, nothing comes. To maintain this position, however, he was forced to deny the testimony of the senses, which show us being in a state of change, of becoming, and he does not scruple to do so. He thus makes a distinction which is henceforth to be of fundamental importance for philosophy, the distinction between sense and reason. True being is known to us only by the reason, the senses present to us a world which is false, which is appearance only, and an illusion. By a curious inconsistency, however, which was apparently unnoticed by himself, Parmenides conceived of this one Being as material, as occupying space, finite and spherical. That this is an inconsistency is clear, for Being is a purely abstract intellectual concept, and cannot have any material characteristics : for it would thus be amenable to sense knowledge and so be not-being, and like all else that is sensed, an illusion. Nevertheless, this inconsistency in his doctrine was the reason why, in fact, there issued from it the two opposing schools of intellectualism and materialism.

Since Being neither arises nor passes away, if we adhere closely to his doctrine that Reality is to be known only by the reason, and not by the senses, we shall conclude that there is only one Being which has no material or sensible qualities, but is eternally the same—an absolute Monism of a type which has become familiar in modern philosophy. If, on the other hand, we accept his statement that Being is material, we are led to the doctrine of the absolute indestructibility of matter ; matter has no beginning and no end, which is materialism. The first aspect of his doctrine represents, however, his most striking and original contribution to philosophy, and therefore we rightly see in him the founder of Intellectualism and Idealism.

### Zeno.

The most outstanding of the disciples of Parmenides was Zeno (born about 489 B.C.), who, in support of the theory that Being is immutable, developed some famous arguments to show that motion is impossible, and that the very idea of it implies contradiction. The best known of these arguments, which are dealt with in Cosmology, is that of Achilles and the tortoise. Achilles and the tortoise run a race, and if the tortoise is given a start, Achilles can never catch it up. For, first, Achilles has to run to the point from which the tortoise started. When he arrives there, the tortoise will have moved to a further point ; and when Achilles reaches this, the tortoise will have gone on still further. This process will be indefinitely repeated, in such a way that the distance between the two will be always diminishing, but never wiped out ; so that Achilles will never catch up the tortoise. This and similar arguments are meant to show that essential contradictions are involved in our ideas of space and time.

### Heracleitus.

The antithesis of this static philosophy of the Eleatics is found, at about the same time, in the dynamic philosophy of Heracleitus (c. 535–475 B.C.). He was an aristocrat of Ephesus, a sardonic man, who despised not only the common run of men, but even men of great reputation, such as Homer

and Hesiod. As Parmenides had done, he sees that all the
world around us is perpetually changing ; but instead of
rejecting this appearance of change as illusory, and asserting
that the reality must be other, he accepts it, as itself the
basic reality. For him there is no stability in the universe,
but all is change. His view is summed up in the laconic
phrase πάντα ῥεῖ. Beneath this flux there is no principle
which is stable and permanent, so that we must not shrink
from affirming that the thing which is, the changing thing,
at the same time is not, since there is nothing which remains
even for a moment beneath the change. This movement,
this Becoming, which is pictured by Heracleitus under the
form of Fire, is all there is, and all differentiations of things
merge into it. Thus, no less than Parmenides, Heracleitus,
the originator of the philosophy of change, is led to a pure
monism ; the assertion that all reality is one and undifferentiated.

This fact suggests two important points with regard to
the nature of philosophy :

1. The human mind tends to reduce all things to a simple
unity ; and that this must be so, we shall see, is accounted for
by S. Thomas' theory of its working. Hence philosophy is
the business of accounting for the many by the one, of bringing particular cases under general laws, and in the last resort
of accounting for all things by one principle, cause and
ground. This effort, pushed to an extreme, ends in Pantheism or Monism, and it is so pressed in the two philosophies
we have just been considering. Extremes meet.

2. But though they are extremes, yet they are antithetic-
ally opposed, since one denies all motion, the other all rest ;
and between these, philosophy has oscillated ever since.
Both owe their attraction to what is, in fact, their weakness,
viz. the denial of one of the elements in the problem. They
are attractive, being clear cut : weak, being inadequate.

This suggests a further point, viz. that the truth is likely
to be found in neither of these, but in a synthesis which combines them, and, in fact, the main trend of philosophy has
been in the direction of such a synthesis, the broad lines of
which were marked out by Plato and Aristotle.

*Empedocles.*

A synthesis of this kind was indeed attempted, almost at once, by Empedocles (*c.* 495–435 B.C.), who seized on Parmenides' principle of the unchangeable character of Being, and, interpreting it in a materialistic sense, asserted that matter is indestructible and eternal. On the other hand, he admitted the truth of the assertion of Heracleitus that change is a reality ; in which case, the change of matter must be, not an absolute coming into being of it, which would be contrary to the Eleatic principle, but a simple mixing and unmixing of it, to form various bodies. There are, according to him, four fundamental kinds of matter which, unchanged in themselves, combine to form the various kinds of bodies. These are earth, air, fire and water, which were later known as the four elements. This theory marks a transition from the more or less idealistic doctrines of the Eleatics and Heracleitus to a fully developed mechanical and materialistic philosophy, elaborated by Democritus and the Atomists.

*The Atomists.*

According to Democritus (*c.* 470–361 B.C.), if we could divide matter far enough, we should ultimately come to indivisible particles which, though extended, are too small to be perceptible by the senses ; these he called atoms Now, since they fill space and have no interstices they constitute the Plenum, and correspond to the ' Being ' of Parmenides. Side by side with the atoms, which have no qualities except to fill space, Democritus acknowledges another reality, the Vacuum, which is also extended. That he must allow the reality of this is clear, since he admits the reality of change, which is nothing but the motion of the unchangeable atoms in space. Hence space must exist and be real, and indeed it has all the reality of atoms, which is nothing else than extension. This Vacuum corresponds to the ' Not-Being ' of Parmenides. Thus, according to Democritus, both Being and Not-Being are real, and are extension. All the motion in the world is determined by the nature of the atoms, which is their size, or weight, since there are no holes in them. Hence the bigger atoms fall faster from the necessity of their nature : and thus, Democritus is led explicitly to rule out any idea of freedom, or directing intention in the constitution of the world, or its development. All comes about by a blind mechanical motion. It originates by chance, and it develops by the necessary law of its nature. In these theories the question as to the origin of the world is, at least obliquely, answered. How did it come to be ? It did not, since matter is eternal and indestructible, and the force which moves it is simply natural to it.

## Anaxagoras.

This answer, however, did not satisfy Anaxagoras (c. 500–428 B.C.) ; for he saw that blind forces and mechanical motion could not produce such an ordered and harmonious universe as that which we see. Nature, moreover, shows design : all, or many, of its operations being directed to the production of ends. Such order and purpose, he thought, could only be produced by an agent which is rational, non-physical and incorporeal—an intelligence or Nous. Aristotle praises him for this entirely original contribution to philosophy : ' he seemed like a sober man in contrast with the random talk of his predecessors.'[1]

He is thus the first to show that philosophy must include, beside the discussion as to the composition and genesis of bodies materially speaking, an investigation as to the ultimate final and efficient causes of the universe ; and moreover the first to make clear the distinction between mind and matter, and between blind mechanical chance and purpose.

Thus closes the first period of philosophic thought in which philosophy has chiefly concerned itself with the attempt to discover the composition of the material world ; and the discussion of its most obvious elements, matter and motion. Thus philosophy, in its infancy, took stock of the world of sense about it, and hardly gave a thought to itself, to man who observes this world, and the mind by whose means he does so. The consideration of these things was

[1] *The Works of Aristotle*, translated into English, Vol. VIII. (Oxford, 1908.) *Metaphysics*, Bk. I, 984$^b$18.

now to be the main business of Greek philosophy, and the link between the new and old is to be found in the introduction of the all-ordering Intelligence postulated by Anaxagorus.

## The Sophists.

Philosophy did not, however, pass at a bound from childhood to mature manhood ; it had first to pass through a period of stagnation and even of decadence—to sow its wild oats.

This is the period of the Sophists, for whom philosophy was a mere means of getting on in the world. It became therefore their slave instead of their mistress, and they did not aim at discovering truth, but only at finding arguments which would flatten out any opponent. This led naturally enough to Scepticism—or doubt as to the possibility of arriving at any knowledge—and Subjectivism—the contention that that is true which appears so to me, or to any individual. Among the Sophists perhaps the most famous are Protagoras and Gorgias. The propositions which the latter undertook to prove : (1) that nothing exists, (2) that if anything exists, it cannot be known and (3) that if it can be known, the knowledge of it cannot be communicated, were typical of Scepticism ; and the dictum of Protagoras, ‘ man is the measure of all things ; of what is, that it is ; of what is not, that it is not ; ’ of Subjectivism. These two, Scepticism and Subjectivism, are twin diseases to which philosophy ever since has been subject.

## Socrates.

A new era of health and vigour opens with the teaching of Socrates after this short period of decadence ; for the Greek mind was still young and strong, and could not long succumb to the enervating cynicism of the Sophists. The spokesman of the revolt was an artisan, a rough and ugly fellow, who loved to argue at the street corners and let the wind of common sense sweep away the pretensions and high-flown arguments of the Sophists. This Socrates, unlike the earlier philosophers, was not so much concerned with the nature,

origin and working of the material world, as with man himself. He regarded philosophy as the means which a man
should use in order to lead the life which will satisfy his
highest aspirations—it was to serve as the guide of life, just
as Christianity, in so far as it lays down a moral law, is
intended to do for us. His interest in it, therefore, was
much more poignant and personal than that of the somewhat
academic speculations which we have just reviewed. Now,
in order that we may lead the ' good life,' we must know
what good is : and Socrates maintained that all knowledge
is knowledge through concepts. Concepts, moreover, are the
notions we have, not of particular things, but of the essences
or natures of things ; and these concepts we express in
definitions which are absolutely fixed and unchangeable.
Hence the Sophistic notion that the truth will vary according
to the mind of the individual is altogether repugnant to
Socrates ; and he insists that it is to be judged by an
absolute standard, not by any subjective impressions. Just
as in measures the State enforces a standard of measurement;
and a draper is not able to assign any number of inches
which he pleases to a yard ; so in the realm of thought we
shall have an absolute concept of Good, by means of which
we are to test the goodness of any particular action. Since
it is absolute and unchangeable it cannot be identified with
what seems to be good for a particular man at a given moment,
viz. what is useful or pleasant for him, but must be equally
applicable to all men at all times ; and so may clash with
what seems good at the moment. He thus vindicated the
supremacy of absolute Good. We know what this good is if
we think rightly. Now, no man can desire what is evil or
bad for him ; if he does but come to the knowledge of the
good, by right thinking, he will follow it. Virtue, therefore,
is to be identified with knowledge, and sin with ignorance.
Hence the attainment of knowledge is of supreme importance,
and consequently, it is necessary to discover the laws of
knowledge in general. The attempt which Socrates made to
do this paved the way for the systematic Logic of Aristotle.
He thus brings within the realm of philosophy three regions
unclaimed, and unexplored, by it before : the investigation

of the essences or natures of things, the enquiry into the
workings of the human mind, and the discussion of right
conduct for man.  It remained for Plato and Aristotle to
perfect and systematise his investigations in these three
regions, and so to develop fully what are now known as the
sciences of Logic, Psychology, Metaphysics and Ethics.

A short account of the work of these two great thinkers is
required in order that we may have a comprehensive idea of
what philosophy meant to the Greeks.

*Plato* (427–347).

Though Plato is one of the greatest philosophers in the
history of the world, his genius and originality did not only,
or even chiefly, consist in the introduction of new ideas ; but
rather in the co-ordination and transformation of the work
of the earlier thinkers.  What is true of Plato in this respect
is true also of all the great philosophers, with the possible
exception of Kant.  Their originality always shows itself
rather in the new perspective in which they viewed the
problems which had been discussed by their predecessors,
and the developments which they gave to them, than in the
propounding of novel doctrines.  At the first glance, the
history of philosophy seems to be but a record of conflicting
opinions without any unity ; but a closer scrutiny will show
that there has been all through it a development of certain
great central ideas, though, of course, with setbacks and
aberrations.  All the great philosophical systems have their
roots deep in the past, and embody a uniform tradition.
This tradition is first found clearly and explicitly in Plato
and Aristotle ; and consequently this philosophy has rightly
been called the ' philosophia perennis.'

So Plato, standing as it were on the shoulders of Parmenides and Socrates, sees even more vividly than they had
done, that the philosopher's work is to contemplate being,
and the essences of things.  Now the characteristic of these
essences is that they are universal.  The idea and the nature
of Man, of Triangle, and so on, apply to all men, all triangles,
regardless of their individual differences.  But Plato asks :
are these ideas merely in our minds, or have they some reality

apart from them ?   He is convinced that they have, though
not in the world known by the senses, for there they are
found particularised and limited.   Thus he concludes that
their reality must lie in some super-sensible world where the
Man-in-Himself, the Triangle-in-Itself must subsist in their
own right.   This the realm of the Ideas which alone is truly
real :  and it follows that the individual things which we
see and handle are not real except in so far as the Ideas are
reflected in them.   They are feeble and deceitful copies of
reality, and the object, not of science, but of opinion.   They
are a number of mirrors reflecting images in the sky, and
indeed distorting ones, such as those convex and concave
ones seen at fairs ; for matter, indeed, distorts the Ideas—
the Reality itself is immaterial—matter is illusory, and is,
in a sense, that which is not.   This theory of the Ideas
involves consequences in other directions ; and especially in
Psychology.   For if, as is the fact, we have knowledge of the
Ideas, this knowledge cannot have come to us by way of the
senses, which tell us only of the illusory material phenomena,
and must, therefore, have come directly from the Ideas
themselves, i.e. the Ideas must be already in our minds
before we begin our sense life, before we were born.   In a
former life, before the soul was imprisoned in the body, it
contemplated the Ideas, and has brought fragments of this
knowledge with it into the world.

> Our birth is but a sleep and a forgetting ;
> The soul that rises with us, our life's star,
>     Hath had elsewhere its setting,
>     And cometh from afar.
>     (Wordsworth.  Ode, " Intimations of Immortality.")

We are thus led to a psychological dualism—man is a soul,
or mind, forcibly united to a body.

Plato, therefore, appears first and foremost as a meta-
physician, considering the fundamental reality and being of
things ;  his psychological and cosmological theories being, in
the main, corollaries which followed from his metaphysical
one.   Nevertheless, he did not regard metaphysics as mere
speculation, for he had a profound belief that, by philosophy,
man can be enabled to live the perfect life.   Thus he expanded

and amplified the moral teaching of Socrates, showing that 'the good life' is to be found, not in pleasure, nor even in virtue, but in union with the Idea of Good ; and it is to this that metaphysical contemplation is directed. So, in the light of his metaphysical principles, he discusses individual and social morality, and the constitution of the perfect society or Republic, where, since the parts are for the good of the whole, all the individuals will be absolutely subordinated to the State.

*Aristotle* (385–322).

For our purpose, which is to discover the nature of philosophy from the conceptions which the great Greek thinkers formed of it, it will not be necessary to set out in detail the various doctrines with which Aristotle enriched it ; but it is sufficient to show that, in his view, the aim of philosophy is to get to the very heart of things ; his doctrine, wide as it is in its scope, being still more remarkable for its profundity. The subject of philosophy, he says, has always been, is now, and always will be the question what is being, what is substance, or as we should say nowadays, what is reality ? In answering this question, philosophy cannot be satisfied with any reply which leaves some being unexplained ; it must reach down to the first causes and reasons of being—of all being, whether material or mental, universal or particular, mutable or immutable. Thus the earlier philosophies had considered *material* being exclusively ; Parmenides and Heracleitus excluded mutable and immutable being respectively ; even Plato had extruded the world of sense and the individual from reality, pronouncing it illusory. So according to Aristotle being is of many kinds, and not all one, as Parmenides would have it. To justify this he works out his great doctrines of the analogy of being, and the categories, which will exclude Pantheism ; of potentiality and act, which will account for motion and change ; of the four causes among which the final cause is first and dominant. It is end which makes the agent act, and determines the form or nature of the thing produced, which form in its turn puts its impress on matter, making it of a certain kind. Now the end to be attained is not something material, but is mental : it is an idea, as is clearly seen in the case of the sculptor carving a statue ; and it is one and the same idea in different states which makes him work, which guides his action, and is embodied in the finished sculpture. Here, then, we see that Aristotle agrees with Plato in asserting that the primary constituent of reality is form or idea, but now it is incarnate in material things, not subsisting separated from them. It is for this reason that Aristotle has been counted as the opponent of Plato : but, though he criticises severely the subsisting forms of Platonism, his aim is not to break down the essential features of Platonic idealism, but rather to complete his master's work. Both agree that reality is fundamentally ideal or mental. Plato, however, since he divorces his Ideas from the world of sense in fact removes all reality from it also, while Aristotle by embodying forms in matter restores reality to material things ; but is obliged to admit that the forms are, when in this state, limited and imperfect. Both form and matter, moreover, owe their very being to the fact that they are directed to the same end, to something other, and more perfect, than themselves, to something which is more detached from matter, more formal and more actual ; and so in the last resort to something wholly formal, wholly actual and perfect, which has, therefore, the nature of mind, or rather of thought. This is the Aristotelean God, from which the whole world hangs suspended by desire : Being, which desires nothing but itself, and thinks nothing but itself, for it is wholly perfect. It is in this way that Aristotle arrives at the ultimate cause and ground of all reality : to search for which is, in his view, the proper business of philosophy.

Since the Thomist philosophy, with which we are to deal, owes more to Aristotle than to any other single thinker, it may not be out of place to add a few details with regard to the life of the man whom S. Thomas calls, without qualification, the Philosopher. Aristotle was born in 385–4 B.C. at Stagira, a seaport of Chalcidice. His father was court doctor to the King of Macedonia, but died while his son was still a boy. He was later sent by his guardian to study at Athens,

where, at the age of seventeen, he joined the Academy—
Plato's school there.  Here he remained as Plato's pupil and
disciple till the latter's death.  He was twice married, and
for five years was tutor to Alexander the Great.  Possibly it
was his life at court which made him more careful of his
personal appearance than are the generality of philosophers,
for it is said that he was noticeably well-dressed.  On
Alexander's succession to the throne of Macedonia he returned
to Athens, where he established a philosophic school in a
place called the Lyceum.  Here his habit of walking up and
down among the trees, discussing abstruse philosophical
questions with his pupils, gained the name of Peripatetics
for his disciples.  In the evening he explained less difficult
subjects to a larger audience.  In 323 there was an outburst
of anti-Macedonian feeling at Athens : and Aristotle, having
been so closely associated with the Macedonian court, was in
some danger.  He therefore retired to the fortress of Chalcis ;
to prevent the Athenians committing another crime against
philosophy, as he said, referring to the execution of Socrates.
He died at Chalcis in the following year.

*Conclusions.*

We are now in a position to draw together the facts which
we have noted in our account of the genesis of philosophy,
and so to determine what philosophy really was in the time
of the Greeks ; which will tell us what it is, in its essence,
to-day.  Now it is evident, in the first place, that all these
investigators were seeking, not a method of making or doing
something, as an artist or an engineer might be, but some sort
of knowledge.  Knowledge in itself, and for its own sake,
seems to be their aim, and they range over a wide tract of
country in their hunt for it.  The Ionians want to know what
the material world is made of ; and answer : material stuff
of one sort or another, which is the uniform basis of all
bodies.  The Pythagoreans, in answer to the same question,
say it is a universal quality of matter : the Eleatics, examining it more searchingly still, say it is the unchangeable being
of matter ; Heracleitus, the constant movement and
becoming of it.  Empedocles and the Atomists try to reconcile

these last two answers, while Anaxagoras points out that there is something in the material world which is not material, viz. order. This must tend to some end and be produced by some mind. So for the first time a new field is opened up for examination by philosophy : it must know what mind is. But man has mind, says Socrates, so philosophy must ask what man is. With Plato the interest of philosophy centres in this question of the nature of mind, and of concepts—of the immaterial ; while with Aristotle the balance is restored and material nature, man, mind and God all come within the scope of the enquiry.

None of these men, it is to be noted, tried to answer these questions by an appeal to any revelation, to myth, or religious knowledge of any kind ; but attempted to extract the answer by using their *reason*; and they used it almost without reference to sensible observation and experiments. Why was this ? Clearly because they were convinced that the thing they sought lay deeper in the heart of the world than the superficial aspect of things, of which alone the senses could tell them. They were seeking the underlying causes of things, and this is the special point of view from which philosophy discusses its multifarious objects, which are dealt with from another aspect, by special sciences, such as chemistry, biology, zoology, and so on. It intends to go further into their nature than these do, and not to rest content until it has uncovered the absolutely fundamental reasons of them all. Thus the early philosophies were not concerned to find out, e.g., of what the world, as at present constituted, is composed, as chemistry is ; but what were its primary constituents : or again, in the case of man, they were not concerned, for example, with his anatomy, but whether, in the last resort, he is spiritual or material, intelligent, and so on. So philosophy is distinguished, on the one hand, from any knowledge which may be gained through religion ; and on the other, from that which may be gained from what we now call the Natural Sciences. Secondly, it uses in its investigations only natural reason, not faith, nor yet sensible experience as such. Thirdly, it excludes nothing from its examination, but includes all things in heaven and earth, man and God, in its enquiry ; and yet is distinguished from all the special sciences which study any of these things, by its special point of view, which is to discover the basic reason of all : and thus philosophy is not to be identified with any of them singly, or all of them together. All this can be summed up in the one phrase, which is the real definition of philosophy : It is the scientific knowledge of all things gained through consideration by the natural light of reason, of their fundamental reasons or causes.

Books to consult :

W. STACE, *A Critical History of Greek Philosophy*. (Macmillan.) To which the foregoing account owes much. It also includes a discussion as to the nature of philosophy.

J. MARITAIN, *Introduction to Philosophy*. (Sheed and Ward.)

BURNET, *Early Greek Philosophy*. (Macmillan.)

W. D. ROSS, *Aristotle*. (Methuen.)

A. E. TAYLOR, *Plato : the Man and his Work*. (Methuen.)

c

# SECTION II

## THE DIVISION OF PHILOSOPHY

ARISTOTLE discusses the division of the sciences in the first chapter of the sixth book of the Metaphysics. Here he divides them into three great classes : practical, productive and theoretical (1025ᵇ25). The first seek knowledge for the conduct of life ; the second in order to make something which is either useful or beautiful ; the third seek knowledge for its own sake. If Logic had to be put within this scheme, it would rank as a theoretical science, but Aristotle considers it to be not a science on its own account, but a necessary preliminary to all knowledge, for, as he remarks : ἄτοπον ἅμα ζητεῖν ἐπιστήμην καὶ τρόπον ἐπιστήμης—'it is absurd to seek at the same time knowledge and the way of attaining knowledge ! ' (Met. 995ᵃ13.) Since, as we have seen, philosophy is scientific knowledge, it will come under the classification given above, though it is evident that philosophy is not productive. The theoretical sciences are, according to Aristotle, physics, which deals with all things which are inseparable from matter, but not unchangeable ; mathematics, which deals with things that are unchangeable though probably not separable, but embodied in matter, and metaphysics, which deals with things that are both separable and unchangeable.

Now Aristotle treats the whole body of knowledge which can be gained of these subject matters as philosophical, since experimental science, as we now have it, had not then been constituted ; but, in process of time, sciences have one by one detached themselves from their parent, philosophy, and set up business on their own account. So Mathematics, Biology, Astronomy, and, last of all, Psychology are now reckoned as independent sciences, leaving behind them, however, sciences which treat of their various spheres purely philosophically ; so that we have, for example, mathematical philosophy, which considers the basis or foundations of Mathematics ; and the philosophy of life and mind which considers the ultimate origin and nature of these. With certain modifications, then, the general scheme which Aristotle lays down for the classification of the philosophical sciences still holds good, and we shall see later that it is the most scientific division which can be made. For this reason, and because it is fairly generally adhered to by Scholastic writers, it will be convenient for us to follow it. We thus begin by considering the material world in general, and then the two great classes of material things, the inanimate and living ones. The first two sections here are often grouped together under the name of Cosmology ; while that of Psychology is given to the third. As Mathematical Philosophy is never treated separately by Scholastics of the present day, it will be unnecessary for us to devote a special section to it, but several questions which really belong to it will be explained in Cosmology. The last part of our explanation deals with Metaphysics. Since this explanation is confined to speculative philosophy, it takes no account of Ethics, which is evidently ' practical ' in Aristotle's sense of the word. (For this last, see Cronin, *The Science of Ethics*.—Gill.)

# II. THE PHILOSOPHY OF NATURE

## Part I.—COSMOLOGY : THE PHILOSOPHY OF INANIMATE NATURE

### INTRODUCTION

As we have seen, Aristotle regards as the object of our study in this part of philosophy, not so much material things *qua* material, but *qua* changeable ; for it is this characteristic particularly which differentiates them from the objects of mathematics. In this he is followed by S. Thomas, who says that physics deals with mobile being, i.e. being which is subject to motion or change. The first question we shall have to ask, therefore, is : What is this mobile or changeable being ? On taking a general view of the world of nature, that which strikes us immediately in it is its variety : the innumerable forms of plant and animal life, the changing clouds, the very stones and kinds of soil are all different. If we look up to the starry sky, the same variety and multiplicity are evident. It is this aspect which is emphasised in the name changeable, or mobile, being which is given to the object of Cosmology, for without variety there could be no change, so that to call this being changeable supposes it to be various. Is this epithet, applied to nature, a correct one ? Such is the first question which we must ask ; and as we have seen, it met with an unhesitating negative from Parmenides. It is, in fact, the central question of Cosmology, and recurs all through it. It will only be completely answered when we have considered it in all its forms, so that at this stage we cannot give more than a preliminary and tentative reply. It is worth doing this, however, in order to strike at the very start the key-note of the whole discussion, and to bring into prominence the principles which must be taken into account in any solution of the cosmological problem. Our reply at this stage will be on the level of ordinary common sense ; and it might be thought that, from this point of view, it is unnecessary even to ask whether the world is composed of a variety of things or not, since it seems obvious that it is ; as Stevenson says :

> The world is so full of a number of things,
> That I'm sure we should all be as happy as kings.

This common-sense view is known, in philosophy, as pluralism. It is, however, not accepted by a great number of those who have given attention to this subject ; who say that all things in the world are of the same kind, and even that they do not differ from one another as units ; so that there are not, for example, many trees, but one tree. This last which, when thus baldly stated, sounds quite absurd, is in fact based on certain theories as to the nature of reality, such as Pantheism, which we shall have to consider later ; when the denial of the numerical distinction of bodies will evidently stand or fall with the theory on which it is based. We may, however, notice at once that we have the testimony of our own consciousness to vouch for our distinction from other men, since we are conscious of initiating our own actions and of doing so, sometimes at least, without any dependence on other men. If, then, we are independent in action, we must be also independent beings, so that there are at least some bodies, viz. our own, which are numerically distinct from each other.

We are here more directly concerned with the opinion that all bodies are of the same nature, than with that which maintains that they do not differ as individuals, for the former view is founded on observation of the material world, not on some preconceived theory of reality. It is an opinion which has been widely held since the advent, or rather the popularisation, of evolutionary ideas. Darwin's theory of the gradual development of one species from another has naturally been extended to the whole world, and an attempt been made to show that everything is but a superficial modification of some primordial matter. This doctrine goes by the name of Materialistic Monism, and was expounded as a scientific theory by Hæckel, and as a philosophical one by Herbert Spencer, to name two out of many. It is also sometimes called Naturalism.

As has been remarked, it is impossible at this stage to do more than to meet this theory at the level of enlightened common sense, and to point out a striking fact of our daily experience. Observing the material world about us, we see groups of bodies which are endowed with characteristics which are found in them, and them only, and which are sharply marked off one from another. Thus living things, with their powers of growth and nutrition, animals, with their characteristics of sense and intelligence, men, with their mark of reason, are striking examples of such groups. Now it is impossible that this distribution of characteristics should be accidental or arbitrary, for unless there were some essential connection between them, and the natures of the things, we should sometimes come across a member of one group which possessed the characteristics of another, e.g. a stone which was able to feed itself and grow. This we never do, however, so that we may conclude that these characteristics spring from the natures of the things themselves, or are, what the the Scholastics call, their properties, and since they are distinct from one another, so also will be the natures which give rise to them.

These simple considerations at least suffice to show that there is a prima facie presumption that the world is not as simple as Materialistic Monism would have us believe ; and we can thus turn to a more detailed consideration of the various theories which have been advanced as to its composition, and the constitution of matter.

# CHAPTER I

History of the Theory—Its Essential Character—Criticism.

THE first of the theories with regard to the constitution of matter to engage our attention is that generally known as Mechanism. In scholastic text-books it is more usually called Atomism, but since this term is ambiguous, for it might be supposed to apply to the Atomic Theory, and the scientific doctrine of atoms, it is better to relinquish it and use the philosophically more appropriate name of Mechanism ; of which the distinctive feature is the denial of specific differences, or differences of nature, between bodies.

The origins of all Atomic and Mechanistic theories are to be found in Leucippus and Democritus. In their view, the question of the divisibility of matter is regarded as of capital importance. Extended concrete substance cannot, it is contended, be infinitely divisible. What, then, remains when it is divided as far as possible ? Not unextended points, for then the extended would be composed of the unextended : nor yet nothing at all, for then bodies would be mere appearances. Therefore, there must remain some extended and indivisible particles, which particles are called atoms. The existence, however, of atoms is not the distinguishing characteristic of the atomic theories ; this consists in the denial that the atoms differ from one another in kind, or if there exist different species of atoms, at least they do not gain or lose anything in combination, but the mere fact of their conjunction and consequent interaction produces an apparent transformation in the composite bodies, as compared with the simple atoms. The theory accounted for everything in the world, including force and intelligence, as the product of extension and the passive movement of the atoms. Such a theory rules out all purpose which, as we shall see, is so marked a feature of Aristotle's view of nature ; and, moreover, avoids the dualism of mind and matter, since it is purely materialistic. It was developed with this object in view by Epicurus, and revived in the first century B.C. by Lucretius, who shared with Epicurus the desire to banish superstitious fear of the gods, and their action on the world from men's minds. After this time, however, such materialistic theories practically disappeared from philosophic thought under the influence of Aristoteleanism, and we do not find any recrudescence of them till the fifteenth century, when they again arose in connection with the metaphysical speculations of Nicholas of Cusa (1401–1464) and others. It was, however, the theories of Giordano Bruno, in the next century, which had the most important influence on the later developments of philosophical atomism ; and which may be taken as the connecting link between the ancient mechanistic theories and the modern.

This modern period opens with the purely mechanistic physics of Descartes (1596–1650) and Gassendi (1592–1655), and with it the reaction against the Aristotelean cosmology comes to a head. According to Descartes all physical phenomena are to be traced to extension and motion, the nature of body being identified by him with spatial extension. He was not, however, an Atomist in the same sense as Democritus, for he regarded all space as one fundamental substance which is infinitely divisible. If, then, body and extension are identical, there will be no vacua within the material universe, since these would be extended, and so be body, not vacuum : and, moreover, the material universe must itself be infinite, since, if it were finite, there would be a vacuum outside it, which would, in its turn, be extended, and so a body, thus forming part of the material universe. Further, if we are to have an absolute plenum, all movement must be rotatory, otherwise there would be a diminution of material substance in one place, and an increase in another. In this rotatory motion particles become rounded, and so produce three elements, elementary fire, air, and earth from which the different parts of the universe are derived. Gassendi, a contemporary of Descartes, had, meanwhile, returned to the theory of the ancients with regard to the atomic structure of the world. In his view, the only principles in nature are empty space and atoms, the latter being composed of one and the same substance, and distinguished only by differences of magnitude, shape, and weight. He found the explanation of all the physical properties of bodies in the motion of the atoms. The English philosopher, Thomas Hobbes, another contemporary of Descartes, expressed similar views.

These general mechanistic theories were greatly strengthened by the practical experiments of Robert Boyle (1626–1691), on the basis of which he attempted to explain all chemical changes mechanically. He insisted on the quantitative determination of weights, thus preparing the way for the modern chemical theory of elements, since he recognised specific weight and chemical reaction as the distinguishing marks of any particular substance.

It is obvious that the main purpose of all these mechanistic theories is to simplify our ideas of matter, by accounting for everything by means of indestructible material units which are all of the same kind, and local motion communicated by impact, thus rendering obsolete all discussion as to the natures and qualities of particular bodies. The idea of a body exerting some active force of its own cannot be embraced in such a scheme ; both because force cannot be regarded as corpuscular, and because it is, moreover, a qualitative, rather than a quantitative, conception. Newton's discovery of the law of gravitation necessarily led, however, to the idea that the atoms exert an attractive force on one another at a distance ; and though this notion was resolutely opposed both by Newton himself and many others, it came gradually to be accepted, and the simple picture of the great world-machine painted by the earlier Atomists was destroyed. It would, nevertheless, be a mistake to suppose that the mechanical view of nature, according to which all material happenings are ruled by a strict mathematical necessity, perished along with it ; for though the conception

of force is not amenable to mathematical treatment, its
effects can be quantitatively expressed ; and thus a mechanical theory, modified by the introduction of dynamical conceptions, for long continued to hold, and probably still does
hold, the field, as the orthodox philosophy of matter,
especially among scientists. The theory so modified will be
considered in the next chapter.

Reduced to their simplest form the earlier mechanical
theories are seen to consist of two propositions :

1. All bodies are composed of material elements of
essentially the same kind—matter is homogeneous.

2. All corporeal properties can be explained by local
motion which is governed by mechanical laws.

When stated in this way the theories are evidently open
to the objections urged against Monism in general, for we
find, both in the organic and in the inorganic world, a variety
of constant and stable types of bodies. We see bodies which
are distinguished from one another by definite and unchanging characteristics : so bodies are by nature liquids, solids,
and gases, under determinate, but different, conditions.
They have differing though constant weights, as, for example,
zinc is lighter than lead. These weights are also known
scientifically to be constant and different for each one of the
chemical elements. Further, the boiling and freezing points
of the different elements exhibit a constant difference. Such
differences, therefore, cannot arise from the circumstances
in which the bodies are placed, but must belong to them by
nature, and be their properties, so that to deny difference
of nature, or specific differences, is to make these bodies
inexplicable.

The second dogma of mechanism is that all the apparent
changes of bodies, and all corporeal phenomena, are to be
explained by the local movement of the atoms. Now, such
local motion alone cannot be a sufficient explanation of the
phenomena, since one of the most striking of these is the
activity or force of bodies. Local motion, however, is a
result of activity, and so cannot be its cause or explanation.[1]
Moreover, local motion, as such, cannot be communicated

[1] Cf. Nys, *Cosmologie*, Vol. I, Sec. 125. (Louvain, 1928.)

from one body to another, for, as M. Meyerson says : ' There can be no movement without a substantial substratum, without something which moves. Movement is in no sense a substance, the most that we can do is to consider it as a *state*. Supposing we accept this latter notion, and consider that this state must last indefinitely, as the principle of inertia requires, how can it break away from one body to attach itself to another ? It would be necessary, as Lotze has very rightly remarked, that this state should exist of itself, between the two, for a moment, even if this moment be infinitely short, becoming thus a true substance, which is absurd. It is consequently quite impossible to conceive of the transmission of movement from atom to atom without the intervention of a special faculty, a mysterious agent.'[1] So it would be like the grin of the Cheshire cat—a grin without a cat.

Lastly, as a philosophical theory, mechanism is inacceptable, since it does not go to the root of the matter ; for, in fact, it does not explain the constitution of either simple or compound bodies : not of simple bodies, since these are the atoms themselves, and no attempt is made to explain the atom : nor of compound bodies, which are homogeneous, having different properties from their elements, as water has different properties from those of oxygen and hydrogen. Neither of these facts is explained by Mechanism, since from the atoms, as conceived of by the Mechanists, there cannot arise a homogeneous compound, for they are complete in themselves, and combine by mere juxtaposition, remaining, in themselves, the same. Nor can a mere juxtaposition of the elements give rise to entirely new properties, but will only give the sum of the properties already existing in the elements.[2]

[1] E. Meyerson, *Identité et Realité* (1912), p. 332.
[2] Cf. Nys, op. cit., Sect. 78–88.

# CHAPTER II

## DYNAMISM

Its Nature—Theories of Leibniz, Boscovich and Kant—Criticism.

SINCE our concern is only with philosophical theories as to the nature of matter, we can omit any consideration of the various modifications which have been imported into Cartesian Mechanism, considered purely as a physical theory ; and turn our attention to the group of philosophical theories which are often generically known as Dynamism. The characteristic tenets of this school are :

1. The assertion of the essential activity of material substance, and indeed of all substance.

2. The denial of extension to the basic principles of bodies.

3. The consequent assertion that all bodies, and all corporeal phenomena, are produced by the grouping and interplay of simple unextended forces.

In virtue of this last view, Dynamism joins hands with Mechanism in holding that bodies are merely aggregates of elements which are in themselves simple, i.e. not having parts of different kinds, and which do not change intrinsically in combination. In all other respects, however, Dynamism is the opposing extreme to Mechanism, since, for the former, the basic principles of the material world are active forces which have no extension, while for Mechanism extension is the very essence of body, and force, which is variable, active, and tending to definite ends, is incompatible with the tenet that all change arises from local motion only.

The initiator of Dynamism is generally acknowledged to have been Leibniz (1646–1716).[1]

He was first ' charmed ' by the mechanical explanation of

[1] Though Fr. Hoenen, S.J., thinks that Dynamism should not be attributed to him. Hoenen, *Cosmologia*, p. 414.

the world, but soon came to see ' that the notion of extended mass taken alone is insufficient, we must also employ the notion of force, a very intelligible notion, though its source may be metaphysical.'[1] Thus he came to abolish extension and matter altogether out of reality. So, in opposition to the ideas of Descartes, who considered the constituent of body to be something passive, viz. extension, he maintained that body is essentially active. From the principle ' that which does not act does not deserve the name of substance ' he soon passed to the statement that active force is the very essence of material beings. He thus spiritualised matter, and decomposed it into an infinite number of infinitesimally small ' bodies ' or elements, which are unextended and simple, i.e. without parts. These he called Monads. They are essentially active, and, in fact, always in action : they can, however, only act internally, not on one another, or on anything outside themselves, since otherwise they would not be simple.[2] He expressed this in the saying : ' The monads have no windows by which anything can enter or go out.' Every being is composed of a whole world of these little ' souls ' : ' A world of creatures, living beings, animals, entelechies, souls, exists in the minutest part of matter. Each portion of matter may be conceived as a garden full of plants or as a pond full of fish. But every branch of a plant, every limb of an animal, and every drop of the fluids within it, is also such a garden, such a pond. . . . Thus there is nothing arid, sterile or dead in the universe.'[3] But since the Monads are simple and unextended, it seems impossible to explain extension and movement by their means. Hence Leibniz denies the reality of these ; they are appearances. Thus in perception we produce the appearances of things which we represent as outside one another. For this representation we have need to construct the fiction of extension ; so that extension is not what we perceive, it is the background which we construct in order to represent indivi- duals as outside one another. ' It is the artifice by which in

---

[1] Leibniz, Art. in *Le Journal des Savants* (1695), quoted by Wildon Carr. *Leibniz*, p. 78. (Benn, Leaders of Philosophy Series.)
[2] Leibniz, *Monadology*, No. 7.  [3] *Ibid.*, Nos. 67, 69.

perceiving a multitude of distinct individuals we represent their togetherness.'[1]  It is clear, however, that the Monads act harmoniously in concord, as if, in fact, they acted on one another ;  so the earth, air, water, etc., all appear to contribute to the growth of a plant, and the plant to grow continuously and harmoniously :  and the same is true of the working of the universe as a whole.  If, then, the Monads do not, in fact, interact, how is this harmony and apparent efficient causality to be accounted for ?  Not being connected intrinsically they must be held together extrinsically by a preestablished harmony, which God, the supreme Monad, had imposed on the universe at its creation, so that the Monads all develop in concord and give the appearance of mutual help and dependence.  As if we had a number of clocks all striking in turn it might be thought that each set the next one on, though, in fact, their striking has been arranged to occur in this order ;  in either case we should have a series of chimes such as that in ' La Boutique Fantasque.'

A somewhat similar theory was proposed in the middle of the eighteenth century by the Jesuit, Boscovich.  This very remarkable man was rather a scientist and mathematician than a philosopher, and his system is less complete from a philosophical point of view than that of Leibniz.  According to him matter consists of a swarm of atoms, each of which occupies a geometrical point of space, is capable of motion, and possesses a certain mass, so that a definite force is required that each atom may acquire a given acceleration. The atoms attract one another, if separated by anything more than a small distance, with a force varying inversely as the square of the distance between them.  At small distances, the force is supposed to be alternately attractive and repulsive ;  and in order to avoid the difficulty of two atoms coalescing in the same place, Boscovich imagines that for all distances below a certain minimum the force is repulsive, and increases indefinitely in proportion as the distance diminishes.  Thus, all actions are actions at a distance, and there is no such thing as actual contact.  It was the idea that

[1] Wildon Carr, *Leibniz*, p. 91.  Leaders of Philosophy Series.  (Benn, 1929.)

the atoms act thus at a distance which led him to abandon the notion that they are extended, since, without contact, the conception of extension seemed unnecessary : and this view was continued by Ampére and Faraday, who regarded the atoms as unextended, or simple centres of force. Here we see clearly that the scheme put forward by Boscovich was rather a scientific hypothesis than a philosophical theory.

The theory of Kant is akin to these, but differs from them in two respects : (1) In accordance with his general principles, he does not allow that we can know what are the constituents of bodies in themselves, but only as they are conceived of by us ; and (2) he will not admit the possibility of a vacuum. As conceived of, then, body, according to Kant, is something mobile which fills a space ; and this filling of space implies a resistance to anything which would penetrate into this space. Now, since all resistance presupposes a force of resistance, and all motion a force which moves, body can only fill a space by means of a motive force, which must consist in a kind of elasticity, and which Kant calls a force of expansion and concentration. It is these plastic forces which constitute bodies as conceived of by us.

The views on the constitution of bodies held by various schools may be exhibited in the following scheme :

Bodies are composed according to :

S. Thomas
of two elements : one potentially extended, and one unextended

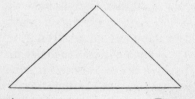

Mechanists  Dynamists
of one extended element  of one unextended element
Kant
|
two elements in idea.

So S. Thomas combines mechanism and dynamism in a positive synthesis : Kant in a negative one.

*Criticism of Dynamism in General.*

1. There can be no doubt that bodies appear to us to be extended, and any theory which is to claim to be satisfactory, must take account this fact, and offer some explanation of it, either by allowing that they really are so, or if it denies this, by advancing some feasible reason to account for their appearing to be so. The first course is not open to the Dynamists, and they cannot offer a satisfactory explanation of the appearance, which will be in accord with their notions as to the nature of bodies ; for their appearance of extension must have some cause. Now this cause cannot be the senses themselves, since, on the Dynamist hypothesis, these are also unextended, and so contain nothing which would cause their objects to appear as extended. Nor can the cause of this appearance be external agents, since these also labour under the same disadvantage : in a word, since, according to the Dynamists, there is nothing in the universe which is extended, there is equally nothing in the universe which could be the cause of an extended appearance. Leibniz's suggestion that we produce it in order to represent a numberof distinct things together is clearly untrue, since the notion of distinction and external position are quite different, that of distinction being wider ; and, moreover, we do not always represent distinct things as outside one another in space as, for example, a series of numbers, or our various thoughts and desires, or immaterial beings, such as angels, or even God and the material world.

2. According to Dynamism, matter is composed of simple forces. Now these forces must be either in contact or not in contact. If they are not in contact they will coalesce, forming one force at a geometrical point, as Boscovich rightly observed. For it is clear that a certain extension is required for contact : if a tangent of a circle touched it at one point only, it would not touch it at all. In this case the plurality of bodies would disappear. If, on the other hand, they are not in contact ; in any one body, the many monads or forces

which compose it will be entirely distinct one from another, as regards their entity, even though they be supposed to act on one another across a vacuum. Hence the unity of such a body will be wholly destroyed. This is also true if they are supposed to coalesce in a point, since this point, which will be the only body, and therefore the only unified body, will be composed of a multitude of forces which will preserve their own entity in it. In either case, therefore, it is impossible to maintain the unity of bodies, on the Dynamist hypothesis. Now, not only is this result in direct contradiction with experience but, if no body is a unity, we can gain no notion of the nature of any body, since it will not have one ; and *a fortiori* shall be unable to determine the nature of body in general, but shall say it is force, which will be a term without any one meaning, and so a mere word to cover our ignorance.

# CHAPTER III

## THE THOMISTIC THEORY OF THE NATURE OF MATTER

Nature and Data of Question—History and Explanation of Hylo-
morphism—The Reasons Advanced to Support it—Additional
Explanations of the Meaning of ' Matter ' and ' Form '—Some
Difficulties Considered.

THE problem of which we are to attempt to find the solution
is : what, in the last resort, is the nature of matter or of
bodies ?  Not of this or that body, but of material things in
general ;  nor yet of what chemical elements bodies may be
composed, for even if we were successful in showing that all
bodies were compounds of one element, such as hydrogen, or
one force, such as electricity, as has been sometimes suggested,
the question would still remain what is the nature of hydrogen and electricity, and we should have our original problem
still on our hands.   The question, therefore, is not a physical
one merely, but both physical and metaphysical.   It is
physical, since the starting point of our enquiry must be the
properties and behaviour of bodies as made known to us by
common and scientific observation.   The experimental or
empirical investigation of material phenomena is the work
of the physicist : and we could take his results as they stand
as the basis of our investigation, were it not that, unfortunately, he often imports theories of a philosophical kind into
them.   Moreover, as we shall see later, there is much disagreement among scientists, and, what is worse, undoubted
error in the views of some of them, as to the nature of scientific investigation.   For it should be observed at the start
that it is impossible for the scientist, as for the philosopher,
to deal with ' brute fact,' i.e. mere disconnected happenings
in the material world :  he is bound to connect them by a
meaning of some kind, bringing them all under a general

law, and it is here that exaggerations and aberrations are apt to creep in. So Newton observed the movements of bodies, and from a mass of observations concluded to the general law that they move as if actuated by a pull which is directly proportionate to their masses and inversely to the square of the distance between them. It was an easy jump, then, to stating that they were attracted, or pulled together, by a force of this kind; though such a transition from observation to theory was, strictly speaking, more than the facts warranted. It follows that it is not possible for the philosopher to assume that physical laws and theories, as enunciated by scientists at any particular epoch, are philosophically true; but in his enquiry he will take as the basis of his investigation the best knowledge available about the material world; and this will include both the knowledge obtained by common observation and that gained by scientific enquiry, the latter being accepted by the philosopher only provisionally, and under certain conditions. For it is to be noticed that scientific knowledge must always be an extension of, and dependent on, common observation, for though the scientist, by reason of the refinement of his instruments, may be able to extend the latter, he must in the last resort rely on his five senses and intellect in using them; so that the philosopher could not accept from the scientist a law or theory which is in contradiction with the evidence of the senses. It is clear, therefore, that this enquiry has a metaphysical as well as a physical side. It must check the empirical observations of the scientist, and of the senses, by considerations of a purely intellectual character, for the object in view is not merely to investigate the phenomena, i.e. those things which can be known by the senses, but something which is outside the sphere of phenomena or appearances, viz. the very nature of things which so appear, and this is knowable only by the intellect. Thus any theory as to the essential constituents of bodies must satisfy four general conditions:

1. It must explain the inner nature of *all* bodies.

2. It must explain not only the unity, but also the essential diversity of bodies.

3. It must explain the dualism of bodies : why they are both active and passive, changing and unchanging (their stability), one and multiple, alike and different.

4. It must take its rise from, and be in full accordance with ascertained facts obtained by observation.

The Thomistic answer to the question : what are the essential constituents of bodies, can be summed up in three statements :

1. There is in bodies a substantial material principle, and substantial formal principle.

2. Both these principles are incomplete substances.

3. The material principle has the same relation to the formal as potentiality to actuality.

What is meant by material and formal principles, or matter and form can be seen roughly by means of an example: the flour, raisins, eggs, etc., are the material principles of the plum pudding, but these have to be combined in the proper proportions, mixed and boiled in a certain way in order to obtain a plum pudding. The result of such combination, mixing, etc., is the formal principle of the pudding, making it a Plum Pudding, differing from all other kinds of pudding. Similarly at the start we may take an example to illustrate what is meant by potentiality and actuality ; as when we say : ' John can read,' i.e. has the capacity or potentiality of reading, and ' John is reading,' i.e. is in the act of reading, is reading actually. We shall shortly see the meanings of these terms more scientifically and precisely ; but before we do this, and pass to the proof of the Thomistic theory, it will be useful to glance at its origin and history.

## The History of the Theory of Matter and Form.

*Matter.* The theory of matter and form, or, as it is often called, Hylomorphism, is due to Aristotle. It is true that Plato had already introduced a notion from which that of matter was derived, in the Timæus, viz. that of Χώρα or ' space.' This is conceived of by him as the screen on which the images of the Ideas or Forms are thrown. In itself it has no form, no determination, no features of any kind. It is not empty space, nor yet in any way the single underlying substance of the universe, it is the reality on which the appearances show, its sole attribute being to support them. Since Plato affirms that the Forms alone are real, he must consequently deny reality to this background of appearances, and so he sometimes calls it ' nothing,' τὸ μὴ ὄν, inasmuch as it is altogether other than the forms. But since it also in some way exists, it is a nothing or not-being, which, in some way, is. It is thought of as being in existence prior, with at least a logical priority, to its determination by the impress of the Forms ; and so may perhaps be compared to the chaos of Genesis, which is itself something, prior to the possession of any definite nature. This obscure being, though far enough removed in some respects from Aristotle's ' matter ' ; since it is altogether immovable and unchangeable, and contrasted with reality which is Form only ; is nevertheless in other ways akin to it, in so far as it suggests the root idea which underlies the Aristotelean ' matter,' of a not-being which in some way is.[1] So long as this entity is thought of as ' other than ' reality, no intelligible meaning can be attached to this phrase ; and Aristotle working on the Platonic notions insists that it too must be real, though formless. Though it can have no *existence* of its own, yet where it exists owing to form being joined with it, it is not identified with form, but has its own *reality*. For reality and existence, though commonly confused, are, as we shall see, two very different things. Aristotle therefore defines it in two ways : positively and negatively. The positive definition, given in the Physics (192[a]31), is : matter is the first subject of each thing, from which, since it is intrinsic, something which is not *per accidens* comes into being.

By the word *first*, it is differentiated from second matter, which is what we ordinarily mean in English when we speak of matter, for this, though the subject of accidents, is yet not the first subject, since there must have been a prior subject of the substantial nature : e.g. cloth can be neither white nor black, till the nature of cloth has been embodied in matter. Cloth in the abstract is of no colour.

The words ' *being intrinsic* ' show that it is not privation,

[1] Cf. R. P. Omez, O.P., *La Notion de* χώρα. *Revue des Sciences Philosophiques et Théologiques* (1925), pp. 433 ff. Taylor, A. E., *Plato*, pp. 456 ff.

but a positive principle which enters into the composition of the complete being.

Lastly, the phrase ' something which is not *per accidens* comes into being ' indicates that the compound of matter and form is not an accidental, but a substantial unity, the two together making up a complete nature, and being joined in one nature ; not as in the case of an accidental union each retaining as its own nature, as, e.g. glass and water in the case of a glass of water. The second and negative definition which he gives is : ' By matter I mean that which in itself is neither a particular thing, nor of a certain quantity, nor assigned to any other of the categories by which being is determined.' (VII Met., 1029ᵃ20.) This definition has received a traditional Latin form as : *materia prima secundum seipsam non est quid, neque quale, neque quantum, neque aliquid eorum quibus ens determinatur*.

It is not any particular thing, for in this case it would be a specifically complete substance ; nor is it in any of the categories, since all presuppose a pre-existing substance, while matter is absolutely first as a subject. Yet, though it is not in any of the categories (i.e. the general classes into which things can be divided) directly, it is reducible to that of substance.

First matter must therefore be carefully distinguished from what is commonly called matter, and which the Scholastics name Second Matter ; since first matter is incomplete in itself, and cannot be known in itself, or by the senses. It can only be known indirectly, by means of form, and cannot be touched, seen, or smelt, being something discoverable only by the intellect. This does not prevent it from being a real substantial entity, though an incomplete and potential one.

The word used by Aristotle (ὕλη) means literally timber, and more specifically ship's timbers. Prof. A. E. Taylor suggests that its selection may be due to a reminiscence of an old Pythagorean fancy which looked on the universe as a ship. It is most nearly rendered in our language by the word ' stuff.'

*Form*. The difference between the Platonic and Aristotelean conceptions is as marked with respect to their notions of Form, as it is with respect to those of matter.

Though both used the same word for form (εἶδος), Plato conceived of it as a nature which was self-subsistent, and separate from matter, though imaged or ' participated ' in it ; while Aristotle strongly maintained that forms must be an integral part of the things to which they give a determinate nature, immersed in the matter of such things, and incapable of being separated from it. In a word, the Platonic forms are essentially discarnate, and immaterial ; while for Aristotle they are incarnate in matter ; so that matter is never found without form, and form is the correlative of matter.

The Aristotelean description of form is therefore : First Act, which constitutes, when joined with first matter, a being which is one in essence, and complete.

The word *act* signifies that form is a positive perfection, and *first* that it is immediately joined to matter in contradistinction to accidental form which presupposes an already constituted thing, which it modifies.

The theory that all bodies are composed of a permanent featureless element, which is matter, and positive determining elements or forms, arose historically speaking from the consideration of the conversion of one substance into another, as in the case of a mixture, such as beer, which apparently has a different nature from that of any of its ingredients, or in the case of conversions of one substance into another, as water into steam, wood into ashes under the influence of fire, or in the case of organic conversions such as that of water and other elements into the juice of the grape. Such changes are known as substantial changes. In recent times doubt has been thrown on the existence of such changes, modern chemical and physical theory seeming to show that they are in fact merely new accidental combinations of the original atoms. Some Scholastics, therefore, as Père Descoqs, S.J., would abandon the classical argument from substantial change, which has always been used to establish the theory of matter and form. It seems, however, that the theory stands or falls with the reality of such changes, the alternative to accepting them being a denial of all essential or specific difference between things. It is to this denial that the current scientific theories would naturally lead, and it is a denial which no Scholastic would make : for, as has been pointed out, the backbone of the philosophy of nature, as conceived by Scholasticism of any type, is the maintenance of the essential differences between bodies, and the rebuttal of monism. Those writers who wish to abandon the argument from substantial change suggest that the series of chemical elements are such specifically distinct natures : but this contention is based on precisely the same grounds as those which lead the Thomists to say that compound natures, such as water and oil, are specifically distinct, viz., that they exhibit constant and sharply distinguished properties.[1] Further, the whole tendency of natural science is to reduce all the chemical elements to a single base, such as hydrogen ; and if scientific results be taken as being applicable as they stand to philosophical discussion, a man who is ready to give up specific differences among compounds, on the ground that science does not recognise them, should also be ready to abandon specific differences altogether, even between simple bodies, if science should not acknowledge them.

The Aristotelean and Thomistic theory as to the constitution of bodies therefore maintains, as we have seen, that their constituents are two principles, which are intrinsic and distinct, viz. matter and form ; and to prove it S. Thomas appeals in the first place to the fact of substantial change, for it is clear that every change implies a subject which changes, and a substantial change, i.e. the change of one substance into another, a substantial subject ; otherwise we should have annihilation and creation, not change. Now, since this subject is to be common to two specifically distinct substances, it must not of itself possess the specific character of either, and will therefore of itself be altogether undetermined and featureless. Such a subject or substratum is what we have called first matter. Similarly, if bodies are substantially mutable, they must include a second principle

[1] Cf. P. Gény, S.J., *De doctrina Hylemorphica*. *Divus Thomas* (*Plac.*), January 1925.

which completes and specifies this quite undifferentiated and potential subject, otherwise they would have no definite character, and so could not change from one character to another. It is further clear that these two principles are really distinct, from the fact that they are separable and separated in the process of change, since the potential subject remains the same, while the form is altered, the prior form disappearing from the subject, which thereupon receives a new form. Hence the subject and the form are separated and distinct.

The *a posteriori* foundation of the theory remains, however, still to be proved, viz. that substantial changes actually occur : or that bodies are substantially mutable. It is necessary to prove this for all bodies, both organic and inorganic, though not that such changes actually occur in every body, since our purpose is to show that it is the nature of body to be capable of such change, even if, as may happen, they have not been subject to it, or the change has not been observed in them. Now, if we prove our general rule for organic bodies, this will afford an *a priori* presumption that it holds good for inorganic bodies also, otherwise, the organic, as mutable, would be inferior to the inorganic which would be immutable. For the immutable is more perfect than the mutable, since that which is absolutely perfect must be wholly unchangeable, and change lessens as perfection grows.

1. Taking, then, the case of organic bodies we have the very simple and evident fact that plants and animals die, and the no less clear fact that the animal and its dead body are specifically distinct, since their operations differ essentially, those of the one being immanent, springing from an intrinsic principle and being directed towards the good of the whole animal, whereas those of the other are transeunt only, the term of decomposition being the disintegration and destruction of the body. Clearly, however, they could not act in these essentially different ways unless they were essentially different in themselves. Similarly, organic things transmute inorganic ones into their own substance in the process of nutrition. Hence, it follows that in the organic realm as a whole, substantial change occurs ; since the

organic bodies either change themselves, or produce substantial changes in the inorganic bodies which they absorb.

2. Passing now to the realm of inorganic matter, we observe the continued formation of elements into new compounds, the elements and compounds being specifically distinct. That the latter part of this statement is true is shown from finality, for things which have different finalistic inclinations or tendencies must be specifically distinct, since such tendency is nothing else than nature itself which is tending to a definite end : hence, where it is different, it follows we have two different natural tendencies, which must therefore be immanent in the things themselves (since nature is immanent), and constitute them as naturally or specifically distinct.

That such different finalistic tendencies do exist in the elements and their compound is an obvious fact of experience ; for all simple bodies act in a certain definite way, and combine according to certain ascertained laws ; and, similarly, composite bodies have their own distinctive actions and laws which differ from those of the simple ones. To take the obvious case of water and its elements to illustrate this, we know that oxygen and hydrogen produce their own distinctive effects, and combine only in certain proportions. Water, however, which is their compound, has its own action which is quite different from either of theirs, and in some ways in opposition to their actions, and it also obeys its own proper laws. Thus all bodies have their own distinctive finalistic tendencies.

3. Another argument to show the fact of substantial change is derived from the unity of bodies.

It is indubitably true that a thing which possesses one, and only one, nature cannot be made of a number of things possessing different natures. Now, if we consider nutrition in plants and animals, we see that they absorb into themselves many things which before absorption have a complete and independent nature of their own, a nature which is lost when they are taken up into the body of the animal or plant which feeds on them : for if not, it would follow that the living thing was but the sum total of the things on which it feeds, and not a complete essential unity on its own account.

If, then, it is such an essential unity, it is clear that the sub-stances on which it feeds undergo a substantial change. Hardly anyone would doubt the essential unity of living things, since all their functions and activities are directed towards the good of the plant or animal as a whole, not to that of some particular part of it. In nutrition, for example, the whole being feeds and is nourished, not the mouth, stomach or any particular organ in isolation. In man, whom we know more intimately than we do any other animal, this is particularly clear, for we say the man, e.g. John, thinks, feels and eats : not that John's brain thinks, John's hands feel, and John's stomach eats. If John were not a unity, but a mere collection of elements and organs, such an attribution of all these functions to him would be altogether illegitimate. We are conscious, however, that it is not so, and the whole human race agrees with us.[1]

Besides this classical argument from the fact of substantial change, there are two other metaphysical arguments which are ordinarily used by Scholastics to prove that bodies are composed of matter and form, i.e. of an undetermined principle which is capable of becoming anything : which S. Thomas calls a *potency* or potentiality ; and a perfecting and determining one, which he calls *act*.

These arguments for their full understanding need more precise acquaintance with metaphysical notions than is possible at this stage ; it is nevertheless worth while to note them here owing to their demonstrative character.

1. The first of these arguments is based on the fact of extension, for it is clear, that since all bodies are extended, they can be divided into parts of the same nature as the original body, as slices of bread are still bread. It is clear, then, that all bodies have a certain capacity for division, or what is the same thing, for multiplication. (Cf. II *Contra Gentiles*, c. 65, Arg. 3.) Such a capacity is, however, what we call a potentiality or potency, and it follows that all bodies possess an element which is potential. They are nevertheless not entirely composed of this element, for they are always

[1] This is more fully discussed in the Psychological section later. *Vied* Ch. IV and Ch. XV.

definite bodies of some kind, i.e. they possess an actual element also ; in other words, all bodies are composed of potency and act, i.e. of matter and form.

2. Again, if we consider a whole species instead of an individual body, we shall be led to the same conclusion : for it is clear that in order that one and the same specific nature may be found in several individuals, it must be differentiated in them in some way, i.e. there must be something which is added to the specific nature in each of them. If each were simply the specific nature, and nothing more, they would not be different individuals. Now, the nature itself is a definite determined thing, i.e. a perfection or an act ; and therefore the individual must possess an element which is different from this act, and at the same time is capable of receiving it. Such a capacity, however, is what we mean by potency, and so the individual is composed of two elements, an actual one and a potential one, i.e. form and matter.

The reason why, in both these arguments, we identify the actual and potential elements in the individual with substantial form and first matter, is that the individual must be a unity and an essential unity, for it is certainly one thing, not two. Now the greatest amount of division that is possible in a unity of this kind is the division into a potency and its immediate act, for if the potency were made actually a substance, any further act would only modify the already existing substance, i.e. it would be an accident ; and the union would be accidental. Undetermined and unactuated potency, such as this, is precisely what we mean by first matter, as the definition given above shows, while its immediate act is substantial form. Consequently, in order to preserve the essential unity of the individual it is necessary for us to say that its potential element is first matter, and its actual element substantial form.

## A Further Consideration of Matter and Form.

We now pass to a consideration of the two principles of bodies, taken individually.

What exactly are first matter and substantial form ? In the first place we ask with regard to first matter : *is it pure potentiality ?* By pure potentiality is meant that which does not contain any act as a part of itself, and that which has not the nature of act in any real order. Now, there are two real orders, those, namely, of essence and existence, and so a two-fold act : act of essence and act of existence, or, as they are often called, formal and entitative act. The first determines what the thing is, the second places the thing outside the state of mere possibility, making it an actually existing thing. So, in the case of a child, every child whether possible or existing is a certain kind of animal, an animal which is capable of loving, thinking, laughing and talking ; of a particular physical shape and organisation, and so on ; but before such a child is conceived it is possible only, it may be born ; but when it is born or conceived, it has not only the formal act which belonged to it when it was still only possible, but in addition the act or perfection of existing, by whose means it makes its appearance in the world, as an actually existing member of a family.

That matter is pure potentiality in the order of essence is universally admitted by Scholastics, i.e. all agree that it has no determined nature of its own, being a mere capacity for receiving form, or in technical language, that it is free of all formal act, and so has no element of form in it, nor is it to be thought of as form, either in itself, or relatively to any real subject which is naturally prior to it. So, no material element, however all-pervasive, or capable of being a substratum in various substances, as oxygen for example, nor even any definite force, such as electricity, can possibly be identified with first matter ; since all have their own original nature or form.[1] It has therefore an unlimited capacity for receiving all material forms ; though not, of course, for receiving those which are wholly immaterial, if there are any such, since these would not be in any way correlative to it. Just as a quart measure can receive any quantity up to a

[1] How easy it is to be entirely mistaken as to the meaning of first matter is exemplified in the following astonishing statement (Haas, *The New Physics*, p. 71) : ' In the modern system of physics electricity no longer stands alongside of matter : it has taken the place of matter. The new physics can descry in electricity that unadulterated primordial something for which scientists sought through thousands of years, and from which all things amenable to sense perception are formed.'

quart, so that, to this extent, its capacity is unlimited ; so
first matter is like a vessel which should be capable of receiving any amount however great ; which would nevertheless
not be capable of receiving anything which was not quantitative. It has an indefinite internal capacity, though externally
it is limited.

Here, however, agreement ends ; for many hold that there
is in matter some entitative act, while others will not allow
it to have any of itself. This question is closely connected
with the more famous one with regard to the real distinction
between essence and existence. Those who deny the real
distinction must hold that the essence of matter is its existence, and since existence is necessarily actual, that this
essence is an entitative act, though an incomplete one. For
they say that it is impossible to conceive of anything being
*real*, unless it has existence which is identified with itself.
This is the opinion of the Scotists, Suarez and others. For
those who hold, with S. Thomas, the real distinction, the
question can only be, whether matter has some existence of
its own, independently of form ; in other words, whether
matter is related to existence immediately, without form
intervening, or whether it receives existence only by the
mediation of form. This latter view, which is universal
among Thomists, is an integral part of the Aristotelean notion
of form, since, for him, existence belongs to form of itself (*per
se*), to matter by means of something else, viz. form (*per
aliud*). The Thomists therefore have to prove that matter
has no existence of its own. To do so they argue once more
from the essential unity of the individual, for if matter has
its own existence, form can only give it an added or secondary
existence, which therefore cannot make it simply existing,
but merely existing in a certain new way. In other words,
it will not make it exist as a substance, but confer an added
accidental existence, so that matter and form together will
not be substance, but substance and accident.

Further, an essential unity cannot have two substantial
existences, which would be the case if matter has its own
existence, as well as form. So, from both points of view, it is
clear that if matter has its own existence, the compound

resulting from matter and form will not be an essential, but only an accidental unity.

This same truth can also be proved as follows : It is clear that if matter can only receive existence by the mediation of form, it has no existence of its own ; and that this is, in fact, the case, we see if we consider that existence can only belong, of itself, either to a complete essence, or, at most, to some actual principle of essence ; since a thing which exists must be a determinate and definite thing, otherwise, we should be in the absurd position of asserting that something altogether indefinite exists. It is, however, clear that matter is neither a complete nature, nor yet an actual principle of nature, since it is defined as a capacity for receiving form, i.e. as a potential principle of nature. It follows, therefore, that we cannot consistently maintain that matter has any existence of its own.

That matter has no formal act, on which all Scholastics agree, is simply another way of stating the definition of it : ' neque quid, neque quale, etc.' ; and it is clear that unless this fundamental notion of matter is adhered to, it is useless to employ the notion at all, since matter which includes formal act will be a mixture of matter and form, so that either we must go on for ever with a series of matters which include form, or else say that at last we come to a matter free from formal act, which is what Aristotle and the Scholastics understand by the expression ' first matter.'

If, then, it be granted that first matter is pure potency, certain other conclusions with regard to it immediately follow :

1. It is metaphysically impossible for matter to exist without form, since it receives its existence by the mediation of form.

2. From which it follows that matter is unknowable apart from form, since that which cannot be, or exist, cannot be known. So all our knowledge of first matter is derived from some compound of matter and form, and Butler rightly derides the pseudo-philosopher who asserts that :

> ' He had first matter seen undressed ;
> He took her naked all alone,
> Before one rag of form was on.'[1]

[1] *Hudibras*, Part I, Canto I.

So matter being a correlative of form is only intelligible with relation to it, we must know of what it is capable if we are to understand its capacity ; just as a Fiji Islander, if confronted with an electric accumulator, and asked what its capacity was, would reply, in all probability, that it could hold about two pints, not knowing that it had a capacity for storing electrical energy, and that this was what it was made for.  He could only understand the accumulator if he understood that of which it was capable.

3. We must further conclude that if matter receives existence from substantial form only, there can be only one substantial form in one compound.  This is a much-debated question, about which more will be said later.[1]  Here it is sufficient to note that there are three main opinions with regard to it.  The first is that of Scotus, who contends that a living body possesses, besides the soul which is united to it, an incomplete and subordinate form, called corporeality (*corporeitas*).  The second view is that of Albert the Great, who was S. Thomas' master, and some modern writers, according to whom the soul would be the primary form of the body, and the forms of the chemical elements would be subsumed by it, retaining their natural reality.  The third opinion is that there is only one substantial form in one compound, and is that of S. Thomas and all Thomists.[2]

As M. Nys says, the reasons given by S. Thomas appear to be decisive.

He argues : one thing has only one substantial being, but substantial being is given by substantial form (as we have just seen), therefore one thing has only one substantial form. Secondly, there is no mean between substantial and accidental form, hence, if there is a first form which gives substantial being, any other which is added to it will find the subject already constituted as a substantial being, and consequently will be accidentally united to it.[3]

4. Since, then, matter is pure potency, and form, act which confers existence on matter, and makes the material

[1] *Vide* pp. 129 ff., Ch. X, Qu. 1.
[2] Cf. Remer, *Cosmologia*, pp. 87 ff. (ed. 4a, 1921).
[3] *Summa Theol.*, Part I, Q. 76, Arts. 3, 4 ;  *de Potentia*, Q. 3, Ch. 3, et 9 ad 9.

thing a being, it follows that form of itself actuates matter, and makes the compound of matter and form a unity. In other words, there is no need, in order that matter and form should be made one, of any unifying medium distinct from them, just as in cabinet-making when parts are dovetailed, there is no need of glue to join them.

From all that has been said of substantial form, it will be obvious that it is not the same as what is commonly called form, in everyday language, as when we speak about the form of a vase. This really means its shape, though there is no doubt a vague reminiscence of the old meaning of form, as that which gives a thing its definite character.

The question is often asked whether this theory of matter and form is compatible with the results of modern science, since spectroscopic investigation has proved, from a scientific point of view, that the chemical elements remain in the molecule, or larger body, intact, and so are not substantially changed, and, even in living things, scientific investigation seems to show that elements absorbed in the process of nutrition are not changed in their natures, but merely used by the living thing to build up its tissues, etc. ; which results would destroy our first argument. What is, perhaps, even more serious, though all of a piece with the denial of substantial change, is that science does not recognise the continuity of matter, nor the unity of bodies ; since, in the scientific view, the atom itself is made up of discontinuous electrons and nuclei, the abandonment of the old notion of the ether making this discontinuity still more apparent. If, however, there is neither continuity nor unity in matter our other two arguments fall to the ground.

To answer these difficulties completely, a treatise on the nature and scope of scientific theories would be required ; but it will be sufficient for our present purpose to note the following considerations :

1. The scientist does not approach the investigation of the physical world with the same aim as the philosopher, for he wishes to observe the *phenomena* accurately, not to discover the ultimate nature of the bodies whose appearances they are. Thus his theories or pictures of bodies, if he presents

E

any, are all directed to the elucidation of the phenomena themselves, not of what lies behind them, if anything does : whereas it is the nature of the underlying reality which is precisely that which interests the philosopher.

2. Exact science can only speak in terms of quantity, neglecting all else, such as nature and quality ; whereas the philosopher has to take every aspect of the physical universe into account.

3. From the account given above of the Thomistic theory of matter, it will be clear that it is essentially a metaphysical theory, which enunciates the elements which bodies must possess if we are to give an intelligible account of matter and motion ; taking all bodies, including our own, into consideration. Such a view is evidently much wider and deeper than the special one of physics, and it follows that the scientific theories and conclusions cannot be transported bodily, and as they stand, into the philosophical theory. Further, the fact that science with its special aim, and using its own proper methods, does not find essential change or continuity in the material world, does not prove that these do not exist there, and if reason demands that we should assert their existence, our conviction of the truth of this assertion is not weakened by the fact that the description which science gives of matter, for its own purposes, does not confirm it : nor would it be strengthened if science did so confirm it. So Fr. D'Arcy says : ' Whatever scientific hypothesis of nature be accepted, evolutionary or static, the principles of S. Thomas find a ready application. They serve to explain the presuppositions of fixity and change, and disclose the two factors which must be assumed and included in any intelligible account. The physical theory of S. Thomas need be taken . . . as only a framework into which a variety of scientific theories can be fitted. It is primarily metaphysical.'[1]

4. If we examine, in the light of these principles, the particular instances in which we have asserted the reality of substantial change and continuity, we shall see that the

[1] M. C. D'Arcy, S.J., *Thomas Aequinas*, pp. 196 ff. Benn, Leaders of Philosophy Series (1930). Cf. P. Gény, S.J., Art. in *Divus Thomas* (*Plac.*), January 1925, pp. 73 ff.

quantity is an accident, or is it to be identified with the
substance of body ? Secondly, what precisely do we mean
by saying that it makes the subject have parts outside
parts, i.e. what is the precise nature of quantity ? This
question is expressed in Scholastic language by asking :
what is its primary formal effect ?

QUESTION I. *Is Quantity Distinct from Substance ?*

Some philosophers, as was to be expected, hold that
quantity is really distinct from substance, and some that it
is not. Among those who admit, at least to some extent, the
truth of the Aristotelean notion of two distinct realities in
bodies, substance and accident, there are still some who
make an exception in the case of quantity. Thus Descartes,
while acknowledging a modal distinction between accident
and substance, i.e. that some accidents affect substance
variably, nevertheless asserted that the nature of physical
body is extension in three dimensions, and so identified its
substance with extension.[1] The distinction of substance
from quantity is also evidently denied by those who do not
recognise the distinction between substance and accidents in
general, as Hume and the Phenomenalist School, together
with the Monists, and the majority of modern philosophers.
The dispute, however, is, in this case, clearly not confined to
the question of quantity.

That substance and quantity are really distinct is the
opinion of all Scholastics, with the possible exception of the
Nominalists ; though they differ in the way in which they
understand this distinction.

Various arguments are used to prove the reality of the
distinction, among which are the following :

1. In order that quantity may be the same as substance,
it is necessary that it should be the same, either as the sum
of the essential parts of corporeal substance, or, at least, as
one of these parts taken separately. This is not the case,
however, for the essential constitutive parts of corporeal

---

[1] *Principes de la philosophie*, Partie I, Ch. LX–LXII. *Œuvres*, Tom. IX,
ed. Adam-Tannery. *Everyman* ed., Vol. 570, p. 188. Cf. *Principes*,
Partie I, *Œuvres*, II, ed. Napoléon Chaix, p. 55, in *Everyman* ed., Sect. 53,
p. 185.

substance are matter and form. Now, it is clear that quantity is not to be identified with matter, since matter is pure potentiality, while quantity is evidently actual ; for it either confers something actual on a subject (if it be distinct from its subject), or is itself actually extended. Nor can quantity be identified with substantial form ; for the characteristic of such form is that it informs the whole of its matter in precisely the same way, since its function is to make the body to be of a particular kind, and so, all of the same kind, otherwise we should have two species of bodies, i.e. two forms. Although form may be divided, yet, since it makes the thing what it is, the whole of any simple body has one and the same form throughout, whereas it evidently does not have the same quantity throughout. A part is not equal to the whole in quantity, but it is the same in form. Lastly, quantity cannot be identified with matter and form taken in conjunction, since together they do not compose some third thing, other than matter and form ; for, as we have seen, the union of matter and form is immediate (cf. p. 50, No. 4) ; and quantity cannot be made up of two elements, one of which is potential and identical with matter, while the other is actual and identical with form ; since, as we saw above, quantity is necessarily and wholly actual. Hence, in no way can quantity be identified with corporeal substance.

2. Another simple but convincing argument is the following :

If quantity were the same as corporeal substance, i.e. were of the very essence of corporeal substance, quantity could not be varied without the nature of the body being varied. In other words, a change in quantity would entail a specific change in the body ; since the change of an essential element must necessarily change the nature of the body. It is clear, however, that quantity can alter, both in different individuals of the same species, and even in the same individual body, by means of addition and division, as well as by condensation and rarefaction, without any such change in the nature of the body following, as a necessary consequence. So a drop of water is water, just as much as a bucketful, or a lake, from which it comes, though evidently

the quantity of water in one drop is not the same as that in
the lake ; or again, a man remains a man even though he
may grow stout or lean. His quantity changes, but his
nature remains the same.

Granted, then, that quantity and substance are not the
same, we have now to consider the way in which this distinction is to be understood ; for some who allow it, yet
regard as properties of substance itself, characteristics
which, others maintain, only accrue to it from the influence
of quantity upon it. Thus :

1. Some think that both quantity and substance have
some extension of themselves, and so have this element in
common, though in different ways. Thus they say that substance has entitative extension, i.e. that corporeal substance
has, in itself, integrating parts ; parts, that is, which taken
together make up the whole ; so that it has such parts before
the coming of quantity to it, the function of quantity being
merely to make these parts capable of filling a place, so
giving impenetrability to the body. This is the view of
Suarez.[1]

2. Others, while agreeing that substance has entitative
extension before the coming of quantity, maintain that the
special function of quantity is to put the parts in order. So
John of S. Thomas.[2]

3. The Thomists, generally, hold that though substance
has no parts of itself, yet it obtains parts on the coming of
quantity to it.

(Note : The ascription by some text-books of the view
that substance does not obtain parts even under quantity to
the Salmanticenses and others, seems to be a mistake.
Cf. Salm., Vol. XVIII, pp. 380 ff.)

The truth of the second part of this statement, inasmuch
as it affirms that quantified substance has parts, is evident,
since quantified substance is extended substance, which,
clearly, has parts. To prove the other part of their statement,
viz. that substance has no entitative parts before the coming
of quantity, the Thomists argue that, if it had, it would be

---

[1] *Disputationes Metaphysicæ*, Disp. XL, Sect. 4.
[2] *Cursus Phil. Logica*, Pars. II, Q. 16, A. 1 (ed. *Vivès*, p. 466).

formally quantified, for to have entitative parts can mean no less than to have parts which are situally distinct, i.e. distinct with respect to position, or order of the parts with respect to the whole, though not necessarily with regard to place, that is to say, with regard to their relation to surrounding bodies ; as the head of a man would not be his feet, even though they were not supposed to have different relations to surrounding bodies. To have parts which are situally distinct, in this sense, is to be formally quantified ; since the proper function of quantity is to introduce into a body a merely numerical distinction of parts, and such merely numerical distinction can only come about by a mere distinction of the parts with respect to their position with regard to the whole. It follows, then, that a substance with entitative parts would be formally quantified, which is clearly impossible when quantity is absent. Thus they contend that to speak of parts which are not produced by quantity is unintelligible. In fact, it seems probable that those who maintain that substance has parts before the coming of quantity, are really making use of an awkward and ambiguous expression, and do not really disagree with those who deny it. For, since both parties agree that corporeal substance is composed of matter and form, and that matter has a positive capacity or potentiality for receiving quantity, or parts, they both allow that it is not simple, in the way that a spiritual substance is, which is absolutely indivisible. To say, however, of a substance whose divisibility consists in a mere passive capacity for division, and so is in itself undivided and indivisible, that it has parts, entitative or other, is clearly an awkward and ambiguous expression ; since to speak in this way implies some actual divisibility, such as is found in a yard of cloth, and even division ; which is a meaning certainly not intended by those who use the expression. It is therefore better to avoid it and say that substance apart from quantity has no parts, and is indivisible, as S. Thomas does.[1]

[1] Cf. II Sent. dist. III, Q. 1, a. 4 ; and *Quodlibet*, IX, a. 6.

QUESTION II. *What is the Nature of Quantity in Itself?*

The question we have just reviewed, on the distinction between substance and quantity, has, of course, shown us that quantity has the nature of accident, and the latter part of it, that its peculiar nature, as distinguished from the other accidents, is to give parts to substance. We now have to try and see in what way it does this ; and, if we do so, we shall have arrived at its definition, since all accidents must be defined by means of the effects which they produce on substance ; and strictly speaking by means of their primary formal effects, i.e. the first effects which they naturally produce. In fact, in ordinary affairs, this is the way in which we judge of the nature of accidents, as a doctor judges the nature of a disease by observing the effects which it produces in his patient—its symptoms—and we are here trying to find the peculiar 'symptoms' of quantity. We must not, however, suppose that its nature consists in the actual positing of this effect ; since, in common with all other accidents, it is that which is naturally *fitted* to be in some subject, not that which actually is in it, and actually affects it. For the nature of a thing is unaffected whether it is actually existing or not ; whiteness would still be whiteness, even if there were none left in the world. Since, in spite of this, the only means we have of judging of its nature is by observing its actual effects—for we have no intellectual X-ray, so to speak, by which we can penetrate into the very heart of it— it is these which we must examine. What, then, are its characteristic effects ?

Consider such an object as a cube of sugar. Since it is quantitatively extended, it occupies a certain three-dimensional portion of space. This extension is measurable and also divisible. Since the cube occupies a certain portion of space, it prevents any other body from occupying it, i.e. it is impenetrable. Now, all these effects presuppose parts in the cube, and parts which are not coincident, but outside one another, and in a certain order ; this being an essential condition for the occupation of space. Thus we have seven characteristics which accompany extended quantity in a material substance, viz. plurality of parts, the order of these parts among themselves, their capacity for filling a space, actual occupation of a space, divisibility, mensurability, and impenetrability.

We want to discover which of these is the first and essential characteristic of quantity ; and it is not easy to do so, since each one of them has some claim to be so considered. Thus, John of S. Thomas holds the view that quantity consists in the ordering of parts among themselves, while Suarez maintains that it is the capacity of the parts for filling a place. The opinion which makes the primary formal effect of quantity to be impenetrability is really the same as this : since a body which is capable of filling a place is *ipso facto* capable of excluding another body from the same place. Neither of these views, however, can be maintained if we accept what was said above as to the absence of parts in substance before the coming of quantity, since to unite parts in order, and, still more to make such parts capable of filling a place, presupposes the existence of such parts.

The same reason rules out the notion that mensurability is the nature of quantity, an opinion said to have been held by S. Albert the Great ; for, in order that a thing may be measurable by an extended measure, such as a foot-rule, it must be extended in itself, i.e. composed of parts which form a continuous body. Scotus is said to have thought that the nature of quantity consisted in divisibility ; this, however, could not be true, as a thing is divisible because it is quantitative, rather than quantitative because it is divisible.

In the minds of all Scholastics, when dealing with this question, there is present a constant theological preoccupation with the dogma of the Eucharist ; and this is particularly evident in their treatment of the view of Durandus that the nature of quantity consists in the actual occupation of a place ; in connection with which they note that, since Christ's body in the Eucharist does not occupy a place, it would be necessary to deny that it is quantitative, a view which they stigmatise as at least erroneous and temerarious, if not heretical. Apart from the theological reason, it is easy to see that the actual occupation of a place by a body is a consequence of its being extended, and having parts in itself, and that, therefore, such occupation cannot be the *primary* formal effect of quantity, and constitute its nature.

Only one conception of its nature therefore remains, viz. that it consists in its capacity for giving to substance a plurality of parts, in doing which it will *ipso facto* put them in order with regard to the whole compound, though not necessarily with regard to place. In other words, the parts will be situally distinct, though not necessarily distinct locally.[1] Some writers, as Remer and Hoenen, call this effect of quantity actual extension of substance, but since this expression might lead to confusion, it is perhaps better avoided ; though the view, intended to be expressed by it, is that now generally held by Thomists ; with the exception of Gredt, who follows John of S. Thomas.[2]

A strong presumption in favour of this Thomist view is already afforded by the manifest insufficiency of all the proposed alternatives, and, if we look at the matter directly, we can see that the primary formal effect of quantity must be that which is the reason and source of all the other properties or effects, which may proceed from it ; for this is what we mean by *primary* effect. For example, if we were enquiring what was the primary effect of alcohol on the human system, we might reply it is the deadening of the nerve-cell junctions (or synapses, as they are called), which, in turn, causes resistance to the passage of nervous energy, and so partial dissociation of the brain ; causing, in its turn, loss of control of the emotions by the intellect, which results in boisterous conduct ; and, progressively, loss of control of the limbs and sense faculties, eventually ending in entire suspension of

---

[1] The two words '*situs*' and '*locus*' have different meanings in the Scholastic vocabulary. The first indicates the distinction and arrangement of the parts of a body among themselves, as for example the arrangement of a man's limbs in sitting or standing ; whereas the word ' place ' implies a relation of the body to external ones, as will presently be explained (cf. Chap. VI, pp. 78 ff.). Of course, in the ordinary way, a change of *situs* would involve a change of location, since if the parts of a body are differently arranged among themselves, they will also be differently arranged with regard to surrounding bodies ; but this need not happen, as we shall shortly see, and in any case it is evident that situation and location in the Scholastic sense are not the same.

[2] Gredt, *Elementa Philosophiæ*, Sect. 315 (ed. 4, 1926).

them, in a heavy sleep.[1] All these latter effects result from the obstruction of the synapses, which, therefore, is primary. We are asking here, not only what is the primary effect of quantity, but what is its primary formal effect, and that will, evidently, be that which proceeds from quantity, and from no other accidental form. Now, these two conditions : that the effect we are looking for must be the source of all other properties proceeding from quantity ; and that by which quantity is distinguished from any other form, are satisfied only in the case of that effect of quantity which is the giving to substance a plurality of parts, on which follows, immediately, their order with respect to the whole ; for it is clear that no other accident gives substance a plurality of ordered parts, and so this property is distinctive of quantity, or formal ; and, moreover, it is primary, since, as we saw above, the other properties of quantity, viz. capacity for filling a place, divisibility, mensurability and impenetrability follow, once the substance has been given such a plurality of parts, and presuppose it. Thus it is evidently the *primary* formal effect of quantity.

The difficulty of this view is, no doubt, chiefly to be found in the fact that we cannot imagine a thing with parts which are numerically distinct one from another, and yet, not distinct as regards place. Undoubtedly, a body which has such parts, which are outside one another as regards itself, is *ipso facto* in a state which makes it able to fill a place ; but in order that it may actually do so, two further conditions are required : (1) that there actually exist other bodies which constitute the place, and (2) that their internal dimensions be actually applied to the external dimensions of the body which is to be in place. For it must be borne in mind that the state of being in a place arises, not from something internal to a body, but from something extrinsic to it, viz. the proximity and juxtaposition of other bodies. Hence, if either of the conditions, mentioned above, is not fulfilled, the body will be extended in itself, and yet not be in any place. So, if we suppose that there existed only one body, it could not be in place, since, owing to the absence of all others

[1] Cf. McDougall, *Abnormal Psychology*, pp. 67–74.

which might surround it, the extrinsic relation of being situated with respect to them, i.e. of being in place, could not arise. Similarly, if a body, which was one of many, were yet not related to them by means of its extension, they would not surround it by means of extension, and so it would not fill the extended place which they form. The difficulty, therefore, is due to the imagination, for we cannot imagine one body joined to another by any other means than by the application of the extension of the one to that of the other, since this is the only union of which the senses tell us. We can, however, understand that there is nothing necessary about this particular mode of union, since it is not necessary that the extension of a body should have any relation to the extension of others, if it is present to them in some other way. It is also extremely clear from the consideration of the unique body (the only one in the world), that for a body to be actually in place is a condition totally distinct from that of being extended in itself.

If, then, as is certainly the case, to be in place and to fill a place is an extrinsic relation added to the nature of extended body, it follows that the exclusion of another body from a place already occupied, is, though a natural consequence of such occupation, as experience shows, nevertheless not a necessary formal effect of extension or quantity. This is another way of saying that such impenetrability is not of the very nature of extended or quantified body, and it is possible to have an extended thing which is not impenetrable.

From our conclusions as to the relationship of substance and quantity, certain other results also follow. First, tha since quantity is not of the essence of material substance, absolutely speaking, it would be possible to have such substance without any quantity, since we can take away from a thing some attribute which does not belong to its nature, without destroying that nature. Substance, however, in this case, would still retain its natural requirement to be quantified, and, in certain cases, it is impossible to conceive of an unquantified, i.e. unextended material substance, as in the case of living things which must be organised, i.e. have parts, in order to live.  If quantity were removed from material substance in this way, the body would not be reduced to a point, as some have supposed, but would simply have no relation to extension ; whereas a point is the beginning of an extension.

A more difficult question arises when we come to consider the possibility of the existence of quantity divorced from substance, for though we might summarily assert that it can so exist, in common with all other accidents (since an accident requires substance only for its support, and consequently if supported, in some other way, can dispense with it), yet certain difficulties peculiar to quantity remain. For quantity immediately affects material substance, and indeed results from the nature of matter.[1]  We must, by all means, avoid thinking of material substance as something inert and passive, on which quantity is imposed from without, like a coat of whitewash on a wall.  On the contrary, quantity, like the qualities of bodies, grows, as it were, from them ; as a plant grows from the ground, being enabled to do so by the nature of the soil.  It seems, then, that the whole *raison d'être* of quantity is to produce extension in substance, and consequently it cannot exist if it does not do so, which would be the case if it were separated from substance.  Now, as we saw, the primary function of quantity is to give extension to substance, but in order to do this, it must be extended in itself.  This accidental extension, therefore, is its true nature, and it may still have a function to fulfil even if deprived of its primary one.

In order to bring out the meaning of the statement that quantity can preserve its nature, and a certain function, even if deprived of the possibility of exercising its primary function owing to the absence of substance, we may, perhaps, be allowed to make use of an illustration, though it is not to be supposed that the two cases are parallel.  The primary function of a doctor is to cure the sick, and in order to do this he must be versed in the medical sciences.  Now, suppose he were in some ' brave new world ' where there were no sick people to cure, he would still continue to be a doctor so long

[1] Cf. *Summa Theol.*, Pars I, Q. 77, a. 6., o. et ad 1um et 3um.

as his scientific competence remained ; and he would also have a function to fulfil, though not his primary one, in so far as he assisted the people to preserve their health, or even to get healthier and healthier. Just as quantity cannot quantify substance if there is no substance, so the doctor cannot cure disease if there is none, but quantity preserves its nature of accidental extension, and the doctor his of medical scientist, and both fulfil a derivative function ; quantity, in virtue of its own essential extension, giving extension to other accidents, and the doctor, in virtue of his medical knowledge, preserving the health of the healthy ; prevention, in his case, being the substitute for cure. If, then, we imagine a case in which it was necessary that the accidents of some substance should remain and be known, when the substance had disappeared, quantity would still have a necessary role to fill, viz. to make them extended, impenetrable, and so on. Hence, it would still have a reason of being. If it be further objected that quantity detached from its subject will not be any particular quantity, since it is not the quantity of anything ; and that, therefore, it is impossible to conceive of it as existing, since only concrete singular things exist ; we notice that quantity is peculiar, among the accidents, inasmuch as it is by quantity that things are distinguished as numerically different, i.e. as individuals.[1] Unlike qualities, such as colour, say the colour white, which, if abstracted from its subject, would give us whiteness, not this white thing ; quantity, even in abstraction, is of a certain definite amount, since its extension is proper to itself, and does not depend on its subject, whereas whiteness, and such-like qualities, are only made individual, particular and definite by being the whiteness, and so on, of a particular subject.

Quantity, then, in our hypothetical case, could exist without its subject, since it would retain its definiteness and individuality, and have a function to perform, even though deprived of its primary one.

---

[1] Cf. Remer, *Cosmologia* (editio sexta), p. 143, Resp. ad 2am diff. *Summa Theologica*, Pars III, Q. 77, a. 2 ; IV Sent. dist. XII, Q. 1, a. 1, Sol. 3, ad 2um, et ad 3um ; V. Metaphysica, Lect. 15.

These considerations throw a little more light on the difficult question of the nature of quantity, and, of course, have their special application in theology, in the question relating to the Eucharistic accidents.

# CHAPTER V

## THE CONTINUUM

Notion of Continuity—Zeno's Arguments—The Divisibility of the
Continuum—Is it Composed of Indivisible Elements ?—Is it
Infinitely Divisible ?—The Parts of the Continuum—The
Indivisibles of the Continuum—Solution of Zeno's Arguments.

WE have already noticed, what is indeed obvious, that there
are two kinds of quantity, continuous and discrete, of which
continuous quantity is a primary kind, while discrete is a
derivative of it. It is, therefore, a natural sequence to pass
from the consideration of quantity in general to that of continuous quantity. No doubt, the analysis of continuous
quantity, or the continuum, was first suggested by observation of the material world, since bodies are, at least in appearance, continuous. The philosophical discussion of it, however, leads us into a region more abstract than that of natural
philosophy ; and indeed this section, like the preceding,
really forms part of the science of mathematical philosophy.

What, then, is the essential feature of continuity ? To
answer this question we notice in the first place the distinction which exists, and which Aristotle points out, between
the continuous and the contiguous ; for two things, or two
parts of the same thing, are continuous, if the extremities in
which they join are the same ; and contiguous, if their
extremities are together, i.e. in the same immediate place.
They are then said to be in contact.[1] Thus the continuum
is a reality which is actually one in extension, stretching out
without any intervals, e.g. a geometrical line. So, to constitute the continuum mere juxtaposition is insufficient, the
parts must be united by a *common* term. As we consider, by

---

[1] Aristotle, *Physics*, 226ᵇ34, 227ª27, 231ª21, 1068ᵇ26, 1069ª14 ; and
S. Thomas in V Phys., Lect. 5 ; VI Phys., Lect. 1 ; in XI Met., Lect. 13,
ed. Cathala, n. 2404–15.

abstraction, one, two, or three dimensions, we arrive at three species of continuum : the line, the surface, and the volume (cube or solid). In the line points are in some way present. Since the point is indivisible, points are called the indivisibles of a line. Both lines and surfaces are indivisible in some respect, the line, namely, with respect to breadth and depth, the surface, with respect to depth only. Thus lines are said to be the indivisibles of surfaces, surfaces of solids.

It is advisable to notice here that there are two genera of continuum, viz. the permanent and successive. The first is, again, of two kinds, the physical continuum, which is natural body ; and the mathematical, whose species, solid, surface, and line, we have just enumerated. The successive continuum is of two kinds : motion and time.

If we now examine this notion of the continuum as uninterrupted extension, it seems that since it is an extension it is divisible without end, in which case it appears that we might have an actually infinite multitude, an hypothesis which few accept, and which presents grave difficulties. (Cf. pp. 107 ff.) If, on the other hand, the continuum is not infinitely divisible, we must come finally to indivisibles, so that in the last resort the divisible continuum will be composed of indivisibles, the extended of the unextended. This difficulty was first recognised, though obscurely, by Zeno, who argued on the assumption that the continuum is composed of indivisibles, and so constructed his famous proofs of the impossibility of motion, which have been referred to in our Introduction (p. 7). Though one of these, the Achilles, may be invalidated by his ' ignorance of the theory of infinite convergent numerical series,' as Whitehead suggests,[1] the others are unassailable, if we admit his premise ; but they stand or fall with it. Thus if we prove that the continuum is not composed only of indivisibles, we shall *ipso facto* refute these arguments.[2] They are as follows :

1. The Dichotomy. In order to travel a distance, a body must first travel half the distance : and half the distance

---

[1] *Process and Reality*, p. 95. The suggestion was first made by Descartes. *Vide Œuvres* (Adam and Tannery), Tom. IV, p. 445.

[2] Aristotle, *Physics*, 239[b]11–[b]30 ; S. Thomas in VI Phys., Lect. 11.

remains to be travelled. Again, since the first half is divisible, it must first travel half of that half, and so to infinity, since a magnitude is divisible to infinity. Infinities, however, cannot be traversed in a finite time, therefore the body will never arrive, nor even can it move from one place to another.

2. The Achilles. Achilles and the tortoise run a race. If the tortoise is given a start, Achilles can never catch it up. For, first he must run to the place from which the tortoise started. When he gets there, the tortoise will have gone to a point further on. Achilles must then run to that point, and the tortoise will have gone still further. This will go on for ever, the tortoise always being ahead, so that Achilles will never catch him up. Since this seems absurd, it is better to say that nothing moves. (Aristotle and S. Thomas omit the picturesque details.)

3. The Arrow. Everything which is in a place either moves or is at rest. Now an arrow in its flight would, at each moment of it, be in its place : therefore at each moment it would either move or be at rest. But it cannot move, for then it would not be in one place, but in two. Therefore it is at rest. If, therefore, it moves at no moment, it does not move in the whole time, and so is at rest.

There is also a fourth argument called the Road. Strictly speaking, only the first two concern us here ; and both assume that the continuum is actually composed of indivisibles. We will therefore first consider this question.

SECTION I. *On the Divisibility of the Continuum.*

QUESTION I. *Is the Continuum Composed of Indivisible Elements ?*

That it is not, is admitted by all philosophers of all schools, with the possible exception of the Pythagoreans, and some Scholastics of the seventeenth century ; for it is, in fact, very obvious that it cannot be so composed. Clearly the indivisibles, inasmuch as they are indivisibles, are unextended. An extended continuum, however, cannot be composed of unextended elements. Moreover, such elements would either

be at a distance from one another, in which case they would
not form a continuum, or in contact, in which case they would
be coincident ; since, having no extremes nor middles, they
must touch in their totality if at all.  So, again, they would
not form an extended continuum, whose parts must be outside one another.  In other words, if we suppose that an
extended continuum is composed of indivisibles which are
outside one another, continuity disappears, and if they are
not outside one another, extension disappears, so that in
neither case can the continuum be composed of indivisibles.

It is useless to suggest that the indivisibles are infinitely
small : for though, in Mathematics, we may speak of an
infiitely small quantity, we mean a quantity whose magnitude is indeterminable.  That such quantities cannot be
infinitely small, in the philosophic sense, is clear from the
fact that they are not nothing, and so must have a finite
magnitude, though an indefinitely small one.  That they
have such a magnitude is seen from the fact that they can be
further divided, which in itself disallows the suggestion that
the indivisibles are of this kind.

Further, the very impossibilities which result from Zeno's
arguments confirm our contention that his hypothesis, viz.
that the continuum is composed of indivisibles, is false ; for,
if it were true, the slowest and quickest movers would move
at the same speed : since the quickest could not pass over
more than one indivisible element of space in less than
one indivisible element of time, i.e. in less than one instant,
since by hypothesis an instant is the least time there is,
otherwise it would be divisible : nor could the slowest take
*more* than a single instant to pass over less than one indivisible element of space, since this is, by hypothesis, the least
space.  Consequently, they would both pass over one
indivisible element of space in the same time, viz. one instant,
and so would travel at the same rate.

QUESTION II.  *Is the Continuum Infinitely Divisible ?*

This conclusion, that the continuum is not composed of
indivisibles, carries with it an important corollary : for if we
never come to ultimate indivisible elements when we divide

the continuum, it must be divisible to infinity. Now, just as
philosophers are practically unanimous in asserting that the
continuum is not composed of indivisibles, so they also agree
that it is divisible to infinity. It is as well to recall here the
distinction between the continuum formally considered,
i.e. as it is one real extension—the mathematical continuum,
and the physical or material continuum, viz. the actual
bodies in the universe, which are extended and endowed
with a variety of accidents. Those who consider the physical
continuum only, hold that it is not infinitely divisible : and
this we do not deny, but rather affirm with S. Thomas : for
the mathematical or abstract continuum is divided into
*proportional* parts, i.e. parts which are some proportion of
the whole, as halves or thirds, which can again be divided
into halves or thirds ; and it is clear that we can go on for
ever taking a half of half, or a third of a third, and so on, so
that this continuum is infinitely divisible. *A priori* we can
see that this may not be true of the physical continuum,
and experience shows that, in fact, it is not : for the physical
continuum is composed of what are known as *aliquot parts*,
determined ones, namely, which when added together make
up the whole. These have a determinate extension, and so
cannot be further divided. The reason of this is that in the
physical continuum we come to a minimum quantity of
matter which is necessary to support a given form, such
minima, for example, as the molecule or atom would be.
Now, if this minimum be further divided we get a body of a
different nature, i.e. the original form disappears, and another
takes its place. So S. Thomas says : ' *Corpus mathematicum
est divisible in infinitum, in quo consideratur sola ratio quanti-
tatis in qua nihil est repugnans divisioni infinitæ. Sed corpus
naturale, quod consideratur sub tota forma, non potest in
infinitum dividi, quia, quando jam ad minimum deducitur,
statim propter debilitatem virtutis convertitur in aliud. Unde
est invenire minimam carnem, sicut dicitur in I. Physicorum,
nec tamen corpus naturale componitur ex mathematicis.*'[1]

[1] *De Sensu et Sensato*, Lect. 15. Cf. *Summa Theol.*, Pars I, Q. 48,
a. 4, ad 3um ; I. II., Q. 85, a. 2.0 ; II Sent. dist. XXX, Q. 2, a. 2.0 ;
III Phys., Lect. 10, a. 9 ; de Potentia IV, a. 1, ad 5um ; IV Sent. dist.
XII, Q. 1, a. 2, Sol. 3.

Thus in the physical continuum we come to ultimate parts which cannot be further divided ; so that this continuum is not infinitely divisible. This seems to be what Fr. Leslie Walker suggests, though he charges Aristotle with denying it : and what is worse, with being ' led astray by appearances.'[1] Thus with regard to the abstract or mathematical continuum, which alone concerns us here, there seem to be few or no philosophers who do not allow that it is divisible to infinity.

That it is so, is seen from what was said above, for we can go on for ever taking a half of a half, and so on. Moreover, it is clear that the whole continuum can be divided, being an extension, and the quotient will be an extension and so divisible, and the same will hold good in all further divisions, so that no end can be put to them.[2]

SECTION II. *The Parts of the Continuum.*

If, then, the continuum is not composed of indivisibles, it must be composed of divisibles, i.e. of extended parts, such as halves, quarters, etc. The name ' parts ' is applied exclusively to such extended portions, and not to the indivisibles. Since, then, such parts exist in the continuum, they may exist there either actually or potentially, i.e. in such a way that they can be made actual parts by division. There are, therefore, two main views corresponding to these two possibilities, while some have tried to reconcile them.

Thus : A. (1) Many teach that the parts exist in act. Plato held this view, according to Prof. Ross, who agrees with him and adds : ' to cut a ball in two is not to bring into existence the common plane of its halves, it is to drive your knife along a plane that is already there.'[3] Similarly, John of S. Thomas, Goudin, and Gredt. These maintain the actual existence of parts without any reservation.

(2) Others say that though the parts are not actually divided, yet they are actually distinct : existing formally as parts joined together by continuing indivisibles. So, Suarez, and others.

[1] *Aristotelean Society's Proceedings*, 1922–3, pp. 98–9.
[2] Cf. Leibniz, Ep. ad P. des Bosses.
[3] Ross, *Aristotle's Metaphysics*, Vol. I, Introd., p. lv.

B. Many others, however, teach that the parts exist only potentially in the continuum : inasmuch as there are in it no actual limits, which serve to separate one part from another. This is the view of Aristotle, as can be seen in VII Met., 1039ª3 ff. ' The double line consists of two halves —potentially : for the actualisation of the halves divides them from one another.' S. Thomas agrees, as in his comment on this passage (Lect. 13) ; also in Lect. 16, and Bk. V, Lect. 21 : ' *Partes sunt in potentia in toto continuo* ' ; and VII Phys., Lect. 9 : ' *Pars autem prout est in toto, non est divisa in actu, sed in potentia tantum* ' ; and IV. Sent. dist. X, Q. 1, a. 3, qª4, sol. 3 ad 1um. : ' *Partes alicujus homogenei continui ante divisionem non habent esse actu sed potentia tantum,*' and many other places.[1]

C. Some try to reconcile these two views, saying that though the parts are not actually in the continuum considered formally as parts, yet considered as realities they are actual in it. So Donat, and Hugon.

The argument which Aristotle and S. Thomas use to prove their opinion is of extreme simplicity and clarity. The first, and most essential characteristic of the continuum as a species of quantity is its unity. If the continuum were not essentially one, we should have, not continuous, but discrete, quantity. This being so, it is impossible that the parts should be actual, since the least that this could mean would be that they are already actual entities, and so actual unities. A number of such unities, however, even if in juxtaposition, could never constitute an entity which was essentially one. It may be useful to quote the very words of S. Thomas,[2] which are lucidity itself : ' *Sicut aliquid est ens, sicut et unum : unum autem est quod est in se indivisum et ab aliis divisum : pars autem prout est in toto, non est divisa in actu sed in potentia tantum, unde non est actu ens neque una, sed in potentia tantum.*' So we may express this simple truth by saying that if the parts are actual entities, they will be actually many, and so cannot at the same time be actually one, or a continuum.

[1] I de Cœlo, Lect. 3, Sect. 6 ; I Phys. Lect. 9, Sect. 8 ; *Summa Theol.,* III Pars, Q. 76, a. 3, ad 1um ; I Pars, Q. 85, a. 8, ad 2um ; Quodlibet I, a. 21.　　　　　　　　　　　[2] VII Phys., Lect. 9, Sec. 5.

It is worth noting that those who take the middle view contend that the matter of which the parts are composed is actually present in the continuum before division, which nobody denies ; consequently, their effort at reconciliation is unsuccessful, for they do not, by this means, solve the question, which is whether the parts considered formally as distinct entities are actual before division. Since, however, they deny that they are actual, their opinion seems to be that of S. Thomas, and the distinction introduced by them only serves to obscure the real nature of the dispute. A confirmatory argument in favour of this same view is derived from the infinite divisibility of the continuum, since if the parts were actually present in the continuum, they would have to be either infinite or finite in number. They cannot, however, be either ; for if they were infinite in number we should have an actually infinite multitude in the genus of quantity, which, as we shall see, is impossible ; and, moreover, they would not be parts but indivisible points, since, if they had any extension, however small, when they were multiplied an infinity of times, they would constitute an infinite magnitude : so that any body, even the smallest, would have an infinite magnitude, which is absurd. Now we have proved, and Suarez agrees, that the continuum is not constituted of indivisibles. So, it is impossible that the parts should be infinite in number. Nor can their number be finite, for, in this case, the continuum would not be divisible to infinity, which we have seen that it is. Hence, it is impossible that the continuum should be composed of actual parts.

SECTION III.  *The Indivisibles of the Continuum.*

In order to complete our analysis of the nature of the continuum, something must be added as to the other elements which are conceived of as being in it, in addition to its parts, viz. the indivisibles. Now, these indivisibles are of two kinds, the *terminating* indivisibles which are thought of as actually limiting the continuum, such as the points at the end of a line ; and the *continuing* indivisibles which are thought of as being within the continuum, and joining together the parts which can be separated at them. We ask, then, whether indivisibles of these two kinds are actually, or only potentially, present in the continuum.

1. There can be little doubt that the terminating indivisibles are actual, since, if the continuum is limited at all, it must be by means of an actual limit. There is, however, difference of opinion as to the nature of this limit, for some regard it as a mere negation, the negation, that is, of further extension, while others think that it is a positive reality, being the reality of the limited body, in so far as this connotes the negation of further extension. A much more general view, however, is that they are something positive, really distinct from the continuum which they terminate, the distinction, of course, not being that of one quantitative thing from another, but of the determinator from the determined, and so a modal distinction, i.e. that which obtains between an entity and some mode of it. This seems, on the whole, to be the most probable opinion, though since all agree that the terminating indivisibles are actually present, for the reason given above, the question is one of lesser importance. The reason for saying that they are positive realities is that where a continuum begins there is something real and positive which was not present before, and where it ends something positive and real ceases. Consequently, the terminating indivisibles being the beginning and end of the continuum, they must be something positive and real. For contact too, it is necessary that bodies should touch by means of indivisibles, otherwise they would interpenetrate. They cannot, however, touch in a negation, for to do so would be, in fact, not to touch, and since the contact is to be real, the indivisibles must be real also. Further, they must be distinct from the continuum itself, since this is divisible, and they are indivisible.

2. With regard to the continuing indivisibles, the Nominalists hold them to be a mental fiction, while some sixteenth and seventeenth century writers, such as John of S. Thomas, whose opinion in recent times has been espoused by others, as Gredt, think that they exist in act, and are really distinct from the parts which they unite. There is little doubt that neither of these views accords with that of Aristotle and S. Thomas, for it seems clear that these considered that they

do not exist in act, but only potentially.  It is, indeed, only another way of saying that the parts of the continuum are potential only, and not actual, since it is clear that if the continuing indivisibles were actual, they would actually determine the parts, and make them actual.  So, if the parts are not actual, as we have already seen to be the case, neither are the continuing indivisibles.

SECTION IV.  *The Arguments of Zeno.*

We are now in a position to see what answer can be made to the arguments of Zeno, against the possibility of motion. In effect, Zeno argues :  You maintain that the continuum is infinitely divisible.  Now, the only things of which there can be an infinity in a lineal continuum are points, and in general, in any continuum, indivisibles ;  for if we suppose that there are an infinite number of extended parts in a continuum, the resultant of these parts will also be infinite.  Hence, a line must be composed of an infinity of points (the Dichotomy and Achilles), time of an infinity of instants (the Arrow). Now, we have proved that the continuum is not composed of indivisibles ;  and not only this, but that though it is infinitely divisible, it is not actually divided at all, and finally that the indivisibles are not actual, but only potential in it.  If this be conceded, Zeno's arguments at once break down, for there will not be an infinity of indivisibles actually in the continuum ;  such indivisibles as there are being only potentially present, and consequently there will be no point which is actually the halfway point of a distance which is being traversed, no actual point in the motion of Achilles where the tortoise was before, no moment in the flight of the arrow actually.  Thus the mover does not divide its trajectory into an infinite number of actual parts, whether proportional or aliquot ;  but into two indeterminate parts, that already traversed, and that about to be traversed ;  which are both continually changing.  If, however, we admit actual indivisibles, and actual parts in the continuum, it seems that the arguments are insoluble, even if it be contended that the number of such parts is finite ;  for the parts must be either extended or unextended :  if they are extended, they are divisible, and if they are unextended, in traversing them a body will not move. So we shall have either an infinite process, or the absence of motion. On S. Thomas's theory, on the contrary, a moving body never arrives at the halfway point, but passes through a potential point, the hero never arrives at the points in the path of the tortoise, but passes through infinity of potential points, the arrow is never at any one point of its flight.

Though it would be true to say that an infinite distance could not be traversed in a finite time, yet it is not true that a distance which is only potentially infinite cannot be traversed in a finite time; for both space and time are infinitely divisible, but not infinitely divided; so that it is possible to pass over an infinitely divisible space in a finite time, since this time is itself infinitely divisible.

# CHAPTER VI

## PLACE AND SPACE

I. Place—Localisation—Kinds of Location. II. Space—Its Nature
—Opinions—Absolutist, Subjectivist, Intermediate Theories—
The Void—Conclusion as to the Nature of Space. III.
The Occupation of Space—Impenetrability—Multilocation.

AT the beginning of our discussion of the continuum, we
noticed that it is of two kinds, permanent and successive.
We must now examine these separately. Now the permanent
continuum is concerned with the extension of bodies, and
bodies, in so far as they are extended, are said to be in space ;
and as occupying a defined portion of it, are said to be in
place. It is necessary therefore to analyse these two notions.

## SECTION I. *On Place.*

Though the notion of place is, in a certain sense, included
in that of space, and dependent on it, yet being one which is
clearer and more familiar to us than that of space, it will be
more convenient to consider it first.

Place is defined by Aristotle as : Τὸ τοῦ περιέχοντος πέρος
ἀκίνητον πρῶτον, i.e. the first unmoved limit of the container.[1]
The word ' unmoved ' indicates that the surface, which
is said to be unmoved, is so formally as a limit ; not
that the interior surface of the container, viz. this or
that vessel which contains the thing which is in place, is
unmoved. Thus, in the case of a ship anchored at sea, though
the water is constantly moving round it, yet the containing
limit of the water, as such, may remain unmoved. How are
we to tell whether it is or not ? Evidently, we must gauge it
either with reference to something which is absolutely immovable, or which at least is unmoved for all practical purposes.
Now, we do not know of any body in the material universe of

[1] Phys., 212ᵃ 20.

which we can say that it is absolutely immovable, but for practical purposes the poles and the centre of the earth are unmoved, and consequently we calculate the place of a body with reference to them. So, S. Thomas says : ' Although this container may move, in so far as it is *this* body, nevertheless as it is considered with respect to the relation which it has to the whole body of the heaven, it is not moved, for any body which succeeds it, has the same order or position with respect to the whole heaven, which the body, which earlier passed away, had.'[1]

Modern Scholastics often distinguish between external and internal place. The former is that of which we have just been speaking, while by the latter they mean the capacity which is circumscribed by the exterior surface of the body, i.e. it is the portion of space which the body occupies, and which exactly corresponds with its real volume. It seems doubtful, however, whether this distinction can be maintained, as it appears that such internal place would not be real.[2] When the word place is used, then, it is to external place that reference is made.

Aristotle distinguishes between the proper and common place of a body : proper place being that which immediately surrounds the thing which is in place, so that it is in contact with it alone ; while common place is that which does not immediately surround the thing, but surrounds it in common with other things ; as in a nest of Chinese boxes, each one containing a smaller one, the proper place of each might be said to be the box next greater than itself, while the common place of all, but the outermost but one, would be the outside box of all.

The accident resulting in a located thing from the fact that it is subject to external place is called ' *ubi* ' or localisation. As to the nature of this accident opinions differ, for some think it is a mere mental relation, and not real at all ; for they think the body must be the same in itself whether it is in one place or another, so that by local motion it acquires

---

[1] IV Phys., Lect. 6, No. 9.
[2] But cf. Nys, *La Notion de l'Espace* (pp. 236–278), who argues at length in favour of this distinction, and the reality of internal place.

nothing but a change of position relatively to other objects. This, indeed, seems to us nowadays the obvious view to take, and accords well with the Cartesian theory of motion mentioned above ; and is probably, as Whitehead suggests, ' the very foundation of the seventeeth century scheme of nature.'[1] Nevertheless, local motion seems to imply more than a mere change of position ; for, supposing, while a body was in motion, all others were to be annihilated ; according to this theory, since it could not change its position relatively to them, its motion would cease : a conclusion which can hardly be accepted since the motion was not caused by the presence of other bodies, and could not therefore be destroyed by their removal. Further, the relation which the located body has to its environment is certainly a real one independent of our thought of it, and consequently requires a real foundation.[2] Now, this foundation cannot be the quantity of the body, as is suggested, for, though it is true that the body is located by means of its quantity, yet it can have different locations while retaining the same quantity. There must, therefore, be, in the body, some additional reality over and above quantity, which is the foundation of this or that localisation, i.e. application of the body to this or that place. For, in so far as contact is made with a second place, a new relationship is acquired by the body. The fact that the foundation of this relation is in the located body, even though the relation is derived from without, owing to the presence of the surrounding bodies, is in no sense a contradiction ; for the foundation and the relation arise simultaneously ; the foundation being the formal cause of the relation, i.e. that by which the relation is constituted, the extrinsic circumscription by the other bodies being the efficient cause of this

---

[1] Whitehead, *Science and the Modern World*, p. 72.

[2] As will be explained more fully later, the Scholastics recognise three elements in a relation : the subject, the term, and the foundation ; all of which, in the case of a real relation, must be real. The subject is that thing *in* which the relation is present, the term that *towards* which it is directed, and the foundation that *by* which the relation is constituted, i.e. the reason why the subject is related to the term. So in the relation of sonship, the subject is the boy who is generated, the term is the parent, and the foundation the fact of being generated. Here, then, the foundation is caused by the act of generation of the parents, while it constitutes the son as standing in a certain relation to them.

foundation. It would, however, be absurd to rush to the
other extreme, and say that this accident was something
absolute, intrinsic to the located body, for it clearly arises as
a result of its quantity being commensurate with those of its
particular surroundings, and hence is something which comes
to it from without, and so is not ' *secundum substantiam, vel
secundum aliquam intrinsecam dispositionem substantiæ* '[1]—
such as quantity or quality—as S. Thomas says repeatedly.
It seems, therefore, that it is a real mode which comes to the
body from without. This theory does not, as the one mentioned above seems to do, render the admission of motion in
a completely empty space impossible, for change of localisation is not here identified with motion, but is considered to be
an effect of it, so that even if there were no localisation, and
consequently no change of it, motion could still continue.[2]

It is worth noticing that the reality of local motion is safe-
guarded by both these theories, since in the first there is a
succession of real contacts, and in the second a connected
succession of real modes by whose means the different real
contacts are effected.

The Scholastics point out that there are several ways in
which a thing may be in place.

First, there is the way of which we have just been speaking,
viz. circumscriptive location, which is predicamental location.
This is the passive circumscription of a body which arises
from its actually being surrounded by a place.

But a thing may also be in place ' not circumscriptively,'
and this either naturally or præternaturally. Naturally
either by operation, i.e. by acting on a place, as an angel
may do ;[3] or by informing a body, which is circumscriptively
in place, as the human soul does. The theologians enumerate
three præternatural modes of being in place, viz. eucharistic-
ally, infernally, and hypostatically.

A thing is said to be definitely in place, if it is so limited to
one place as not to be able to be at the same time in another.
Evidently it is only bodies which are in place circumscriptively, and, as we shall see shortly, they must also be in

---

[1] XII Met. S. Thomas, Lect. 7 (ed. Cathala, 2530).
[2] Cf. Nys, op. cit., pp. 254, 264 f.
[3] *Summa Theol.*, Pars I, Q. 52, a. 1.

place definitively, i.e. they cannot be in two places at once.

Owing to the importance of the subject, we may perhaps be allowed to notice that the body of Christ in the Eucharist is in place neither circumscriptively nor definitively, as is plain from the definitions given. It is only metaphorically that we say that It is in place ; indeed it is only those things which are in place circumscriptively, which are in place properly speaking, so that an angel, or the human soul are only in place metaphorically, in somewhat the same way as when we speak of a discussion or remark being ' in or out of place,'[1]

From what has been said, it will be seen that there is a very close connection between the notions of place and space ; and we are thus naturally led to consider the latter.

## SECTION II. *On Space.*

Although the greatest divergence of opinion is to be found among philosophers as to the nature of space, yet these opinions are linked together by the degree of reality which they attribute to it ; and may be classified under three heads : the theories (1) of those who emphasise this reality, (2) of those who emphasise its ideal character, and (3) of those who preserve the balance between the two. The last group of opinions will have a *prima facie* claim to be preferred as being a mean which preserves the truths pointed out by both the other groups.

The difficulty of the question consists in this, that if we make something real of space in itself, we shall be logically led to say that space without bodies is something real, or that absolute space is something real, which is a purely gratuitous assertion, based on no evidence ; and one, more-over, which would make space itself unintelligible ; since, if all bodies are removed, leaving real space behind, this space must be immaterial. It is, however, the function of space to be the location of bodies, and apart from this function we seem to have no conception of it. It is, moreover, clear that the material cannot be located in the immaterial, and so by

---

[1] Cf. Salmanticenses, *De Angelis*, Vol. IV, pp. 83 ff.

making space real we deprive it of its only meaning, and render it unintelligible. On the other hand, if we say that space is not real, we shall seem to contradict common sense, to speak in a way which is in disagreement with scientific language, and to deprive the material world of its objectivity.

Can these and similar objections on one side, or the other, be met, or must we try to reconcile the two views ? Such is the question to be answered.

I. Turning, then, to the first group of opinions, of those, namely, who insist on the reality of space ; we find among the Greek philosophers some who regarded *space as absolute*.

1. Thus Democritus, and others who took a similar view of nature, taught that space is the vacuum, or a universal receptacle, which is distinct from bodies, but in which they move. Similarly, some Peripatetics taught that space is a kind of immense sphere which surrounds all bodies. Gassendi, in the seventeenth century, reviving the old Atomism, adopted this view of space, but tried to rid it of some of its absurdities, by denying to it the character of absolute necessity, which had been given it, and saying that it has a reality which does not come within our categories, being neither substance nor accident. Locke (1632–1704) also seems to incline to the ultra-realist opinion, which would substantialise space, though his way of speaking is by no means free of ambiguity.[1] He, like Gassendi, suggests that space may be thought of as a substance, granting that ' substance ' be taken in a different sense from that in which we ordinarily use it. The word, he says, has already three different senses as applied to God, spirits, and bodies : why not add a fourth to apply to space ?

If we examine these notions one by one we shall see that all of them involve inconsistencies. So the suggestion that space, the receptacle of bodies, is the vacuum, is untenable, since the bodies are extended, and so their receptacle must be extended also. The vacuum, however, of the Atomists was unextended, and so cannot be space. Even if it were thought of as extended, it would need a further receptacle

---

[1] Cf. *Essay on the Human Understanding*, Bk. II, Ch. XIII, Nos. 5 ff., especially No. 22 ; and Nys, op. cit., pp. 37 ff.

G

or vacuum to contain it, and so we should have an unending series of vacua containing one another, without ever arriving at an ultimate space. This last objection militates equally against Gassendi's view, for whom the receptacle of bodies was extended, and the very reason which, in his opinion, makes it necessary to imagine a first receptacle, viz. that an extended thing must be received in something, would apply with equal force to this receptacle itself, and so on to infinity. Further, this space was thought of as eternal independent being. Such being, however, would be unproduced, and pure act, which is in direct contradiction with the notion of space as the receptacle of bodies, which must necessarily imply a universal potentiality for receiving them.

2. Such views as these seem to deify space, and this idea that space is an attribute of the Deity, is found explicitly in the opinion of Newton and Clarke, though the latter, under the pressure of the objections of Leibniz, modified his original position to some extent. Thus Newton identifies it with God's omnipresence, and Clarke with His immensity. So, in a curious passage, Newton writes : ' Is not the sensory of animals that place to which the sensitive substance is present, and into which the sensible species of things are carried through the nerves and the brain, that there they may be perceived by their immediate presence to that substance ? And these things being rightly dispatched, does it not appear from phenomena that there is a Being incorporeal, living, intelligent, omnipresent, who, in infinite space, as it were in his sensory, sees the things themselves intimately, and thoroughly perceives them, and comprehends them wholly by their immediate presence to himself ; of which things the images only (i.e. on the retina) carried through the organs of sense into our little sensoriums, are then seen and beheld by that which in us perceives and thinks.'[1]  Now, if there is one thing which is clear about the divine attributes, such as omnipresence and immensity, it is that they must be identical with the divine nature, and so an absolute unity. This is in evident conflict with that most fundamental character-

[1] Opticks, pp. 344 ff. (quoted by Burtt, *Metaphysical Foundations of Modern Science*, p. 258).

istic of space which is its extension and divisibility. Moreover, such a theory would lead straight to Pantheism, since space is an attribute of bodies, and so can only be held to be also an attribute of God by Pantheists.

This is, in fact, the view adopted in the pantheistic philosophy of Spinoza. Starting with the Cartesian notion that the nature of bodies consists of their triple extension, he follows him also in asserting that there is only a logical distinction between space and extension. There are, he considers, two aspects in which space is viewed by us. In the first place, we imagine it as composed of parts, and so divisible, and, in fact, divided : its parts being what we call bodies. Secondly, the intellectual consideration of space shows us that it is, in fact, a common reality, viz. substantial extension in three dimensions, which is everywhere the same, absolutely indivisible, and positively infinite. Such an entity can be nothing else than an attribute of God.[1] Now, we cannot concede the second part of this theory, since it is clear that extension implies a non-coincidence of parts, and is therefore essentially divisible.

A theory having marked affinities with those of Newton and Spinoza has recently been evolved by Professor S. Alexander in his work, *Space, Time and Deity*, according to whom the whole universe, whose reality is Space-Time, which is progressively evolving, is to be identified with God.[2] This idea is open to the objections raised against Spinoza, and, in addition, God is represented as progressing or evolving, and, in fact, never coming to be. Such a ' Being ' is evidently imperfect and finite, so that the name God is applied to it equivocally, i.e. in a wholly different sense to that intended by Theists when using the word. Alexander's God is not their God.

II. The Second Group. The Ultra-Subjectivist theories.

1. If the Absolutist views of space thus fail to satisfy us, perhaps we may find a more adequate idea of it among the Subjectivist theories. The first of them to claim our attention is that of Kant. According to him, we cannot know

---

[1] Spinoza, *Ethica*, Pars I, Prop. 15, Scholium.
[2] Vol. II, pp. 428 ff.

whether the external world has those characteristics which we attribute to it, and so whether ' things-in-themselves ' are extended, distant from one another, and so on : all we can say is that they appear to be so to us. Now this spatial appearance might derive either from the things, or from us. Just as to a man crossing to France in a Channel steamer the sea might appear yellow ; and this appearance might be caused either by the flood waters of some river running into it and discolouring it, or to the disturbed state of the man's liver ; so, in the case of space, the spatial appearance might be due either to things sensed being spatial, or to the constitution of our senses ; and Kant argues that we see that this latter supposition is the true one from the fact that space is a general form, which applies universally to the whole material world. Now, the thing-in-itself is singular, and so cannot contain, or transmit to us the universal. Hence this form must be part of the constitution of our minds or senses. What, then, is space ? It is a part of the pattern of our senses, and so Kant calls it an ' *a priori* form of the sensibility.' It is *a priori*, in a way somewhat similar to that in which the shape of a ' castle pudding ' may be said to be given *a priori* : it is that particular shape because of the mould in which it is made. So the senses, having a particular mould (of space and time), turn out the objects marked with this mould or pattern. It is seen to be *a priori*, since it *logically* precedes any sensible experience ; in saying which, Kant wishes it to be clear that he does not think that it really precedes it, as if we could know space before we know sense-objects : but it is present in the sensibility in a similar way to that in which an image on a photographic film may be said to be present in it before the film is developed : as soon as the acids are applied to it the image will come up. Similarly, as soon as the sense-objects are applied to the sensibility, the forms of space and time will, as it were, develop up. Further, he calls it ' pure,' since it is not derived from any experience ; and finally, it is necessary, as being an essential condition of all sensible experience.

The most fundamental criticism of this view is that which shows the inconsistency in Kant's distinction between appearance and reality, between phenomena and things-in-themselves ; for, according to Kant, not only is space phenomenal and *a priori*, but the same is true of the notions of cause and existence, which he calls *a priori* categories of the mind. The reality, therefore, can be neither a cause nor existing. If this be so, we are faced with a contradiction, for our sensations, though not their forms, are in Kant's view caused by the thing in itself ; which must therefore exist. But, according to him, as we said, it can neither exist nor cause, if existence and causality apply only to phenomena. Further, on Kant's theory, it is impossible to give any coherent account of the change and movement which we perceive among bodies. For this movement, even if it is only phenomenal, is at least a real phenomenon which must therefore have some cause. This could only be the *a priori* form of space, or some influence external to the senses. Now, Kant's theory will not admit of either of these explanations of its source ; for, in the first place, the *a priori* form is logically prior to all phenomena, and essentially static, since it is a form of our nature, from which it receives its function of making the phenomena appear as extended in three dimensions, and only three. Hence, though it may imply relative position, it cannot give us *change* of position, direction, distance, etc., which are things quite extraneous to the form of space as such ; which would equally well be preserved in an entirely static world, implying, as it does, nothing more than three-dimensional extension. In the second place, it is even more impossible that the appearance of spatial change should be derived from external influences, for, in this case, the *a priori* character of the space-form would be destroyed.[1]

2. A second view of the ultra-subjectivist type is that of Leibniz, who thought of space as ' something purely relative . . . as an order of coexistences. Space denotes, in terms of possibility, the order of those things which exist at the same time, in so far as they exist together ; leaving on one side

[1] Cf. Nys, op. cit., p. 79. For a detailed criticism of Kant's theory see Pritchard. Kant's *Theory of Knowledge*, Chaps. III and IV, and Nys, Ch. II.

their way of existing. Whenever we see several things together, we are conscious of such an order of the things among themselves.'[1]

Consistently, therefore, with his cosmological theory, according to which the world is composed of unextended monads, he banishes space altogether from reality, and makes of it something purely mental or ideal.[2]

We already noticed one radical defect of this theory, when we showed that it is impossible for the notion, or appearance, of extension—and so of space—to arise in our minds unless there be some spatial extension somewhere in reality : but we may mention here some difficulties which belong peculiarly to this view of space. For, in the first place, the coexistence of things, and *a fortiori* the order of coexistences, presupposes space, since they are said to coexist precisely because they appear to exist together in different parts of space. Consequently, since the order of coexistences presupposes space, it cannot constitute it. In the second place, the attributes of space must apply to the order of coexistences if these two are identical. Now, space is said to be full, empty, and equal to the located thing, none of which predicates can be applied to the order of coexistences, since an order, or relation, cannot be full, empty or equal. In the third place, things which coexist must be bound together by some common link, which cannot be true of the Leibnizian coexistents, seeing that they are simple monads without extension. In Leibniz's view the monads do not interact in any way, but are like the puppets in a marionette show, which appear to bow and speak to one another, but are, in fact, controlled entirely by the showman : they are not related to one another, but to the man behind the scenes. In a similar way, the monads have no connection with one another, but only with God, who destined them by pre-established harmony to act in a certain way. So there is no common link between them, and they cannot be said, in any direct sense, to coexist. Leibniz, in fact, recognised the gravity of this difficulty, and tried to meet it—and other cognate ones—by his elusive doctrine of

---

[1] Correspondence with Clarke, third letter of Leibniz, No. 4.
[2] Cf. Nys, op. cit., pp. 121 f. Wildon Carr, *Leibniz*, pp. 156 ff.

the ' *vinculum substantiale*,' a real substantial link, and a reality other than the monads, from which alone continuity is said to arise. This seems rather to add to the difficulty, than diminish it, since it is not easy to see how it can be reconciled with the independence of the monads, which is a central doctrine of Leibnizianism. The notion of the *vinculum substantiale* was introduced in an attempt to reconcile his theory with the Scholastic idea that bodies, e.g. of animals, are unities *per se*, not mere aggregates.[1]

Lastly, space would still be preserved if there were only one body in the world ; but, evidently, in this case, there would be no order of coexistences, and consequently these cannot be identified.

III. The Intermediate Theories. We now turn to the intermediate theories, which make space neither a reality on its own account, nor yet wholly ideal.

1. The first of these is the view of Descartes, Balmes, and Palmieri, which identifies space with extension. They say that when we think of space, we abstract from the extension of bodies, and give to space a generic unity, without division, so that we can speak of bodies moving *in space*. Consequently, our notion of space has no counterpart in nature, but is nevertheless based on something found in nature, viz. the extension of bodies.

Hence, space is, according to these philosophers, abstract extension. We have called this an intermediate view, and indeed it does seem to try and mediate between the extreme realists and the extreme idealists. Unfortunately, however, like so many peacemakers, it only succeeds in receiving the blows which the rivals aim at one another. For, if space be identical with corporeal extension, it will certainly be real, and in Descartes' system, an absolute reality ; since there can never be a vacuum ; and so matter must be indefinitely extended. Space, then, from this point of view, will be an absolute, infinite, real being, and open to all the attacks which the idealists make on the ultra-real views of space, such as those of Clarke and Spinoza. On the other hand,

---

[1] Cf. *Epistola ad Patrem des Bosses*, 29 May, 1716 ; and Latta, *Monadology*, etc., pp. 118 ff. (Oxford Univ. Press.)

since this theory denies that our conception of space corresponds to anything found in nature, it seems to make of space something purely mental, and so falls a victim to the blows which the realists aim at the idealists, such as Leibniz or Kant. Apart from the awkward position in which it finds itself, as combining the disadvantages of both the other theories, the notion that space is to be *identified* with extension will not bear investigation, for though it is true that there are many characteristics, such as stretching out, being measurable, divisible, and so on, which belong both to space and extension, yet space has at least one characteristic which is contrary to that of extension ; for we conceive of space as that which is filled and occupied by bodies, while extension is that by means of which a body fills or occupies space. Consequently, far from being formally identified, space and extension are formally opposed, as the filled and the filler, the occupied and the occupier. The truth, therefore, is that these two are not identical, but that the notion of space includes that of extension.

2. The second of these intermediate opinions is that of Suarez and many other Scholastics, as de Backer, Dario, and others, according to whom space is a logical being with a real foundation. They conceive it, in itself, as an empty receptacle which is capable of containing bodies, real space being that portion of absolute space which is occupied by real bodies. This opinion, like the last, is attacked from two sides ; since Nys,[1] as it seems justly, accuses it of taking away all reality from space, while others say that it gives it too much. For, according to Suarez, absolute space is not real, and what is called real space in this theory is merely a portion of this absolute or imaginary space ; and so will be as ideal as it is, since the portions of such ideal space cannot become real from the mere fact that real bodies are present in them, nor from any of their properties, since in this view the parts of space are carefully distinguished from any of the realities of the bodies which occupy them. Space, then, on this view, appears to remain a purely ideal entity, a conception which seems irreconcilable with the notion of space

[1] Cf. Nys, op. cit., pp. 177 ff.

as the receptacle of bodies, and the field of their real motion.

On the other hand, Hoenen maintains that the theory is ultra-realist, as making a reality of absolute or imaginary space, since, in this opinion, it is held that a single body would have in itself a determinate localisation in space, irrespective of any extrinsic relations to others, so that even if there were only one body in the world, it would be localised in space ; and so could, properly speaking, have local motion through the variation of this intrinsic location.[1] There is, in fact, an inconsistency in this theory, for either absolute space must be allowed to be real, in which case Hoenen's criticism is justified ; or else, as is, in fact, done by those who hold this view, its reality must be denied, and it then becomes impossible to say that a single body will of itself be really present in any part of it ; and space will be something wholly ideal. Since, then, absolute space is not allowed to be real, it seems that the criticism of Nys is justified.

3. We now pass to the opinion which regards space as the interval between bodies. Even here we have a divergence of views, for some hold that space is the interval between the confines of a single body, others that it is constituted by the relation of distance which holds between several bodies, which relation rests on the accidents which localise these bodies. The latter is the view of Nys, and can be explained as follows :

(a) Since all are agreed in conceiving space as the receptacle of real bodies, we start our investigation with this conception. Now, it seems clear that such a receptacle must be a three-dimensional relation of distance containing them, i.e. a three-dimensional relation of distance which connects the related terms ; and so is such a relation between real bodies, the foundations of this relation being the localising accidents which give to the bodies a certain situation in the universe. That the receptacle must be three-dimensional is clear, since it must be able to contain the bodies, which are themselves three-dimensional. This condition is not only the necessary one for such a receptacle, it is also sufficient, since

[1] Cf. Hoenen, *Cosmologia*, pp. 109 f.

to contain or surround a body requires nothing but such extension, the composition of the receptacle in other ways being irrelevant.[1]

Apart, however, from the difficulty, touched on when we were dealing with place, of allowing that the accidents which localise a body are something which it has of itself intrinsically, and which are not derived from its relation to others (and of such a kind are supposed to be the foundations of the relation of distance in this theory) there is another difficulty in it, inasmuch as it would follow from it that a single body was not in space, which seems to be at variance with the common view of space, and our ordinary expressions with regard to it, as when we say : ' This street ' or ' this room is spacious.' To this it might perhaps be replied that though we may imagine a single body to be in space, yet, in fact, considering the essential elements of the notion of space, viz. that it is a receptacle, and a distance capable of being traversed, neither of these conditions would be fulfilled in the case of a single body : for, being single, it could not be received in anything, since there is nothing else, and a thing cannot be received in itself ; nor would the distance included between its limits be capable of being traversed, for it would either have to be traversed by some body other than itself, which is impossible, since, by hypothesis, no other body exists, or else by some part of itself, in which case the body would be broken up and would no longer be one body. Neither of these replies is, however, really satisfactory, for even though a single body could not be actually traversed owing to the absence of anything to traverse it, yet this evidently arises from something extrinsic, and not essential to the body itself, which, as being extended, still retains its capacity for being traversed. So it would be as absurd to say that an absolute desert was incapable of being traversed because there was nothing to traverse it ; as that a man living alone in a hermitage had lost the power of speech because he had no one to talk to. Further, with regard to the non-fulfilment of the second necessary condition, viz. that it must be received in something, we notice that its

[1] Cf. Nys, op. cit., pp. 216–287.

outside surface would afford a receptacle for it ; for this, though only modally distinct from the thing itself, is yet sufficiently distinct for our purpose, since this surface can be considered as a container instead of part of the content ; and we are all agreed that space is not a receptacle, which is a reality, on its own account, apart from the bodies which it contains.

(b) We turn, therefore, to the second way of regarding space as an interval of distance. This is that space is formally constituted by the dimensions of the containing body in so far as the relation of distance is considered in them. This theory follows directly from the idea of space as the receptacle of bodies ; since a receptacle of a body is that whose dimensions are of sufficient extent to circumscribe it : so that space will be constituted by the dimensions of the containing body, considered as enclosing an extension, i.e. precisely with reference to the relation of extension.

What may be considered to be a serious objection to this theory is that it makes the existence of the void not only physically, but even metaphysically impossible ; for it is clear that a body cannot contain nothing ; since to assert this would be equivalent to saying that it does not contain— it is not a receptacle—which is to deny the initial concept of space. Hence, in a void space would vanish, and with space distance. So, if two bodies were separated by a void, they would be separated by no distance, and so would not be separated ; so that the existence of a void becomes metaphysically impossible.

### On the Void.

This question of the void has been one of the most constantly discussed problems in the history of natural philosophy, and it is therefore worth while examining it a little more fully. Both Plato and Aristotle rejected the idea that there is, in fact, any empty space in the world : and the latter seems to have regarded it as impossible that there should be. Most of his arguments are based on his mistaken idea of ' natural movement ' ; according to which ' light ' and ' heavy ' are qualities belonging to different kinds of bodies, so that some bodies naturally move upwards, others downwards ; and both these, and his other, arguments are all directed to show that it is *physically* impossible that there should be a vacuum. S. Thomas, as it seems, shared these views, and even added one reason which might be taken to mean that he regarded a vacuum as metaphysically impossible, for he says : ' *Cum de ratione vacui sit, quod sit spatium corporis præter corpora, sequitur quod vacuum non sit* '[1]—in other words, the notion of a vacuum is self-contradictory. Since, however, in the whole of this section, the view of the Platonists, which he regards as mistaken, is being considered, it is not clear that this statement should be taken absolutely, but it may be only ' *ad hominem.*' The absolute impossibility of a vacuum was, without doubt, of necessity maintained by Descartes, since he identifies extension with body, so that any extension will be *ipso facto* corporeal. He was followed in this view by Spinoza and Balmes, and also by Leibniz, though for a different reason.[2]

Apart from the false Cartesian presuppositions as to the nature of body, it is clear that if the material universe is finite, an hypothesis which is faced by no metaphysical contradiction, there must be a certain kind of void outside it, which some call a negative void ; so that a void is possible, absolutely speaking. The discussion here, however, is concerned with the possibility of a void within the confines of the material universe, and regarding the matter without prejudice, there seems to be no conclusive reason for saying that such a void is impossible ; since it would only imply that there should be no matter within a certain area, this area remaining, nevertheless, surrounded by bodies. Against this it is argued : (1) that in this case the interior surfaces of the body (or bodies) which surrounded the void would come together, or (2) if not, at least there would be no determinate distance across the void. The first consequence clearly does not follow, since bodies are not kept apart by the matter which separates them, but simply are apart by being localised at different points in space. Neither is the second a necessary consequence of a void, for since, if there was one

[1] IV Phys., Lect. 10, No. 8.    [2] Cf. Nys, op. cit., p. 386.

there would be a determinate circumference round it, there would also be a determinate distance diametrically across it. We are, then, led to the conclusion that an internal void is possible.

Whether there is, in fact, any void within the material universe is a question which is even less easily answered. Generally speaking, physicists from the time of Aristotle down to the present day have agreed in saying that there is not. The pre-Newtonian scientists held this opinion, either on the grounds put forward by Aristotle, or later, on the basis of the Cartesian mechanics. Even when this latter view was not accepted in its entirety, a void was rejected, as it was by Newton, on the ground of the impossibility of action at a distance. Consequently, modern scientists have supposed that there is an all-pervading ether, which acts as the carrier of light, and electro-magnetic, waves. Even though, in the universe of Einstein, the hypothesis of a luminiferous ether is no longer necessary, its place will be taken by Space-Time. It would, nevertheless, be unwise to build up a philosophical theory on the basis of these specu-lations, and therefore rash to assert, on their authority, that there is no void in the material universe. In any case, it seems clear that a theory which makes the void metaphysic-ally impossible cannot be regarded as a satisfactory account of the nature of space. If, then, the second view, given above, is to be taken literally, it is ruled out ; and it seems that a modification of the first view is required. We wish, then, to construct a theory which will allow of a single body (if there were only one in the universe) being spatial or in space, since there seems to be no valid reason for denying that it would be : and, secondly, to eliminate the intrinsic localising accidents which, according to the first theory, are the foundations of the relation of distance which constitutes space, while admitting with this theory, or at least not excluding, the possibility of a vacuum. To satisfy these conditions, we shall refuse to say that space is a relation of distance between several bodies, and at the same time admit that it is a relation, not something absolute, as the second theory maintains. It will, therefore, be a relation which will

hold as well in a single body as in several.  Moreover, there
is no doubt that the basis of our concept of space is extension.
Hence, it will be a relation of extension or distance.  Now, it
is clear that the only relation of distance which is to be found
in a single body is that between its extremities ;  and space
being conceived as the receptacle of body, it will be, as it
were, an envelope enclosing the extremities of the body, and
will be formally constituted by the three-dimensional relation of distance between the extremities of real body.  Thus,
from the point of view of the concept which we form of it,
space will be distinct from the body which it encloses, though,
in fact, their extent will be the same, and an empty space
will be identical in extent with the interior dimensions of the
bodies which enclose it.  This explanation thus seems to
include all the data which we have as to the nature of space,
for it will be a receptacle of real bodies, it will be found as the
container of a single body, and empty space will be not
impossible ;  being constituted by the relation of distance
between the extremities of the real body or bodies which
enclose it.  The space of a single body (if there were only
one) would be constituted by the relation of distance between
its own extremities, considered ideally as enveloping or containing it.  It is clear that, if this view be taken, space will
be a logical being, not a reality on its own account ;  having,
nevertheless, a basis in reality, since there is, in nature, real
extension, or continuous quantity.  The relation of distance,
as conceived of, is not however found in nature, and is the
absence of contact, a condition which is verified both in a
vacuum and a plenum.  That space is indeed such a logical
being is very generally held by Scholastics.

SECTION III.    *On the Occupation of Space.*

(*a*)  *On Impenetrability.*

If one body occupies a portion of space in such a way as
to fill it, it seems clear that it will exclude another from
occupying the same portion.  We are familiar enough with
such impenetrability in ordinary life, for we know that we
cannot occupy the same place as another man, or any other
solid object.  The question, considered philosophically, is,

however, much wider than this, since it is the question whether it is possible for two bodies to occupy the same place at the same time, i.e. whether compenetration is possible. Thus, we are not concerned with what is usually known as penetrability, which occurs when one body enters into the pores or interstices of another, as when a sponge is filled with water ; for, in this case, the body which is penetrated does not occupy the space of its interstices, and therefore there is no question of two bodies occupying the same place. Nor is our question confined to any particular kind of bodies, such as solids or liquids, but is quite general, relating to any kind of bodies.[1]

As a preliminary to dealing with the possibility of compenetration, something must be said as to the question of fact ; viz. whether it is a fact that any matter is continuous, for if it is not, the whole question of the possibility of compenetration falls to the ground, since it is clear that if no body has continuous extension, none will occupy a place, so that we cannot ask whether any other can occupy it at the same time.

That the question comes to be asked at all is due to current physical theories, in which matter is regarded as composed of discontinuous molecules, molecules of discontinuous atoms, atoms of discontinuous electrons and protons. The electrons within the atom are said to be such that they cannot have both velocity and position in an exact sense.[2] It seems, therefore, that they cannot have continuous extension, and the same would be true, no doubt, of the nucleus ; and so, in this theory, all continuous extension appears to be taken away from the world.[3] On the other hand, we have a theory which is the antithesis of this, and asserts that all through the universe there is an absolutely continuous ether which

---

[1] Fr. McWilliams in his *Cosmology* (p. 94) says that ' compenetration . . . means the presence together of two *absolutely solid* bodies in the same place.' If this were to be taken to mean that the question is confined to solids, as opposed to liquids or gases, it would no doubt be a mistake. But the context seems to show that his meaning is that the question does not relate to solids in this sense, but to continuous bodies, or, to the parts of discontinuous, or porous ones, which are continuous.

[2] Eddington, *Nature of the Physical World*, pp. 220 ff.

[3] Cf. Whitehead, *Science and the Modern World*, pp. 122 ff.

is thought of as the carrier of light, and electro-magnetic waves. This ether pervades the atom, and even the nucleus and electron of which the atom is composed. These, then, may be either knots or coagulations in the ether itself, in which case there would be only one body in the world—the ether—and so no chance of compenetration ; or else they may be bodies other than the ether, in which case compenetration is a fact. Science, therefore, in different moods, or in accordance with different theories, seems to say : (1) that the question of compenetration is illegitimate, since there are no extended bodies, i.e. having continuous extension, (2) that it cannot occur, since there is one continuously extended body, and only one, and (3) that it does occur. The apparent contradictions here are reconciled by taking now one view of matter, now another ; and by denying material character to the ether.[1] This last denial would clear up the affair, if we knew what matter itself is, for it is clear that we cannot attach any meaning to the statement : ' the ether is not material,' unless we know what the predicate means. Now, this is just what we do not know ; and we therefore have to be content to use that theory which suits us best, i.e. which is simplest, in investigating any particular class of phenomena. But whatever may be the divergences of view as to the nature of matter and the ether, all the theories agree in making the elements of matter separate from one another in space, i.e. in saying that there is a distance or extension between them. Now, it is clear that if the ether were supposed to be material, we should have a number of continuously extended portions of it ; and so some continuous body in the universe ; and if it is not material, it is impossible to measure it by physical means, since all our measuring instruments are, of necessity, material ; so that it would be illegitimate to assert that it is extended. It seems to be a curious position to deny extension to material objects which can be measured, and to assert it of an immaterial one which cannot. From the point of view of physics, therefore, the position is not unsatisfactory, for we can use any hypothesis which suits us at the

[1] Cf. Eddington, op. cit., pp. 31 f.

moment ; but from the point of view of philosophy, if these hypotheses are to be taken as telling us of the nature of bodies, it is intolerable, and lands us in contradictions : and our only course would be to deny any extension at all to the physical world ; since it is absurd to assert that unextended points, having no position, are separated from one another in space. If bodies, or their elements, are not extended, the spaces between them cannot be either. In this case, however, we are faced with the insuperable difficulty of explaining the illusion of extension, as it is then thought to be, and all the other difficulties of the Leibnizian theory. We are therefore compelled to reject the notion that there is no extension in the world, and to assert the continuous extension of both simple and compound bodies, unless such extension can be shown not to exist in a particular case. In doing so, we shall not be rejecting the scientific theories, as scientific, i.e. as giving the simplest and most comprehensive account of phenomena yet discovered, but we shall be reject-ing them as philosophical ones, which they were never intended to be : and we do so for the excellent reason that they are, in this sense, contradictory in themselves, and lead to impossible conclusions. If it be true, then, that some bodies have continuous extension, it is possible to ask whether two of them can occupy, i.e. make their dimensions exactly correspond with the same place at the same time. That they actually do so, and therefore, that it is possible for them to do so, is held by some scientists, as Lodge, who con-sider that the ether is a kind of matter which permeates other bodies ;[1] but there is here almost certainly some confusion of ideas. Among philosophers, apart from the Dynamists, who deny the legitimacy of the question, none hold that bodies actually do compenetrate, and almost all that it is in some way, either physically or metaphysically, impossible for them to do so.

Descartes and his school necessarily thought that it is metaphysically impossible, for, if the nature of body is

[1] Cf. Lodge, *Ether and Reality*, Ch. II, pp. 38 ff. Though he seems to deny that the ether is ' matter,' yet he says that material particles are probably formed out of it. So the ether is other than the particles, and yet the particles consist of ether.

H

extension, where there is a single extension there must be a single body, so that two bodies occupying the same place would *ipso facto* be one : in other words, the supposition is unthinkable.

Locke thinks it physically impossible, since ' this resistance, whereby it ' (i.e. a body) ' keeps other bodies out of the space which it possesses, is so great, that no force, how great soever, can surmount it.'[1]

Though among Scholastics there is general agreement as to the possibility, absolutely speaking, of compenetration, there is considerable difference of opinion as to the nature of that property of bodies which makes them naturally impenetrable. Some consider it to be an active force, as Palmieri and Hoenen, others as a simple consequence of continuous extension ; and this latter opinion is that of the majority, following S. Thomas. Indeed, this view seems much more consonant both with common sense and the present state of knowledge than the other ; with common sense, since it is difficult to see how a body can preserve an unbroken continuity of its boundaries if another one, which is also continuous, forces its way into it ; and with our knowledge of nature, for in fact no compenetration is known in nature, but only the passage of small bodies through the pores of other bodies, and, moreover, the smallest scientific bodies, atoms and electrons ($\alpha$-*particles*, etc.) are said to vary in their power of penetration. So the $\alpha$, $\beta$, and $\gamma$ rays are progressively more penetrating, and this in proportion as they possess more of the character of waves, and less of corpuscles. This would seem to accord better with the idea that the cause of impenetrability is the corpuscular or continuous nature of a body rather than the activity exerted by the body to be penetrated.

Whatever interpretation is to be put upon the facts, in so far as they are known, philosophical considerations seem clearly to indicate that impenetrability naturally results from the extension of bodies ; since if, as we have seen, it is

---

[1] Locke, *An Essay concerning Human Understanding*, Bk. II, Ch. IV Sect. 3. Fr. Dario, S.J., and Fr. Hugon, O.P., represent Locke as holding it to be metaphysically impossible, but this does not seem to be the case. *Vide* Dario, *Cosmologia*, p. 143 ; Hugon, *Cursus Phil.*, Vol. II, p. 197.

the function of quantity to give material substance parts outside parts, it will naturally follow that one part will be outside the place of another. Now, this relationship of the parts of quantity with regard to place is evidently something extrinsic to quantity itself, since the nature of quantity is merely to have parts outside parts in the whole, without reference to place. Consequently, absolutely speaking, no contradiction is involved in this natural consequence of quantity, which is impenetrability, being removed ; for the essential character of quantity, the having parts outside parts would still remain, even though the parts of the quantities of the two bodies would occupy the same place. Hence compenetration, though naturally impossible, is not metaphysically so, and consequently could be effected by an agent who had sufficient power, such as God ; granted that the distinction of the bodies, which is ordinarily secured by distinction of place, could be preserved ; a condition which is capable of fulfilment in the case of bodies of different material constitution ; though impossible for purely geometrical volumes, which, if equal, can only be distinguished by position.

## (b) On Multilocation.

If two bodies cannot naturally be in one place together ; what is to be said on the question whether one body can be in two or more places simultaneously ? Is such multilocation possible ? This question admits of solution much more easily than the last. We must bear in mind the distinction made above (pp. 81 f.) between circumscriptive and non-circumscriptive presence in a place. That non-circumscriptive presence (which, as we have seen, is only analogically called location) by a thing in several places at once, is possible, is universally admitted, for there is clearly no contradiction involved in a body being circumscriptively in one place, and yet joined to another in some other way. With regard to circumscriptive presence, on the contrary, there is a difference of opinion, for Suarez holds that it is not absolutely or metaphysically impossible, in which view he is followed by Dario, among recent writers. The opinion of S. Thomas is quite clear, since he says plainly that bilocation involves a contradiction, which is to say that it is metaphysically impossible.[1]  The reason for this latter view seems absolutely convincing, since it is quite impossible for a thing, while retaining its own dimensions to be twice, or three times, as large as it is. That this would be the case, if a body were circumscriptively in more than one place at the same time, is clear, since circumscriptive location is brought about by the dimensions of the located body corresponding with those of the containing one ;  so that if a body were in several places at once, its dimensions would correspond with those of several containing bodies at once ;  and its dimension, say A, would be at the same time A + B, . . . which is contrary to the principle of identity.  If we want to bring this vividly before the imagination, we may picture a man sitting in two contiguous places at once.  The space occupied by him would thus be double what it was when he was sitting in the usual way, and yet his dimensions would remain the same, and so could not occupy more space than they did before.  Without swelling out he is twice as big, which is absurd.

[1] Quodlibet III, Arts. 1 and 2 ;  IV Sent. dist. XLIV, Q. 2, a, 2, sol. 3, ad 4um.

# CHAPTER VII

## THE LIMITS OF QUANTITY

The Infinite—Its Kinds—The Possibility of Actually Infinite
Quantity—Of an Actually Infinite Multitude.

ONE question still remains to be discussed with reference to
quantity, viz. whether it is necessarily limited, or is it
possible for it to be infinite ; for the infinite is that which
has no term or limit. In order to grasp the exact bearing of
this question, we must first see the various ways in which
this term ' infinite ' can be understood.

1. So the Scholastics distinguish in the first place between
the *privative* and *negative* infinite, the former being that
which, though capable of being terminated, yet is not actually
terminated ; while the latter is that which is incapable of
being terminated ; which incapacity may be due to its entire
perfection, when we have what is sometimes known as the
positive infinite (or to its imperfection).

2. Again, they divide the infinite into the *categorematical*
and *syncategorematical*. The first is that which is unlimited
in act, and so is called the actual infinite ; and the second,
that which is capable of receiving one act after another
without end. So it is finite in act, and infinite potentially
only, and is called the potential infinite, or the indefinite.

3. A third division is into the infinite *simply speaking*,
and in some particular respect (*secundum quid*). The infinite
simply speaking is that which is altogether unlimited, and
possesses every possible perfection. It is known also as the
absolute infinite. The infinite *secundum quid* is that which
in some direction has no term, and thus possesses some particular perfection in an unlimited degree. This is also called
the relative infinite.

The question we are asking here is whether it is possible
to have an actual infinite with respect to quantity.

That the syncategorematical infinite, both in magnitude
and multitude, is possible, is sufficiently clear, for no reason
can be assigned why we should stop at any particular magnitude in a series, and say there could not be a greater ; and the
same applies to a series of individuals—there could always
be one more ; and we have seen, too, that the continuum is
divisible to infinity.  Our question, therefore, is confined to
the possibility of the categorematical infinite.

Aristotle defines the privative infinite, of which we are
here speaking, as follows : ἄπειρόν μὲν οὖν ἐστιν οὗ χατὰ
ποσὸν λαμβάνουσιν αἰεί τι λαβεῖν ἔστιν ἔξω (207ᵃ7),[1] which
may be rendered : ' so then the infinite is that of which
any quantity being taken, there always remains something to be taken outside ' (this quantity) ; a definition
which is approved of by S. Thomas, who rejects with
Aristotle the definition of infinity which makes it ' that
outside which there is nothing ' : since what is essential to
infinity is that it should be inexhaustible, not that there
should be nothing greater than it.  It has been suggested[2]
that this is rather the definition of the indefinite, but this
does not seem to be the case, for in the indefinite, when a part
has been taken, there does not remain something more to be
taken, but only something potential ; and it is that which is
potentially, not actually, inexhaustible.

There is no general agreement as to the possibility of an
actually infinite magnitude and multitude within the genus of
quantity, but the majority of Scholastics following Aristotle
and S. Thomas deny the possibility of either.

(a) That an actually infinite discrete quantity, or number,
is impossible, is easily seen, since every actual number is
closed by its last unit, for if it had not a last unit, it would
not be actual but potential ; as the series of ordinal numbers
1, 2, 3, 4, etc. . . . n. is a potential whole, not an actual
one ; and so is potentially infinite, or indefinite, not actually
infinite.  What is actually infinite cannot be closed by a last
unit, or it would not be infinite, and consequently no number
can be actually infinite.

[1] Cf. S. Thomas in III Phys., Lect. 11.
[2] Vide Dario, Cosmologia, p. 114.

(*b*) Turning to the question of an actually infinite continuous quantity, or magnitude, we notice that this might be an attribute either of natural or mathematical body. But it can be seen that the supposition that either has such an attribute leads to contradiction.

1. Considering natural body, we see that its quantity is an intrinsic accident, which will therefore take its rise from its substantial form, since it is this which gives a thing its intrinsic nature. Now, it is clear that every natural body, when it is actual, will have a certain determined substantial form, since form is its act, and that a determined form cannot be the source of what is not determined, but infinite. Hence, no natural body can have an actually infinite extension or quantity.

2. Just as natural body, when actual, has a certain determined form, so has mathematical body, though, in this case, the form is its shape. Now, shape is the outline of the mathematical figure, and is therefore its termination or boundary. Consequently, every mathematical body is terminated and finite, and the supposition that it is not, is in contradiction with the very notion of mathematical body.[1]

We see, then, that it is impossible to find actual infinity either in number (multitude within the genus of quantity), or in magnitude.

Though, strictly speaking, we are here concerned only with the possibility of an actually infinite quantity ; since we have spoken several times of multitude within the genus of quantity, it is implied that we might have a multitude outside that genus, and the question suggests itself whether such a multitude could be actually infinite ; so that it is convenient to discuss it here.

By a multitude we mean a collection of distinct beings ; if these are quantitative, it will be a multitude within the genus of quantity ; if not, it will be outside it. Now, quantity is an accident found only in material substances, so that a collection of quantitative beings will be a collection of material ones. Hence, the question here asked is whether we can

[1] Cf. S. Thomas, *Summa Theol.*, Pars I, Q. 7, a. 3.

have a collection of immaterial beings which is actually infinite.

The earlier Thomists, as Capreolus,[1] affirm that the notion of an actually infinite multitude involves an intrinsic contradiction ; and this seems to have been the generally accepted view among the great Thomist writers, such as John of S. Thomas ;[2] though there is always much doubt whether they are not speaking only of quantitative multitude. In any case many recent writers, as Hugon,[3] are definitely opposed to the possibility of any kind of actually infinite multitude. Nevertheless, the contrary view has lately begun to find favour, as with Mercier,[4] Nys,[5] Remer,[6] and Geny.

The opinion of S. Thomas is not altogether clear, but it seems that we can trace a development of his thought in this matter. In the *Summa* he denies the possibility of an actually infinite multitude.[7] This was written[8] in the years 1267–1268. Nevertheless, the argument on which he founds this assertion is pronounced by him, two years earlier, in his commentary on the Physics (III Phys., Lect. 8, *circa* 1265) to be a probable one only. Thus it is not surprising to find that in the *Questiones Quodlibetales* (IX, a. 1, XII, a. 2), written in 1264–1268, he distinguishes between the absolute and ordinated power of God, and seems to allow that, with respect to the former, an actually infinite multitude is not impossible, though he says that the view which denies its possibility ' seems truer.' Finally, in the essay *De Æternitate Mundi* (1270), he absolutely affirms that no proof of the impossibility of an actually infinite multitude has yet been given : ' *Et tamen non est adhuc demonstratum quod Deus non possit facere infinita esse in actu.*' With regard to the statements in the *Summa*, we may perhaps apply to them the distinction made in the *Quodlibets*, and say that they ' should

---

[1] *Capreolus* (ed. Paban-Pégues), Vol. II, p. 537.
[2] John of S. Thomas, *Cursus Phil. Phil. Nat.*, Part I, Q. 15, a. 3.
[3] Hugon, *Cursus Phil.*, Vol. V, pp. 193 ff.
[4] Mercier, *Métaphysique Générale*, pp. 193 ff.
[5] Nys, *La notion d'Espace*, pp. 335 ff.
[6] Remer and Geny, *Cosmologia*, Nos. 119 ff.
[7] *Summa Theol.*, Pars I, Q. 7, a. 4 ; Pars I, Q. 7, a. 3, ad 4um ; I.46,2, ad 6 and 7.
[8] The chronology of these writings is that of Mandonnet, *Bibliographie Thomiste*, pp. xii ff.

be understood not absolutely, having regard to nothing but the power of God which is limited only by the principle of contradiction, but bearing in mind the normal conditions of quantitative beings, and the action of God, which pre-supposes the concord or harmony of all His attributes.'[1]

The chief argument against the possibility of an actually infinite multitude is that such a multitude could not be added to, being infinite, and yet since it is actually infinite, it must contain a definite number of individuals, otherwise it would be only potentially infinite, not actually so ; it would be indefinite. If, however, it contains a definite number of individuals, we could always add one more ; so that it both could and could not be added to, which is absurd. Further, if we supposed that there existed an actually infinite multi-tude of spiritual beings, there would be a still greater multi-tude of their thoughts, volitions, etc., so that we should have two infinities of which one was greater than the other ; so that the lesser could not be infinite. The idea, then, of an actually infinite multitude is, it is argued, self-contradictory ; since such a multitude, though infinite, must contain a definite, i.e. a limited or finite, number of individuals.

The fallacy of this argument seems to be that we are not here dealing with individuals which are numerable, and con-sequently the idea of number introduced into the argument is out of place.

In favour of the possibility it is argued :

1. That the ideas of infinite and multitude are not contra-dictory ; since the second implies only a collection of dis-tinct individuals, while the first denies that this collection has any limits.

2. God knows all possible things, actually and distinctly. There is, however, an infinity of possibles, so that God knows an actually infinite multitude, distinctly and actually.

3. If creation from eternity is possible, there seems to be no reason why there should not be an actual infinity of creatures. This series would be infinite *a parte ante*, though limited *a parte post*, i.e. at the ' now ' ; just as the series of our thoughts and volitions, on the hypothesis of individual

[1] Pégues, *Commentaire Littérale de la Somme Théol.* in I.,7,3, and 4.

immortality, is infinite *a parte post*, though limited *a parte ante*, if our souls were created at our conception.

Whatever is to be said on this difficult problem, we must certainly avoid confusing multitude with number. As Cardinal Mercier says : ' The question of the possibility of an infinite multitude is certainly open to dispute, but the debate cannot be cut short by the summary consideration that every collection of unities is essentially finite. To confuse multitude and number is to solve the question by begging it.'[1]

Note : S. Thomas remarks in the *Contra Gentiles* (Bk. II, Ch. 81) that Aristotle in the *Physics* (III Phys, V, 13 ff. : S. Th. Lect, 9), and in the *De Cœlo et Mundo* (I *De Cœlo*, V ff. ; S. Th. Lect. 9 ff.), proves that there is no actually infinite multitude of corporeal beings, but not that there is none of incorporeal ones. This was written between 1258 and 1260.

[1] Mercier, *Métaphysique Générale*, p. 196.

# CHAPTER VIII

## THE QUALITY OF BODIES, OR MOTION

The Nature of Motion—Action at a Distance—The Nature of
Gravitational Action.

SECTION I. *On the Nature of Motion.*

AFTER the consideration of the quantity of bodies, we now
turn to that of their common quality, which is change. The
word 'motion' was used by Aristotle and S. Thomas to
express this; but its signification is evidently not the same
as that of mutation, or the transit from one state to another,
for mutation may be either intrinsic or extrinsic; and in
both cases there are some kinds of mutation which cannot
properly be called motions. For extrinsic mutation may be
either metaphysical, as creation and annihilation, which are
not motions properly speaking, since in both there is only
one term: or physical. In this latter case the change may
be either substantial or accidental; the first being of two
kinds: generation and corruption; while the second
embraces both instantaneous change, which is accidental
generation and corruption, and which again, not being continuous is not motion properly so called; as well as successive, which includes local motion, alteration, and increase (or
growth).

Motion, in the sense of successive physical mutation, is
defined by Aristotle as 'the act of that which is in potency
as such.'[1] Obviously, when a thing is merely in potency to
something it has not begun to change; when it is actually
something, it has ceased to change, if it ever has changed;
so that in order that it may be in motion it must be neither
wholly actual, nor wholly potential, but in some intermediate

---

[1] III Phys., 1; 201ª10.

state, i.e. will be the actualisation of that which is in potency, or of the potential. But this is not sufficient for actual present change, for it may have begun a motion towards some term, and never attained it, but have stopped half-way. In this case, though it is in potency to the term, and in process of being actualised, it is not changing. Hence, the words ' as such ' are added in the definition, meaning that the potency is being actualised, or is actually tending to some further act.[1]

Now motion, which is confined, strictly speaking, to that kind of change which is successive—since, as S. Thomas says,[2] it requires time—is always produced by some agent. So we are led to the consideration of action, of which the correlative is called ' passion.' Action, moreover, is of two kinds : immanent, whose source and term are in the agent, and transeunt, which produces an effect in something other than the agent.

There was, in the Middle Ages, a vigorous dispute as to the subject of action, some maintaining that action was in the agent, others that it was in the thing acted on—the patient ; the first view being held by the Scotists, Cajetan, and others ; the second by the majority of Thomists, such as Capreolus, and by Suarez. It is not necessary for us to enter in detail into this discussion, which seems to be largely a controversy about words and phrases ; since Scholastics now generally agree that the contending views can be recon-ciled, and all the factors of the situation satisfactorily accounted for, by saying that there are in action two form-alities, one by which the agent is actuated, and another which is in the term, and actualises the patient ; so that the complete formula, with regard to the subject of action, will be that action is initially in the agent, and completely in the patient. It is, in fact, clear that the agent is the cause of action, and originates it ; and no less clear that it is the patient which is altered, and so, that the action, as producing its effect, which is action properly so called, is in the patient. So S. Thomas says : ' An act, which is in reality the same, belongs to two things in different ways : for it belongs to

---

[1] Cf. Ross, *Aristotle*, p. 81.    [2] V Phys., I, Lect. 1.

the agent inasmuch as it is *from* it, and to the patient inasmuch as it is *in* it.'[1]

## Section II.  *On Action at a Distance.*

Having determined the way in which it is most correct to speak of the subject of action, we next have to consider its necessary conditions.  Now, it is suggested that presence is not such a condition, but as this matter has given rise to a good deal of controversy, it is well to see what can be said about it.

### Preliminary Notions.

It is obvious that when we say that two things are present to one another, we mean that they are not separated from one another in some particular respect.  If we are dealing with quantitative things, this non-separation, with regard to quantity or extension, is called contact.

Now, presence is of two kinds :  virtual and formal ;  for, as between an agent and its effect, it may happen, either that the very substance of the agent is present to the effect, when we have formal presence, as in the case of the soul and the body which it informs ;  or that the agent is present to the effect, not in its own substance, but by means of its power, as in the case of a man whose thoughts produce effects in others, such as those of a statesman, a philosopher, or a religious teacher.  The Scholastics call the presence, in these two cases, immediacy of suppositum, and immediacy of power, respectively.

Quantitative presence is divided in a similar way.  So we have mass contact when the extremities of two bodies are together, and virtual contact, when there is immediacy of power only, between two things.

It is clear that mass contact can only occur in the case of two bodies, whereas there may be virtual contact between two things, of which one is quantitative, or corporeal, and the other not quantitative, or spiritual.

The statement ' action at a distance is impossible,' may be taken in one or other of two senses as meaning either that we

[1] III Phys., Lect. 5, 10.

cannot have action between two bodies without mass contact, or that such action is impossible without either mass or virtual contact. The word ' cannot ' is also ambiguous, since it may imply physical impossibility, i.e. that we have no warrant in nature for saying that it can occur, or metaphysical and absolute impossibility. How easy it is to confuse these meanings can be seen in a remark by Dr. Schiller : ' Such action ' (i.e. at a distance) ' our scientists persist in regarding as impossible. . . . If metaphysics had been consulted, it would have been obvious that no special medium was required to make interaction possible between bodies that coexist, seeing that their coexistence is an ample guarantee of their connection and of the possibility of their interaction.'[1] This, at least, is obvious, that Schiller is maintaining that such action is metaphysically possible, and the scientists that it is physically impossible—opinions by no means incompatible.

Three distinct views may therefore be held on this subject :

1. That action between bodies without mass contact is both metaphysically and physically impossible. This appears to have been the view of Aristotle and S. Thomas, though the latter, at any rate, does not seem to have stated it explicitly. It was also held by Suarez,[2] and is still maintained by modern Scholastics.

2. That action without mass contact between bodies is physically impossible, but that its metaphysical impossibility has not been proved. This is the view put forward by Nys.[3]

3. That such action is both physically and metaphysically possible.

Those who hold this last view, further maintain that such action occurs ; and it is an opinion which has found favour both with great scientists such as Faraday, as well as with philosophers as Leibniz.

That mass contact between bodies is a metaphysically

---

[1] Schiller, *Riddles of the Sphinx*, p. 66.
[2] Suarez, *Metaphysical Disputations*, Disp. 18, Sect. 8, nn. 1 and 13.
[3] Nys, *Cosmologie*, Vol. I, Sect. 199.

necessary condition of action appears to be a proposition incapable of proof ; nevertheless, arguments derived from our knowledge of natural laws seem to show that action does not take place between two bodies without such contact : in other words, that, as far as our knowledge of nature at present extends, it is probably true to say that mass contact is physically necessary.  That some kind of contact is absolutely necessary for action of any sort between two things is really a truism, as we shall see ; and it seems to be in this sense that the axiom ' action at a distance is impossible ' should be understood.

With regard to the physical necessity, there are some probable arguments which show that the laws of nature, as at present known to us, are not consistent with the view that action between bodies can take place without mass contact.

First, we may argue from the law of the inverse square, which governs the actions of bodies in such a way that the intensity of the action varies inversely as the square of the distance between them, and so diminishes as the distance increases.  It follows that they cannot act on one another at a distance, i.e. without mass contact, since a material force can only be diminished by a material resistance which, in this hypothesis, would be lacking, since the bodies would be supposed to act across a space void of matter.  Since, then, there would be nothing to diminish the force with which they act on one another, it would not be diminished ; unless we are ready to posit an effect without a cause, or invoke spirits, or other unknown forces to account for the unaccountable.

Secondly, such action is not a natural mode of action, since bodies are naturally in a place, and just as the being of a body is naturally circumscribed by a definite place, so also is its action, on the basis of the general principle that the mode of action of anything corresponds to its mode of being.

As against this opinion the following objection may be urged.  Gravitation is propagated instantaneously, or, at least, with a velocity which has been estimated to be at least fifty million times that of light ; all bodies appear to be absolutely transparent to gravitational action ; and it is not subject to any kind of reflection or refraction. It seems also to be independent of the structure, or the physical and chemical conditions of the bodies between which it acts : its energy is unchangeable and inexhaustible. Hence, it appears that gravitation acts without being in any way affected by the medium through which it may appear to pass ; i.e. that it acts at a distance.

This serious difficulty may perhaps be met on the lines of the classical physics by supposing that gravitation is due to waves in the ether of space, which, by hypothesis, is omnipresent ; waves which can penetrate intervening matter even more easily than can the long waves of wireless telegraphy.[1] Another solution, however, has been suggested by the theory of Einstein. The connecting link between the two is to be found in a sentence written by Fitzgerald in 1894 : ' Gravity is probably due to a change in the structure of the ether, produced by the presence of matter.'[2]  In the developed theory of Einstein there are in space-time natural paths, along which bodies move naturally ; the structure of space-time being such that it will only allow of certain definite configurations.  Such a state of affairs is familiar to us in bodies with which we are constantly dealing in everyday experience, as in the shapes taken by liquids in motion, or to use Eddington's example, in a piece of cloth which is gathered into puckers ; the part between the puckers being capable only of a definite configuration, or, conversely, if the part between the puckers is to lie flat, the puckers themselves must be of a particular kind.[3]  Similarly, in this view space-time allows of certain curvatures only, and since these curvatures are the matter in it, the bodies must be so arranged in it that they will not create any unallowable ones ; or, it would be better to say that they will *appear* to arrange themselves in this way.  Their doing so is their falling to the earth, their passage round the sun, and so on,  So, in following the intrinsic laws of space-time, and of matter, they will naturally

---

[1] Cf. Lodge, *Ether and Reality*, pp. 44, 60, and Ch. IV.
[2] *Scientific Writings*, p. 313.
[3] Eddington, *Nature of the Physical World*, pp. 127 f.

move in certain paths. Just as in Newtonian physics we imagine bodies to move naturally along straight lines in three-dimensional space, when not acted on by any forces, since such paths will be the shortest distance between two points ; so in the curved four-dimensional continuum of space-time, the bodies will still tend to take the shortest track, but this track will no longer be a straight line, but a curve. Hence, the earth circling round the sun, the stone falling to the ground, are not, according to this view, pulled out of their natural paths by some force, but are simply following that path in space-time which is the shortest, and does not entail their inducing in it any unallowable curvature. So gravitation is not a force which acts between bodies, but the appearance of pull is simply due to the fact that in the regions near matter space-time is curved, and the natural paths of bodies are therefore curved also. This way of regarding gravitation, therefore, describes it, not by way of cause and effect, as Newton did, but simply as the statement of a situation : space-time being of a particular kind, and only amenable to certain configurations, bodies move in a definite fashion. So the idea of gravitation as a force is got rid of, and with it the objection that it is a force which acts at a distance ; for it is clear that if there is no gravitational action between bodies at all, there cannot be action at a distance which is gravitational.

To turn to the proposition : 'some sort of presence is required for action between things,' it can hardly be denied that we are justified in calling it a truism. For, if one thing acts on another, it influences it in some way, and so has some connection with it, or is not altogether separated from it. To say that a thing can act at a distance in this sense is an obvious absurdity, since it is equivalent to saying that it can influence the thing on which it acts, while it remains in every way separate and disconnected from it, and so not influencing it. That, if there is not mass contact, there must be some medium through which the action shall pass is not, and cannot be, proved by this and similar arguments.

So, in a word, we may say that there seems to be no metaphysical impossibility involved in action between two bodies without mass contact, but that physically it is probable that the laws of nature do not allow of it.

For the whole question, see Nys, *Cosmologie*, Vol. I, pp. 256 ff. Also : Hugon, *Cursus Philosophiæ Thomisticæ*, Vol. VI, pp. 142 ff.

Note : The explanation given above of Einstein's account of gravitation is, of course, entirely inadequate. All that is necessary to grasp here is that, according to Einstein, gravitation is not regarded as a pull or force, and so cannot be an example of a pull which acts at a distance. A fuller explanation is given by Eddington in the work referred to, and this is probably the most intelligible account of a non-technical kind. (Eddington, *Nature of the Physical World*, Chaps. VI and VII.)

# CHAPTER IX

## THE MEASURE OF MOTION, WHICH IS TIME

Duration—Eternity, Ævum, and Time—Division of Time—Non-Thomistic Views as to the Nature of Time—Newton, Kant, Leibniz, Bergson.

THE word 'motion' no doubt means, properly speaking, successive motion for which time is required, by which motion itself is measured; and so the consideration of motion naturally leads us to that of time. The whole question as to the nature of time is a very thorny one, for as soon as we begin to submit it to analysis, time, which seems such an obvious fact of our lives, eludes us, and has 'softly and silently vanished away.' This is due to the nature of our thought which can only deal with things which are fixed and permanent, whereas time is essentially fluid and impermanent. Nevertheless, though we cannot give a clear-cut answer to the question—what is time?—and, indeed, such an answer would be its own refutation—we can discover a good deal as to its nature by careful consideration.

First, then, it is clear that time is a species of duration : and to say a thing endures is to say that it continues to exist, so that duration is permanence in existence, and it might be thought that duration is either to be identified with the thing which endures, or, if not, at least is the same as its existence. Neither of these opinions, however, is tenable without qualification, for, in the first place, the hold which anything has on existence is not something which belongs to it of its very nature, otherwise, so long as its nature was not altered, it could not cease to exist, which is contrary to experience ; since things do come into being and pass away, which they could not do if existence was their very nature. It is clear that this conclusion would not be conceded by those, such as Suarez, who identify essence and existence ; but, even if this be done, duration is, in the second place, not precisely the same as existence, and so, as the nature of the thing, for to say that a thing exists durably or permanently is to say more than that it simply exists.

Whatever differences of opinion there may be as to the relation of duration to the enduring thing, the Scholastics all agree in distinguishing three kinds of duration : eternity, ævum and time ; the first being the duration of a thing which is altogether unchangeable, the second that of a thing which is subject to accidental change, though it remains immutable in its substance, the third the duration of a thing which is subject both to substantial and to accidental change.

Eternity is defined by Boethius as ' *interminabilis vitæ tota simul et perfecta possessio.*'[1] The words ' *tota simul* ' exclude the idea of succession, and the word ' *perfecta* ' the idea of the temporal ' now,' in which possession of life and existence is imperfect, since it is essentially transitory. Eternity is, strictly speaking, interminable, since it has neither beginning nor end. Since there is absolute immutability in eternity, it is clear that there is no succession in an eternal being, nor even are things which succeed one another successive with regard to it, since, having no beginning or end, it includes and embraces them all. ' Just as,' says John of S. Thomas, ' if there were a tree of such a size as to stretch out over all the waters of a river, it would coexist with all the parts of the river together, even though these succeeded one another.'[2] Time, on the other hand, is intimately connected with succession, of which we get our first notion when we notice local motion, since the moving thing passes through a succession of places. Now, it is clear that such movement takes place in time, and at first sight it might seem that time is simply the motion of some body. So the day seems to be the revolution of the earth on its axis ; and the year its passage round the sun. But a little reflection will show us that though time and motion are closely connected, yet they

---

[1] *Philosophiæ Consolatio*, Lib. V, Ch. VI, 10.
[2] *Phil. Nat.*, Q. 18, A. 1, diff. 3.

are not to be identified, and this for two reasons : first, because motion is something which belongs to the thing which is moving, whereas time affects all things everywhere ; and, secondly, because motion can be fast or slow, but time is not.[1] If time varied with the movement, as it would have to do if they were the same, we could never say of anything that it moved quickly or slowly ; and the fact that we can do so shows that we compare the motion with time, for we say that one motion is quicker than another, if it takes a shorter time to traverse the same distance. Hence motion is measured by time.

Again, though time implies succession, this latter is not the same as time, since some successions are non-temporal, e.g. the succession in the series of ordinal numbers. Nevertheless, since time implies succession, we shall have to state its successive character in our definition of it. All these elements were included in the Aristotelean definition of time, which was adopted by S. Thomas, and is now generally accepted by Scholastics, viz. : Time is the number of movement in respect of before and after. τοῦτο γάρ ἐστιν ὁ χρόνος, ἀριθμὸς κινήσεως κατὰ τὸ πρότερον καὶ ὕστερον.[2]

The word ἀριθμος here (i.e. number) is equivalent to measure, for all quantity is measurable, and measure is expressed by number. Time is the measure of movement only, that which is immobile is not in time ; and, further, by this phrase we affirm that time is not the same as movement, since it is its measure.

Lastly, the words ' in respect of before and after ' indicate that time does not apply to movement precisely as movement, but in so far as it is successive. Hence the words do not merely repeat the notion of time which they are intended to explain, as Plotinus thought,[3] but indicate expressly its successive character.

In this definition, as indeed in our everyday conceptions, time is thought of as a unity ; but it is difficult to see on what such a unity can be founded, for the motions of which it is the measure are multiple. The Aristotelean physics

[1] Cf. Aristotle, *Physics*, 218b9.    [2] Aristotle, *Physics*, 219b1.
[3] Inge, *The Philosophy of Plotinus*, Vol. I, p. 171.

gave, at least, a partial answer to this question, since Aristotle regarded motion in a circle as the primary kind of local movement, and thought that the celestial sphere moved uniformly.  Hence, in his view, there is one uniform motion which dominates all others, and so one from which the unity of time can be derived.[1]  It is from this notion that we derive our way of speaking of time, and the changes of human affairs, as cyclical.  It is, however, clear to us at the present day, that there is in nature no known movement which is absolutely uniform, and consequently none which can be taken to standardise and unify time.  Nevertheless, such a movement can be readily conceived of, and was, in fact, used in Newtonian physics, under the name of mathematical time.  It is evidently a mental fiction.

If, then, we must abandon the hope of finding any absolute time, we nevertheless are well acquainted with relative times, and so can continue, with regard to the things whose motion is measured by them, to speak of them as being in time.

What, then, are these things which are in time ?

As Aristotle points out, ' to be in time,' may have three senses :  (1) to be when time is, (2) to be a part or attribute of time, and (3) to be measurable by time.[2]  The first of these senses can obviously be ruled out at once, it is simply an ambiguity of expression.  Of the other two senses the second applies to past, present, and future, which are, in a wide sense, parts of time ;  the third to events which are measurable by time ;  i.e. all things whose being is mutable or subject to change.

### The Division of Time.

There are two kinds of time :  imaginary and real, the first being external to the material universe, and containing within itself all durations.  The second is the measure of real motion.  We have seen that this absolute imaginary time is a mere mental fiction, and we shall shortly see what is to be said as to the extra-mental existence of ' real time.'  This

---

[1] Aristotle, *Physics*, 223b12–224a2 ;  cf. S. Thomas, loc. cit., and in IV Phys., Lect. 17, No. 4.
[2] Aristotle, *Physics*, 221a7 *sqq.* ;  S. Thomas in IV Phys., Lect. 15, No. 3.

last is of two kinds : time as duration, and time as a measure. The first is also called intrinsic, and the second extrinsic, time. Extrinsic time is also of two kinds : primary and secondary. Primary time is the measure of the motion of the earth, secondary being the measure of any particular motion, such as that of a clock, or clock-time. Primary time is again divided into sidereal, apparent, and mean time. The sidereal day is the interval between two consecutive southings of a particular star. Apparent time is derived from the motion of the sun, the solar day being defined as the interval between two consecutive southings of the sun. This interval is by no means constant, owing to the inclination of the ecliptic to the equator, and the lack of uniformity in the velocity of the sun. The mean time is the average of the apparent time, the maximum divergence being about sixteen minutes.

We are now faced with the difficult question of the extra mental status of time. Aristotle raised the question whether there would be time if there were not soul (mind), but gave no definite answer to it.[1] We have to enquire as to the objectivity both of time as a duration—which is the continued existence of motion—and of time as a measure, whose definition is the number of movement in respect of before and after. At first sight it appears as if time as a duration were something which exists quite apart from the mind, but a little reflection shows that all that can be said to exist in this way is the moving thing and its successive states ; the *continued* existence of motion not being found in nature. For it is clear that a car running along a road, though its motion is continuous, is yet to be found in reality at only one potential point of its course at any one (potential) moment ; whereas to have continued or enduring existence it would either have to be fixed at one point, not passing through a potential point, or stretching out from one point to another, in which case it would be in two places at once. There is a striking passage in S. Thomas' commentary on the *Physics*, which deserves to be quoted.[2] He says : ' The notion ' (the word used is ' ratio,' which means both nature

---

[1] Aristotle, *Physics*, 223ᵃ21–29.      [2] In III Phys., Lect. 5, No. 17.

and notion) ' of movement is made complete, not only by
what there is of motion in nature, but also by what the mind
apprehends. For, of motion, nothing more exists in nature
than an imperfect act, which is a kind of beginning, in the
thing which is moved, of a perfect act. Thus, in a thing
which is turning white, there is already some whiteness. In
order, however, that such imperfect act should have the
nature of movement, it is further required that we should
conceive it as a mean between two extremes, of which the
preceding one bears to it the relation of potency to act, and
the one which follows it that of act to potency : which is the
reason that we call motion the act of that which is in potency.'

Thus the duration of motion is not a reality found in
nature apart from the mind. It is our mind, which is endowed
with memory, which gives unity and so being to motion, and
to the duration of motion, as a whole. Further, its duration
is the foundation of time as a measure, since only in so far
as it is an enduring whole does it lend itself to measurement.
This conclusion is strengthened by considering the attempts
that have been made to account for the existence of time :
for some, as Suarez, have maintained that time exists by
reason of its parts, the past and future, which continually
flow on. It is, however, difficult to see how a thing can exist
by reason of parts which do not exist themselves ; for the
past is already dead, and the future is not yet born. Consequently, S. Thomas and his school affirm that in so far as
time exists, it does so by reason of the present instant,
which is not a part of time, but the indivisible link of its
parts, the past and future. This instant must exist since it
is the measure of unity of a definite state of the moving
thing, and without such definite state the moving thing itself
could not exist. It is, however, present only in so far as it is
considered by the mind in relation to the past and future ;
and it is clear that it cannot make the past and future exist,
since the past cannot exist in the present, and to speak of the
present presupposes that the future is not yet existing. So
we are brought back to our former conclusion that neither
time as a duration, nor time as a measure, exist, or are real,
apart from the mind. This, however, should not blind us to

the fact that there is an element of time which has such extra-mental existence, viz. the indivisible of time, the instant. So S. Thomas says : ' If motion had some fixed existence in things, as a stone or a horse have, it would be possible to say absolutely that just as, even if the soul does not exist, there exists a number of stones, so, even if the soul does not exist, there would be a number of motion which is time. But motion has no fixed existence in things, and in things there is found nothing actual of motion, except a certain indivisible of motion, which is the division of motion : but the totality of motion is comprehended through the consideration of the soul which compares the former to the latter disposition of the moving thing. So, therefore, time also has no existence outside the soul, except with regard to its indivisible, but the very totality of time is comprehended through the order-ing of the soul which enumerates before and after in motion.'[1] So, he adds, time has an imperfect existence only, apart from the mind, just as motion itself has.

Taken then as a whole duration or measure, it exists in the mind only.[2]  In this delicate doctrine as to the existence of time, it is essential not to overlook either the objective or subjective element in it : both of which must be preserved in their proper proportions. Those who dissent from the Thomist view do so, in fact, because they ascribe undue weight to one or other of these elements, and so fall into two classes which may, for convenience, be called Ultra-Realist and Subjectivist.

*Non-Thomistic Views of the Nature of Time.*

Though it does not come within the scope of this explana-tion to set out extraneous opinions for their own sake, yet, in this case, a short review of the principal ones will serve to clarify the meaning, and emphasise the balance and sanity of the Thomist view.

I. *The Ultra-Realist view* is represented in the first place by Gassendi, who, basing his theories on those of Epicurus, considered time to be something which is neither substance

[1] In IV Phys., Lect. 23, No. 5.
[2] Cf. Nys, *La Notion du Temps*, pp. 59 f., No. 38.

nor accident, and which is eternal and uncreated.  Newton and Clarke, in a somewhat similar way, held that time is a divine attribute.  Gassendi, however, as a theist, was in an impossible position, since there cannot be two uncreated and eternal beings ;  and the Newtonian view is faced with the difficulty that the divine attributes are immutable, and there is no succession in them, whereas time is essentially successive. The elaborate theory of space-time put forward recently by Professor Alexander seems to have affinities with these views. He considers it to be the fundamental stuff of the universe from which Deity is progressively emerging.  It seems difficult to regard this view as other than pantheistic, though its author has repudiated this interpretation of it.

## II.  *The Subjectivist Views.*

1.  Kant regarded time as an *a priori* intuition of the sensibility, something, that is, which belongs to the very texture of our senses :  so that, for him, it is purely subjective.  This is evidently false if we recognise motion as a real foundation of time ;  and moreover it is contrary to experience, since, in observing some extended sensible object, such as a landscape, our observations are successive, while the landscape appears as a static whole.  If, however, succession were something which directly affected our sensibility alone, both it and its objects ought to be affected by it, or neither of them ;  so that, on Kant's hypothesis, it should be impossible for us to have a successive knowledge of a simultaneous whole.[1]

2.  Leibniz at least inclines to over-emphasise the subjective character of time :  for he defines it as the ' order of successions.'[2]  He remarks that a thing of which no part ever exists cannot exist ;  and in the case of time, nothing exists except the present instant, which is not a part of time ; and concludes that time cannot be other than an ideal being. It will be seen that this view has close affinity with that of S. Thomas ;  for they are at one in recognising the purely mental character of absolute time, and also that the only element of time which exists in nature is the instant.

---

[1] Cf. Nys, op. cit., p. 226, No. 138.
[2] Cf. 3rd letter to Clarke and 5th letter to Clarke (on Par. 10).

S. Thomas, however, notices what Leibniz overlooks, that this instant is the number of the motion of the body, and corresponds to the indivisible of motion, which, though the only actuality in motion, is at the same time potential to the further process of motion, so that time exists as a perfect and actual being ideally only, but as an imperfect and potential one in things. It seems, therefore, not unjust to Leibniz to say that his teaching on this point is not so well balanced as that of S. Thomas, and that his theory is of the subjectivist type, though not of so extreme a kind as that of Kant. Further, in his definition and view of time, Leibniz loses sight of its essential continuity ; for the definition does not take account of the fact that time requires continuous motion, as well as the permanence of the thing which moves. Order does not necessarily imply either of these, for there can be order among discontinuous things, and, consequently, apart from the permanence of the thing which is subject to order. Hence, Leibniz's definition does not discriminate between that by which the motion of material things is measured, and that which applies to the motion of pure spirits : which latter is discrete, not continuous.

Lastly, to define time as the order of successions is a loose way of speaking, for order is a consequence of succession, and so of time, rather than constitutive of successive duration, or time. There is order in the succession of things because of the motion by which the things succeed one another, not conversely : for it is not true to say that there is motion because there is order.

### III. *Bergson's Theory of Time*.

According to Bergson, there are two kinds of time, homogeneous and heterogeneous. The latter is the time of our experience, and is named by him ' *la durée*,' to which no English expression exactly corresponds. Homogeneous time, which is what we ordinarily mean when we use the word time, is, in his view, merely space, on to which the mind projects psychological time, the succession of our conscious states, thus making it appear to be a successive and continuous reality. In fact, it is nothing but an illusion for there is no true succession in things which are said to be measured by time, since one state has entirely disappeared when another appears. So he writes : ' Doubtless exterior things change, but their moments only succeed one another with respect to a consciousness which remembers them. We observe outside us, at any given moment, a collection of simultaneous positions ; nothing remains of the former simultaneities.'[1]

Hence, the only time which is not illusory, and which he regards as real, is the heterogeneous time, or succession, which accompanies the development of our conscious states. Such development is purely qualitative, and its parts can only be qualitatively, never quantitatively, distinguished, so that they are absolutely heterogeneous ; for it is clear that all our psychic acts are unextended—it is impossible to have a yard of thought—and so if distinct their distinction can be qualitative only.

There can be no question as to the subjective character of this theory ; and to make of time an affection of our conscious states is to contradict completely the common-sense notion of it, which undoubtedly attaches it to bodies. What is more, it is only the permanent which changes, and the permanent endures : so that it is inconsistent to admit that things change and to deny their duration. Moreover, if time attaches only to our conscious states, each one of us will live in his own time, and there will be no unique sense in which two events can be said to be simultaneous. This, however, is to deny time, not to explain it, for the notion of time surely implies, at least, the possibility of comparing the position of two events in the world process. Without this capacity, it is altogether useless. Of the characteristics of time, as all men conceive it, viz. as measuring events, as having parts, past, present, and future, and as continuous, the only one which is, in the end, retained by this theory is the last, and that illegitimately ; for Bergsonian time is, in fact, the series of irreducible different qualities, which, therefore, can never form a unity or continuity. Much more might be added in criticism of the theory, but these remarks

[1] *Essai sur les donnés de la conscience*, p. 173.

may suffice to show that it is irreconcilable with common sense, and inconsistent in itself ; though highly ingenious, and devised with the best of intentions, viz. to rescue living things, and especially conscious processes from the grip of a deterministic mechanism.

(For a fuller discussion, see Nys, *La Notion du Temps*.)

Note.   The theory of Einstein with respect to the relativity of space and time is well known : but it would be to go beyond the limits of a simple explanation of Scholastic philosophy to attempt to explain and comment on it here.   The reader may be referred to Einstein's own explanation of it in his book, *The Theory of Relativity* (Methuen) ; and there are many other explanations of it in English, such as those given by Professor Eddington in various works, e.g. *The Nature of the Physical World*.   Scholastic comments on it can be found in Nys' monographs on Space and Time, cited above ; and a good discussion of it from a metaphysical point of view is contained in Maritain's *Reflexions sur l'intelligence*.   The *Prælectiones Cosmologiæ*, by Fr. Dario, S.J. (Paris : Beauchesne) can also be consulted.

# CHAPTER X

## SUBSTANTIAL CHANGE IN GENERAL

Meaning of Substantial Change—The Plurality of Forms—The
Source of the New Substantial Form in Generation.

IN considering the quality of the material world (mobile
being), which is motion, we have seen what is meant by
motion in general, and how material beings are affected
extrinsically by their motion through space. We now turn
to that motion, or change, which is intrinsic to them. Such
change is of two kinds : substantial, by which their very
nature is changed, and accidental, by which their qualities
are altered. There are two questions which require separate
treatment with regard to substantial change, that of substantial change in general, and that of the particular kind of
substantial change which occurs when two or more simple
elements combine to form a chemical compound.

With regard to substantial change in general, we notice
that the changing of one substance into another involves
both the appearance of a new substance, and the disappearance of the old. It is therefore called by Aristotle generation
(γένεσις) and corruption (φθορά).

Generation is defined as the change by means of which
some real subject, which before the change did not have
existence, receives it ; while corruption is the change by
means of which some real subject, which before the change
had existence, loses it. The real subject referred to in both
cases is the compound of matter and form. So, for example,
assuming for the moment that wood and the carbon which
results from burning it are substances of different natures,
we have the carbon receiving existence, which it did not
have before, and the wood losing that which it had. The
coming-into-being of the carbon is the passing-out-of-being

of the wood, so that the Scholastics say that the generation
of one thing is the corruption of another.  Thus, that which
is produced by generation is the concrete thing, in our
example, the carbon.  This carbon is, moreover, a certain
nature which exists, and one which comes into being as a
result of generation ;  so that it is clear that the nature of
carbon is itself a product of generation ;  not, however, as
that which is directly generated in itself, but as a constituent
of the concrete thing.  So the Scholastics call it the ' *terminus
qui generationis* ' as contrasted with the ' *terminus quod*,'
the thing which is generated.  The nature itself is made of a
definite and specific kind by the substantial form, which is
therefore also a *terminus qui* of generation.  It is clear,
further, that there is no moment of time between the disappearance of one nature, one form, and the coming of
another, since the disappearance of one is the appearance of
the other.  Nevertheless, in substantial change the first form
does disappear entirely, according to the teaching of S.
Thomas ;  so that, in his view, matter is stripped of all
substantial form in this process.  The truth of this opinion
has been, and still is, hotly contested ;  and we must pause
to consider it more fully.

QUESTION I.  *On the Plurality of Forms.*

Whether we admit S. Thomas' view or not will depend
on whether we allow a plurality of forms in one being.  Until
the time of S. Thomas the possibility of there being many
substantial forms in a thing, which still remained essentially
one, and indeed that there actually were many such forms,
was generally admitted by Scholastics.  S. Thomas, however,
always held firmly to the opposite opinion,[1] being, as Professor Taylor says, ' too sound an Aristotelean ' to admit
such plurality.[2]  The views of his opponents on this question,
and so on the process of substantial change, were of two
kinds, of which the first is that some substantial form does
remain throughout the change.  So Avicebron (Ibn Gebirol),
according to S. Thomas,[3] held that in a man there would be a

[1] But cf. Fr. Roland-Gosselin's edition of *De Ente et Essentia*, pp. 110 ff.
[2] *Platonism and its Influence*, p. 127.
[3] *De Spiritualibus Creaturis*, Art. 3.

hierarchy of forms, beginning with the form of substance, to which is added that of corporeality, then of vegetative life, then of sensitive life, and finally of intellectual life. Scotus admitted a form of corporeality in living things, and taught that it remains on the departure of the soul ;[1] while Albert the Great held that the forms of the elements remain in a mixture, subsumed under the form of the mixture, which is new ; as the Greeks in the Trojan horse were subsumed under the form of horse, though they did not lose their own forms, if we may use a very inadequate example. A similar view was held by Avicenna and Averroes.

The second way of regarding this process of change is that of Suarez, who, though allowing that no substantial form remains throughout the change, yet, since he holds that accidents are individuals of themselves, not by reason of the substances in which they inhere,[2] is able to grant that the accidents of the generated thing are the same individual ones as those which were found in the corrupted thing. Apart from this, his opinion is practically the same as that of S. Thomas. Those who differ from S. Thomas maintain that his position is unintelligible, for they say that if there be no form remaining, we shall have absolute indetermination, which is the same as nothing. This is, in fact, the denial of the reality of pure potency : and as we have already seen neither Scotus nor Suarez is willing to admit that matter is pure potency without *any* act (cf., p. 48). Further, they object that when one form disappears there will be a moment, if not in time, at least in the order of intelligibility, when the subject of the first form, lacking that form, will vanish ; since the Thomists admit that matter cannot exist without form. Hence, in order that we may have a common subject it must be furnished with a form independent of those which it loses or acquires in the change. Apart from these theoretical objections, it has recently been urged by Fr. Descoqs,[3] and others, that the facts show that the subject of change is not first, but second, matter.

---

[1] In IV Sent. dist. XI, Q. 3, A. 2.
[2] *Disputationes Metaphysicæ*, Disp. V.
[3] *Essai Critique sur l'Hylémorphisme*, pp. 31 ff.

The Thomists reply that they are compelled to adhere to their doctrine that at the moment of change no substantial or accidental form remains by irresistible metaphysical arguments. With regard to substantial form, it is evident that if it be true that there can be only one substantial form in one compound, since change of substance or nature must mean that the old nature passes away and a new one takes its place, and substantial form is that which makes a thing to be of a definite kind substantially, this too will pass away at the moment of change, and if it is the only one, none will be left. The question, therefore, resolves itself into that concerning the plurality of substantial forms in a body which is an essential unity ; as we have already stated. Though we mentioned shortly, at an earlier stage (*vid.* p. 50), the reasons which St. Thomas gives for excluding a plurality of forms, as a corollary to our discussion of the potentiality of matter, it is necessary to examine the question rather more fully here, as it is one of the main arches of the Thomist structure, and is a characteristic architectural feature of it.

There are two questions to be asked : first, What do we mean by the phrase : ' a being which is essentially one ' ? and, second, Are there any such beings ?

Can we say, in answer to the first question, that we mean a being whose nature is itself a compound of several, so that E, its nature, is compounded of $E_1$, $E_2$, $E_3$, . . . etc. ? This is surely impossible, for the thing will have these natures $E_1$, etc., either all at once or in succession. If it has them all at once, it clearly has a number of natures, since, by hypothesis, they are different, and therefore cannot have a single nature. If it has them successively, when it has nature $E_1$, it will already be a definite and determinate kind of being ; and so cannot be made a definite being by having a nature $E_2$ added to it. For, just as it is true to say that nothing gives what it has not already got, so also is it true that nothing gets or receives what it has already. This is true even in the accidental order, as for example, it is impossible to make a man a millionaire if he already is one ; and it is certainly true in the substantial, a man cannot be made a man, a determinate nature cannot be made a determinate

K

nature. To doubt this would indeed be to doubt the principle of identity—being is being—from which follows the principle of Parmenides : ' from being, being cannot come to be, since it already is,' which, with the precision imported into it by Aristotle, becomes : ' from being in act, being in act cannot come to be.' And this is precisely the case in point, since being which has an essence is an actual being, and so by the addition of another essence cannot become one. It is already constituted as a substantial nature, so that any addition to it can only modify that nature, not constitute it. So S. Thomas says : ' *Quod advenit alicui post esse completum, advenit ei accidentaliter.*' (*Contra Gentiles*, Lib. II, c. 58.) So it is clear that by essential unity we must mean that the thing which has it, has one nature only, for no kind of compound of natures will satisfy the conditions. But it might be said : ' No doubt in the abstract essential unity means that there is a single nature, but in the concrete existing thing is it not possible that several natures should so fit in with one another that all should be united in the bond of a single existence, thus giving us a substantial unity ; in other words, that though there may be several substantial forms in a body, yet it may exist as a unity ? ' If we consider this we see that it is impossible to agree with this suggestion, for substantial form is that which, when it is joined to matter, makes a compound which is capable of receiving existence, neither form nor matter being capable of doing so in separation, since they are only principles of being. If, then, the compound receives existence—as it must do in order to be a concrete thing—the existence which it receives will be existence without any qualification or addition, making it pass from the realm of mere possibilities to that of actual existing things, for if it does not do this the thing will not pass out of the abstract order. If, however, it does do it, any further existence cannot do it, since it is already done, and so any further existence will be only existence of a particular kind, as to be white, etc. Hence, in order to have a single substantial existence, and so a substantial unity we must have one substantial form, and one only.[1]

[1] Cf. P. Geny, S.J., *Gregorianum*, 1925, Vol. VI, pp. 126 f. ; and *Divus Thomas (Plac.)*, 1925, pp. 72 f.

But, are there in the world any beings which possess
essential unity of this kind ?[1] We must certainly answer
this affirmatively, both because of our consciousness which
affirms that we are such unities ourselves, and the intolerable
consequences which follow from splitting up human nature
into two or more natures—from what is called psychological
dualism—and because in the world of inanimate matter, if
we were to deny such essential unity to everything, it is
clear that nothing could be quantitative, since, having no
one nature, there could not be parts of one nature, and
nothing would be quantitative and extended. The hypothesis of Leibniz was precisely that of the plurality of monads,
of substantial forms, and we agree with him that this must
logically lead to a denial of extension : a denial which we
have seen to be impossible, and which, in any case, no
Scholastic, not even those who hold the doctrine of the
plurality of forms, would admit. Thus, the individual in the
organic and inorganic worlds must be granted to have a
unity of nature, an essential unity, otherwise the world as we
know it becomes inexplicable.

S. Thomas argues against the plurality of forms in the
following passages, among others :

*Summa Theologica*, Part I, Q. 76, Arts. 3, 4, 6, ad 1um, 8 ;
Part III, Q. 1, A. 5, ad 1um. *Contra Gentiles*, Lib. II, Caps.
57, 58. *Questio Disp. De Spiritualibus Creaturis*, A. 1, ad
9um ; A. 3 ; *Q. Disp. de Anima*, A. 9 et 11 ; *Quodlibet I*,
A. 6 ; *Quodlibet XI*, A. 5 ; *de Substantiis Separatis*, Cap. 6 ;
from the last of which the following passage may be quoted :

' To make an end of the matter, the aforesaid position '
(i.e. that there are a plurality of forms) ' destroys the first
principles of philosophy, by removing unity from individuals,
and consequently both true entity, and the diversity of
things. For if another act supervenes to something which
exists in act, the whole will not be a unity *per se*, but only
*per accidens*, for the reason that two acts or forms are in
themselves diverse, and agree only in the subject ; to be
one, however, through the unity of the subject is to be one
*per accidens*.'

[1] Cf. Geny, *Divus Thomas*, loc. cit., p. 74.

Thus he always appeals to the principle : 'substantial form gives existence simply speaking '; so that anything added can only give accidental existence, with the result that nothing can have more than one substantial form.

It follows immediately from this that the opinion of Suarez, that the same individual accidents remain throughout a substantial change, cannot be maintained ; for if substantial form disappears at the moment of change, the subsistence of the first subject which constitutes its capacity for sustaining itself also disappears, since this is caused by substantial form. So, evidently, if the substance ceases to be self-sustaining, it *ipso facto* becomes incapable of sustaining or supporting anything else, such as accidents, which must therefore disappear also ; to suppose the contrary would be like supposing that you could hang your hat on a nail that wasn't there.

Are we, then, to suppose that nothing at all of the substance which undergoes substantial change is to be found in the new substance which comes into being, with the exception of the absolutely undetermined first matter ?   This does not at all follow, for we can see that though the replacement of one substantial form by another is instantaneous, yet the process which leads up to this change is a gradual one : since the first substance is gradually changed by the modification of its qualities until it arrives at the state in which the new substantial form, which is to take possession, is required as the source of these modified qualities.   The accidents introduced in this way into the changing substance are called by the Scholastics the previous dispositions, since they dispose the subject to be informed by a new form ; and these remain virtually through the change, since the matter which has been brought, by their means, to the point at which it calls out, as it were, for the new form, remains throughout the change.   It never has the chance to fall into complete indetermination, since the new form takes possession of it as the old one disappears.   They are like children playing 'musical chairs,' where one child holds on to the coat-tails of another, so as to be able to occupy immediately the chair which the other has vacated.   Consequently, the

new form will produce in the substance accidental dispositions which are the exact counterpart of those which the
subject had, immediately before the change, when the old
substantial form was present. These dispositions will, however, be numerically distinct from the previous ones, since we
now have a new subject. They are called the proximate
dispositions. Can these latter be said to precede the substantial form ? The answer is, that, regarded from different
points of view, they precede and follow it. Inasmuch as
they prepare the subject for the reception of the substantial
form, they precede it ; for, from this point of view, they are
the same as the previous dispositions, which affected the
matter which the new substantial form takes possession of ;
but they follow it, inasmuch as it is due to the new substantial form that they are able to be supported as entities of a
certain nature. Thus they precede it in the genus of material
disposing cause, and follow it in the genus of formal cause :
according to the general principle : ' *causæ ad invicem sunt
causæ in diverso genere* '—causes which are mutual causes are
causes in different genera. From the point of view of time,
they neither precede nor follow the new substantial form, but
are contemporaneous with its coming, since this occurs instantaneously. Hence, we see that matter is never left wholly
undetermined, even for a moment, whether in the order of
time, or that of intelligibility. If difficulty be experienced
in conceiving how a thing may both precede and follow
another, and yet be simultaneous with it, the following
example, though inadequate, may be a help. In an ecclesi-
astical procession the dignitaries walk at the rear of it, and
so follow it ; nevertheless they precede all the other members of the procession in dignity, and are at the same time
simultaneous with them all in walking, since the whole procession moves together at the same time. Thus they follow
in space, precede in dignity, and are simultaneous in time.

QUESTION II. *The Source of the New Substantial Form in
Generation.*

What has been said about the ' dispositions ' introduced
into the changing body will suggest that the new substantial

form takes its rise from the changing material thing itself; and this is, in fact, the Thomistic opinion, which is expressed in the phrase : 'material forms are produced (*educuntur*) from the potentiality of matter.' The process may be likened—if proper care be taken not to press the comparison too far—to the felling of a tree. Little by little, as the axe bites into the trunk, the tree becomes less capable of preserving its upright position, until finally the moment comes when it is unable to stand any longer ; a slight stroke, the tree wavers and comes crashing down. Similarly, a body which is undergoing a substantial change has its capacity for preserving its original nature gradually weakened until finally it, as it were, topples over into the arms of the new form, which comes to it, not from without, but from within, as a result of its natural propensities having been gradually altered. This process is held by S. Thomas to be verified only in the case of material forms, not of spiritual ones ; since only the former are dependent on matter for their existence, and consequently these alone can be dependent on it for their actual coming into being. Evidently, also, the process applies only to substantial generation, not to the beginning of all things.

There are, however, two other opposing theories as to the way in which substantial forms come to be ; between which the Aristotelean theory stands as on an eminence, preserving the truth of both, and filling in their lacunæ.

So, some thought that all forms actually existed in matter, but lay hid in it ; while others supposed that they were not in matter at all, but were created whenever substantial change occurred.

The first view is, according to S. Thomas,[1] erroneous, as we have already seen ; the error arising from a failure to distinguish between potency and act ; since the forms are potentially only in the matter, not actually ; while the second is also erroneous, since it implies that a form is, in itself, a complete being, not a principle of being. It is, in fact, the new compound which comes to be, not form alone, as we noticed earlier (cf. p. 129).

[1] Cf. *Summa Theologica*, Pars I, Q. 45, a. 8 ; and VII Metaphys., Lect. 7, ed. Cathala, Nos. 1430 and 1431.

It is, however, not easy to see how the new substantial form is made actual, if, as we have just said, it is only potentially in matter, and is not created ; for since matter contains it only potentially, it cannot make it actual ; and the efficient cause, or agent, by whose means the change is brought about, seems also incapable of doing this.  The principle of causality demands that a cause must contain the effect at least virtually, and that in a way which is at least equal in perfection to the effect itself.  This condition is not, however, verified in the case of many of the agents which appear to produce substantial changes, as heat or electricity, which can hardly be said to contain virtually the forms of the bodies produced by their means.  And how can a bullet be thought to contain virtually the forms which appear in the dead body of the man whom it kills ?  So, neither matter nor yet the agent seem to be causes which are capable of producing the new substantial forms.  Besides this, there is a further difficulty in supposing that the new form is produced by the agent, since the action of an agent is an accident, and so cannot produce substance.  Aristotle thought that the ' heavenly bodies ' exercise a general influence on all terrestrial operations, and that they are beings of a higher order than earthly bodies, so that their power virtually contained all earthly forms.  This view is obviously untenable, but some Scholastics, thinking that an absolutely general cause of a higher order to that of parti-cular material substances is required, have substituted for the influence of the ' first heaven ' either that of God, or of the all-pervading ether.  The first is the suggestion of M. Nys in his *Cosmologie* ;[1]  the second that of Remer.[2]

In M. Nys' view the Divine action is required at the moment when the forms appear, not by way of creation, but as giving to the generative forces the necessary perfec-tion ; while Remer thinks that the ether of space, being the subject of all physical action, may be considered as a universal agent, and so as containing virtually, and on the same level as themselves, the forms of all other bodies.

[1] Nys, *Cosmologie*, Tome II, pp. 178 ff.
[2] Remer, *Cosmologia*, ed. 4a (1921), pp. 83 ff., No. 54, *versus finem*.

Neither of these suggestions, however, seems altogether satisfactory, for to invoke a special action of God every time a generation takes place, and when unable to see any natural explanation of a natural event, to cut the knot by asserting that it must be due to the action of God, seems to make of Him a ' *Deus ex machina*.' It is as if a savage, falling into a river, and being swept away by it, were to say ' the god of the river has got hold of me,' not knowing the law of gravitation ; but what is pardonable in a savage is hardly so in a philosopher.

Nor is Remer's theory much more probable, for even if there be a material ether of the kind supposed, which is highly doubtful, its characteristics are so negative, since it is thought of merely as the medium whereby electro-magnetic waves are transmitted, that it can hardly be considered to be an active agent of the kind required.

The solution seems rather to be found in a careful and strictly philosophical consideration of the parts played in the process of substantial change by the material which undergoes it, and the agent which modifies this material, as well as by the active character of substance itself. According to this view, the agent which introduces into the changing bodies the dispositions favourable to the coming of the new substantial forms does not produce or effect these forms, but merely gives the matter that actuation which is necessary for the transformation of its capacity for them into actual possession of them. So, absolutely speaking, a sculptor has no need formally to possess the form of the statue which he is carving ; nor even virtually, except in the sense that he has the power, both mental, by reason of his artistic conception, and physical, so to manipulate his material that in it the statue may appear. The statue which results depends therefore both on the material used, e.g. whether it be marble or wood, and on the power of the sculptor. Similarly, in the case of natural agents, both the matter which is being changed, and the agent which is introducing modifications into it, concur in the production of the new substantial compound, though in different ways : for the agent modifies the substance, which, when so modified, gives birth, as it were, to the new form. It is, therefore, the material substance, as modified by the agent, which possesses virtually the new form which is to arise in it ; and the objections raised to the virtual possession of this form by the efficient cause of the change fall to the ground. That this is true seems to be borne out by the fact that a random application of the efficient cause will not produce the new substance ; the old must be modified in a particular manner, i.e. the modifications must be such as to bring it to the state in which it possesses the new form virtually. So, an electrical current has to be applied to oxygen and hydrogen in a particular way in order to make them combine into water ; and it is only certain lesions or diseases which cause death. Thus, it is not necessary to suppose that electricity or a bullet possess virtually the forms which are educed by their means, except in the sense that they are necessary in order to modify the material in a suitable manner. But it will still be objected that the actions which cause such modifications are accidents, and cannot therefore produce substantial forms, but only accidental ones, viz. these very modifications. This, however, is easily answered, since they are the actions of substance, and are naturally united to it, in such a way that it acts with and through them. The power manifested in the action of any agent is not the power of the action, but that of the agent ; being nothing else than the power or force of the active substance. So, as Cajetan says : ' *Accidentalis vis non sua, sed substantiæ est virtus* ' ; so there is no reason why it should not produce a substantial actuation. The substance does not lie inert or inactive under accidents which act for it, like sentries who drive away intruders from the sleeping camp ; but they are, as Cajetan puts it, ' *organa conjuncta*,' whose whole efficacy is that of the substance whose ' organs ' they are. Thus, as far as virtual possession of the new form is concerned, we can say that this is found in the changing material ; and as far as it is necessary that this material should receive a new substantial actuation, passing from the capacity for being a new substance to being it actually, such actuation is derived from the agent, whose accidents act with its own substantial power. So the formal or specific character of the substantial form is educed from the potentiality of matter ; while its substantial character is derived from the substantial agent, imparting its substantial power to its accidents.

These remarks seem to express Cajetan's view as he suggests it in his commentaries on the first part of the *Summa*. Cf. *Comm. in Iam Partem*, Q. 54, A. 3 ; Nos. 8, 16, and 17 ; in Part I., Q. 77, A. 1 ; No. 13. Cf. Goudin, *Physica*, Pars I, Disp. 2, Q. 4, A. 3 *versus finem*.

# CHAPTER XI

## SUBSTANTIAL CHANGE IN CHEMICAL COMPOSITION :
### THE QUESTION OF MIXTURES

Current Scientific Views—Philosophical Views—Thomist Opinions
as to the Permanence of the Elements and Qualities in Mixtures.

IN the general discussion of the theory of matter and form
we noticed that some modern Scholastics refuse to admit
that substantial change actually occurs, owing to the difficulties which have arisen from the discoveries made in
modern times by physical science.   These difficulties are
particularly acute with regard to inorganic chemical compounds, which the Scholastics call ' mixtures '—though the
name is not absolutely confined to the inorganic realm—and
some authors who are willing to allow substantial change to
organic things refuse to admit it in the case of the inorganic.
In the present discussion we shall confine ourselves to a
consideration of inorganic bodies ; and even so it will be
impossible to consider in detail all the difficulties which can
be raised from the point of view of physical science, since we
are concerned to unwind the thread which may lead a begin-
ner safely through the labyrinth of Scholastic philosophy,
not to examine all the obscurities of its caverns ; and because
such a consideration would entail a course of physical science
which is outside the scope of a brief philosophical summary,
such as the present.   We will therefore try to see what are
the main philosophical ideas and principles which lead to the
solution of these difficulties.

As is well known, all inorganic bodies are regarded by
science as aggregates of smaller ones, composite bodies being
collections of molecules, which are themselves collections of
two or more particles of the simple elements, which are
called atoms.   In both cases, therefore, gross matter, whether

composite—what is called by the Scholastics a mixture—or simple, which we may take for the present as meaning the chemical elements, is composed of a number of discrete particles in juxtaposition. Even so, we have not come to the end of the division of matter as envisaged by physics, for the atom itself is regarded as being composed of parts : the proton, which is a positive electric charge, and electrons, which are negative unit charges. The number of these electrons is held to vary in the different chemical elements ; beginning with hydrogen, which has one electron, and so a positive unit charge as proton, up to uranium which has ninety-two electrons. Hence, according to this view, all matter is fundamentally the same, being composed of a greater or less number of electrical units.

Faced by this theory, which seems well-established scientifically, some Scholastics thought that the traditional view, that inorganic substances differ in kind, ought to be abandoned, and along with it, of course, the idea of the essential unity of inorganic bodies. Some of these writers thought that the essential unity of organic beings (i.e. living ones) could still be maintained, but others more logically (e.g. P. Descoqs, S.J.) abandoned this also. For, in fact, if the reasons which cause us to give up the idea that the elements of inorganic matter do not remain actually in the compound,—and so the essential unity of compounds,—are peremptory in the inorganic realm, they will be so also when these substances, exhibiting the same characteristics, are found in living things, as is in fact the case. The theory, however, that living things are not essential unities leads to very serious difficulties both philosophical, and, as Professor J. S. Haldane has pointed out, scientific. Nevertheless, it is such thorough-going sacrifice of unity which the scientific theory, if it is to be taken at its face value, seems to demand

We are therefore led to ask whether the traditional view may not, after all, be the true one : i.e. whether chemically simple bodies, those, namely, which are not composed of other chemical elements, do actually persist as such when they join together to form a compound.

What are known by the physicists as the chemica

elements, of which ninety-two are supposed to exist, and of which ninety have at present been discovered, are not in fact all chemically simple, though they are usually treated as if they were.  For our purpose it will be sufficient to consider them as simple, since, if we can show that these elements cannot retain their own nature in composition, the same reasons will apply to the constituents of those elements which are, in fact, composite.

Since the chemical elements naturally combine with one another, those which do so must have a natural tendency to do so, or, as it is called, have affinity for one another.  Their power to combine is known as their valency, so that an atom which combines with one, two, three, etc., atoms of another element is called mono-valent, di-valent, tri-valent, and so on.  The result of such a combination will be an equilibrium, and the question is, how is this equilibrium to be explained philosophically.

Broadly speaking, there are two opinions at present in vogue among Scholastic writers.  The first is that of the pluriformists who trace their philosophical descent to S. Albert the Great.  The second is the Thomistic view, which maintains that in many compounds the elements of which it is made up do not remain substantially, or as such, when mixed together.  They are not present in the mixture actually and formally, but virtually only, by means of a persistence of their qualities.

The opponents of this view urge, in addition to the general scientific argument touched on above, the further consideration that it is difficult, if not impossible, to see why a chemical compound possessed of a single form or nature which is different from those of its elements, should invariably be able to be resolved again into these elements, as we know that in fact it can be ; and moreover, why, if it is an undifferentiated unity, different agents acting on it do not produce different effects, whereas, in fact, such different agents as electricity, heat, or even a blow, all produce the same effect of resolving the compound once more into its constituent elements.  All these phenomena, they contend, are easily and naturally explained on the hypothesis that the compound is a mere aggregate of atoms. In addition many other arguments are brought forward against the Thomistic opinion, such as the impossibility of accidental forms producing substantial ones, of which we spoke above : as well as many special difficulties relating to particular classes of chemical substances. We must, therefore, see what answer the Thomists make to these objections, and why in spite of them, they are so determined in maintaining that the elements do not remain actually in the mixture.

To explain the resolution of the chemical compound into its elements, modern Thomists develop further what they mean by saying that the elements remain virtually in the mixture.

This virtual permanence of the elements may mean either :

1. That neither their substance nor their qualities remain formally in the mixture, or :

2. That while the substances do not remain formally, the qualities do so ; and this again may be understood in two senses :

(a) That the qualities which remain are homogeneous throughout the whole mixture or compound, or :

(b) That they are localised in different parts of it, so that the compound is heterogeneous with respect to its qualities, having one quality in one part, and another in another.

(1) With regard to the first view, it is further explained as follows : The chemical compound is perfectly homogeneous, and contains all the material bases of the elements, which are moulded into a higher unity by means of the one specific principle. This form of the compound is virtually many, inasmuch as it takes the place of the various substantial forms of the elements. The qualities of the elements are thought to persist virtually in the compound in so far as their opposing qualities are represented in it by some third quality which is their mean, and the mean qualities so formed are considered to be distributed evenly throughout the whole compound, in such a way that it has a single electrical force, a single luminous force, a single calorific force, and so on ; which single forces represent, though, of course, they are not the same as the corresponding forces o

the elements. The compound is thus perfectly homogeneous, both substantially and accidentally.

(2) (*a*) The second view in its first form is that put forward by Fr. J. Gredt, O.S.B.[1] It differs from the view just given in that he holds that the qualities of the elements remain formally in the compound, i.e. that the electrical force of each of the elements occurs again in the compound, and is not replaced by a single third quality which is their mean. Nevertheless, it agrees with the previous view in maintaining that these qualities are evenly distributed throughout the whole mass of the compound. Thus the intensity of the qualities of the elements will be diminished until a state of equilibrium is reached, owing to the action of the elements on one another, but the nature of these qualities will remain the same. Hence the compound will have a single substantial form, and a variety of qualities which are of the same kind as those of the elements. These qualities have a uniform intensity which is less than the intensity of the qualities of the elements, the qualities themselves being found equally, both as regards their natures and their intensities, in all parts of the compound, which will thus be perfectly homogeneous, both substantially and accidentally. This qualitative homogeneity is, however, mitigated to some extent by the admission of a quantitative heterogeneity in the compound, i.e. a heterogeneity of structure.

(2) (*b*) The second form of the second view goes further in the admission of accidental heterogeneity within the compound ; for, while still maintaining that there is a single substantial form in the compound, it allows that its qualities are of the same nature as those of the elements, and, moreover, that they are found in the mixture in groups, which are localised in different parts of it. As regards their intensity, it agrees with the previous view. This is the theory proposed by M. Nys.[2]

The view that the qualities remain formally in the mixture, as opposed to that which says they remain virtually only, by

[1] *Elementa Philosophiæ* (ed. 4), Vol. I, Nos. 405–408.
[2] Nys, *Cosmologie* (ed. 4), Vol. II, pp. 206 ff., Nos. 169 ff.

means of some third mean quality, is now almost universally accepted among Thomists : for the reason that it seems impossible on the latter view to account for the reappearance of the elements at the dissolution of the compound. For it is a principle of hylomorphism that a form cannot appear except in matter which is predisposed to receive it. The theory of the mean quality, however, renders such predisposition absolutely impossible, for if the compound is altogether homogeneous, both substantially and accidentally, it is impossible that it should be predisposed in one part in a different way to that in which it is predisposed in another ; and so the appearance of two or more distinct forms is excluded.

To show that the elements do not retain their own nature in the mixture, or, in other words, that the mixture is a new entity with a nature of its own, distinct from those of its components, the Thomists argue from its distinctive characteristics and operations. If we find in any body, or class of bodies, characteristics peculiar to that body or class, and such as are found in no others, it is permissible, and indeed unavoidable, to conclude that such characteristics are properties of it, since, if they did not arise from the very nature of the body—which is the meaning of the word property—they would be without reason of being ; for, as they are constant, they must owe their being to some constant factor in the situation, and the only constant one is the natures of the bodies themselves. Now, in mixtures, this is just what we do find, for along with some qualities which were present in their elements we also find many which were not present there, and are really new ; qualities, moreover, which attach to certain mixtures exclusively and constantly. Such are colour, taste, scent, chemical affinities, etc. For example, some compounds such as sulphate of barium, are stable and absolutely inert, though its elements are very active,[1] and new characteristics are produced by hydration, which renders acids capable of dissolving metals, etc., which their components could not do. M. Nys says that thousands of such modifications, which are more or less pro-

[1] Cf. Nys, *Cosmologie*, Vol. II, p. 231.

found, have been observed, and the reader may be referred to his work for many more examples.[1] We shall decide whether any substance which is under consideration is a true compound, in accordance with our observation of such changes in particular mixtures; and it is also to be noted that what is important, from the philosophical point of view, in the properties observed in compounds is not their physical analysis, but the way in which they operate. Scientifically speaking, all we can know of these properties is such aspects of them as are amenable to quantitative treatment, and so are measurable, but the philosopher ought to take into account their operation as a whole, including the effects which they produce on other bodies; since their operation and mode of working taken as a whole is the only means we have of discovering their nature. Science, by reason of its method, which is mathematical, does not find it necessary to take account of the ends towards which things tend, or their purposes, nor even why they occur in the way they do, but philosophy must consider all these elements, if it is to arrive at a balanced view of the natures of things. If this is done, we shall find that the compounds often behave in a way very different from that of their elements; and naturally tend to different ends. These considerations, then, as to the operations and intrinsic tendencies of the elements and compounds show that the elements are specifically distinct one from another, and the compounds also from their elements. It is altogether illogical to admit a specific distinction among the elements, and to deny it as between elements and compounds, since the same criterion which assures us of the one, viz. diversity of operations, is equally decisive in the case of the other.

If, then, the elements are specifically changed when they combine, so that they do not remain in the compound formally, how are we to explain the fact that the compound shows many of their characteristics, or the sum of them, such as weight, and is always resolvable into them again?

As we have already seen, the Thomists agree in saying that the qualities of the elements remain formally, i.e.

[1] Nys, op. cit., Vol. II, pp. 227-239.

L

retaining their original nature, in the compound. If they did not, they would either be represented by a quality which is their mean, or potentially only, or not at all. The last hypothesis makes it quite impossible to explain how it is that many qualities of the compound are merely the sum of those of the elements, the fact that the spectrum of the molecule shows the characteristic spectra of the elements, and the fact that the compound is always resolvable into its elements. If they remain potentially only, different external agents, which dissolve the compound, would produce different results, since the only determining factor in this case would be the agent. This, however, is not the case, for whatever agent be employed, the resulting elements are always the same. We have already seen that the theory of a mean quality cannot be maintained, and so we must conclude that the qualities remain in the compound formally. If this be so is it sufficient, in order to account for the facts, to say that they are distributed evenly and homogeneously throughout the whole compound, their capacity for reappearance in the solution of it being accounted for by its being heterogeneous in structure, i.e. that there is a difference of arrangement of parts in one portion of the compound from that in another? It seems very improbable that such a heterogeneity as this is sufficient, since it is quantitative only, and thus seems to be inadequate as a predisposition for the appearance of substantial forms which differ in kind, and which must, therefore, be prepared for by qualitative differences. It does not seem possible to regard inanimate bodies as wholly unified and unorganised, as was done in the Middle Ages, but rather we find in them an organisation which is comparable to that of living things, though less elaborate. Thus, the view which ascribes to the molecule different qualities in its different parts appears more consonant with the known facts, and on a wide view more acceptable, than that which denies it : since we shall recognise right through the material world, from the atom up to the highest forms of life, a continually increasing heterogeneity of structure and quality, along with a consistent homogeneity of nature. To maintain such a gradual ascent is merely an expansion of the Thomistic notion of the scale of being of which Milton speaks in *Paradise Lost* (Bk. V, lines 468 ff.) :

> To whom the winged Hierarch repli'd.
> O Adam, one Almightie is, from whom
> All things proceed, and up to him return,
> If not depraved from good, created all
> Such to perfection, one first matter all,
> Indu'd with various forms, various degrees
> Of substance, and in things that live, of life ;
> But more refin'd, more spirituous, and pure,
> As neerer to him plac't, or neerer tending
> Each in their several active Sphears assignd,
> Till body up to spirit work, in bounds
> Proportiond to each kind.  So from the root
> Springs lighter the green stalk, from thence the leaves
> More ærie, last the bright consummate floure
> Spirits odorous breathes :  flours and thir fruit
> Man's nourishment, by gradual scale sublim'd
> To vital spirits aspire, to animal
> To intellectual, give both life and sense,
> Fansie and understanding, whence the soule
> Reason receives, and reason is her being.

Somewhat the same idea, though carried much farther, is held as true by Professor Whitehead, who says : ' The doctrine which I am maintaining is that the whole concept of materialism only applies to very abstract entities, the products of logical discernment.  The concrete enduring entities are organisms, so that the plan of the *whole* influences the very characters of the various subordinate organisms which enter into it.  In the case of an animal, the mental states enter into the plan of the total organism and thus modify the plans of the successive subordinate organisms until the ultimate smallest organisms, such as electrons, are reached.  Thus an electron within a living body is different from an electron outside it, by reason of the plan of the body. . . . But the principle of modification is perfectly general throughout nature, and represents no property peculiar to living bodies.'[1]

The difficulties arising from the existence of isomeric and polymeric substances,[2] as well as the phenomena of allotropy,[3]

[1] *Science and the Modern World*, pp. 98 ff. ; cf. pp. 164 ff. Cf. also Nys, Vol. II, pp. 200 ff. ; Geny in *Gregorianum* (1922), pp. 458 f. ; *Divus Thomas (Plac.)* (1925), p. 77.
[2] Cf. Nys, Vol. II, pp. 268 ff.     [3] *Ibid.*, Vol. I, pp. 240 f.

can be explained on these principles ; while the assertion that atomic weight, mass, etc., remain constant does not affect our conclusion, since we maintain that the same matter remains throughout the change, and so those accidents which are quantitive, and thus directly associated with matter, will naturally remain unchanged also.

In general it is true to say that all the facts which science takes as proving the essential discontinuity of matter—since this is the simplest hypothesis, and therefore for science the truest—can equally well be accounted for by substantial homogeneity, together with accidental heterogeneity. We are led to adopt this latter view from the philosophical consideration of the natural intrinsic tendencies of bodies and their relations with the rest of the material universe : considerations which natural science does not, and ought not, to take into account ;[1] dealing as it does only with measurable phenomena.

[1] Examples of the application of these principles are to be found in Hœnen's *Cosmologia*, pp. 350–404 ; e.g. p. 368 with regard to Bragg's experiments. See also his *Summary*, pp. 401 ff.

# CHAPTER XII

## THE INDIVIDUAL

Its Nature—Opinions—Explanation of the Thomist View—Reasons in its Favour—Meaning of 'Materia Signata'—Some Difficulties Considered.

So far, we have been concerned with general natures ; first of material substances, and then of its various species and accidental characteristics ; and we now have to turn to the individuals which belong to these species. It is with such individuals that our knowledge begins, and the whole process of generalisation has as its object and end the understanding of them. It will, however, only allow us to have knowledge of them with regard to those features which they possess in common with other individuals, leaving us still in ignorance as to what it is that constitutes them as individuals, or as differentiated from other concrete substances ; for the individual, while undifferentiated in itself, is yet distinguished from others, as S. Thomas says.[1] If what has been said about the essential unity of the atom and molecule be true, these bodies, at least, when taken singly, will be true individuals ; even if we are obliged to deny or doubt the individuality of larger masses of inanimate matter ;[2] and we wish to discover what it is precisely which is the root of their unity and of their distinction from other bodies of the same nature as themselves. This question as to the root of numerical unity is known as the problem of the principle of individuation, and is one of the most recalcitrant and obscure of the many difficult problems discussed in mathematical philosophy.

The history of the consideration of this problem may be

[1] *Summa Theol.*, Pars I, Q. 29, a. 4.
[2] For a full discussion of this question see Nys, *Cosmologie*, Vol. II, pp. 281–294.

said to begin with Aristotle who regarded the individual as containing reality in itself, in contrast to Plato, who looked upon the subsisting Forms as constituting reality. The former finds in the individual two kinds of unity, a unity of nature, which it shares with other individuals, and a unity which is all its own. The first is specific, and the second numerical, unity. Specific unity is, in his view, derived from form, since form is that which makes the substance to be determinately what it is. What, then, is it which is the source of the numerical unity of individuation ? Few passages, and those ambiguous, can be cited in which individuation seems to be ascribed to form ;[1] while there are numbers in which it is distinctly attributed to matter. So he says : ' The whole thing, such and such a form in this flesh and these bones, is Callias or Socrates ; and they are different owing to their matter (for this is different), but the same in species, for the species is indivisible.'[2] So it is no doubt true to say that Aristotle thought that things which differ numerically within the same species do so in matter only, and so by reason of it.

The question does not make much progress till we come to the Arabian philosophers of the Middle Ages ; though Boethius, in touching on it incidentally, seems generally to ascribe individuation to accidents. ' Ea vero quæ individua sunt et solo numero discrepunt, solis accidentibus distant.'[3]

Passing then to the Arabians, Avicenna (980–1037), or rather his translator, first introduces us to a term which was to become famous in discussions of this question, by using the word ' signatum ' as synonymous with ' determinate individual,' which thence comes to be applied to any determinate reality. Thus we hear both of ' forma,' and of ' materia,' ' signata.' Since a nature, he contends, is not of itself individual, the relation between it and individuality is an accidental one, and therefore we must look for its source not in essence, but among the accidents, such as quantity, quality, place, and time. Nevertheless, a definite theory of

---

[1] Cf. Met., 1038b14 ; 1071a27–29 ; Phys., 412a6–9.

[2] Met., 1034a5–8 ; cf. 1016b32 ; 1035b27–31 ; 1054a34 ; 1074a31–34 ; Phys., 278a7–b3.

[3] In Isagogen Porphyrii, ed. Brandt, pp. 241, 9 ; cf. De Trinitate, I.

individuation is not worked out by Avicenna, though his
dicta about it should logically lead to the conclusion that its
source lies in matter which is determined by spatial dimensions. No doubt this latent conclusion was perceived by the
penetrating mind of S. Thomas : who, however, was also
much influenced in this question by another writer of the
same race—Averroes (1126–1198). According to Averroes,
known in the Middle Ages as the Commentator, from his
exhaustive commentaries on Aristotle, matter is in itself
numerically one, since being undetermined, it cannot be
many. Nevertheless, it is divisible, and that which makes it
so must be quantity, i.e. the three dimensions of the continuum. Hence matter must be conceived as carrying with
it, not this or that three-dimensional extension, but extension in general—'unterminated extension or dimensions.'
So first matter is in potency to a determination by three
dimensions in general, which potency is logically prior to that
which it has for being determined by a specific form.

The theories of Avicenna and Averroes seem to have had a
predominant influence on the thought of S. Thomas (1224–
1274) ; which vacillates in a remarkable fashion between their
explanations. He never, as it seems, had the least doubt
with regard to the Aristotelean theory of individuation by
means of matter ; but he hesitates for some time as to the
way in which this general theory should be understood.
After accepting, at first, the expressions and theory of
Avicenna that the principle of individuation is matter
designated by determined dimensions,[1] he abandons it in
favour of the Averroist opinion that it is matter affected by
unterminated dimensions which is this principle.[2] He makes
considerable use of this second theory, only in the end to
throw it over and return once more to the view that the
dimensions are determined ones.[3]

The reason of this change of opinion is almost certainly to
be found in S. Thomas' keener realisation of all the consequences which flow from the strict acceptance of the
doctrine of the uniqueness of substantial form : since the

[1] *De ente et essentia*, Cap. 2.
[2] In *Boethium de Trinitate*, Q. 4, A. 2, et ad 3um.
[3] e.g. *Quodlibet*, XI., a. 6, ad 2um.

Averroist theory really implies some real priority of the unterminated dimensions to substantial form.

A few words must be added with respect to the subsequent history of this discussion in the Schools, though it is impossible to treat it fully, or to examine non-Scholastic views of individuation.

*Scotus* (1265(?)–1308) held that the source of individuation is the numerical determination of the form and matter of the compound, by which they become *this* form and *this* matter. He maintains, further, that it is distinguished from the nature of the thing by a formal distinction *a parte rei*, i.e. it is not wholly identified as a reality with the nature. He says it is the ' *ultima realitas entis* ' ;[1] and though not substantial form is yet of the nature of a formality as determining the thing to be ' this.' He calls it ' *hæcceitas* ' or ' thisness ' ; so that a thing is this by its thisness, it is an individual by means of the last reality of its being : a conclusion which is not very illuminating.

*Ockham* (*c.* 1300–1348), and the *Nominalists* generally, necessarily regard the question as to the principle of individuation as meaningless, since they do not admit as realities independent of the mind any universal or specific natures, but only individual things or phenomena. Hence the individual is distinct of itself, and not multiplied in the species, the latter being either a mere concept or a group name.

*Suarez* (1548–1617) considers, in opposition to Scotus, that the principle of individuation can only be logically distinguished from the individual being. Every being, even an incomplete one, is individual of itself, by reason of its entity. He is particularly determined in his opposition to the Thomist thesis which would see in a part of the nature only, viz. matter affected by quantity, the principle of individuation.[2]

It is essential to notice that in this enquiry we are not

---

[1] *Opus Oxoniense*, II, dist. III, Q. 2, No. 15.

[2] *Disp. Metaph.*, V, Sect. 3. Cf. *Mahieu*, François Suarez, pp. 112 ff. The greater part of the foregoing account of the history of this problem is derived from Fr. Roland-Gosselin's masterly analysis in his edition of the *De ente et essentia* ; particularly with regard to S. Thomas' opinions.

looking for the proximate cause of individuation, but its root or first cause ; nor yet do we wish to discover how individuals are to be distinguished by it, how we recognise them as distinct individuals, but how they are distinguished from one another in themselves.[1]

The Thomist school all answer this question by saying that the principle is matter signed or sealed by quantity : which at this stage we may take as meaning matter which has a relation to quantity—Wicksteed describes it as ' earmarked by quantity '[2]—though later we will examine this phrase more closely.  It is necessary to discuss this question fairly fully since S. Thomas' view on this subject is at the very heart of his metaphysical system, to such an extent that its abandonment would seem to involve the abandonment of his whole conception of the universe ; and conversely a real grasp of it will greatly help to an understanding of the whole of his philosophy.  We have already had occasion to notice that the theory of matter and form is a particular case of the Aristotelean division of being into potency and act—though almost certainly not a derivative of it—and this thesis is another special case of that theory.  For multiplication implies a distinction, and so a restriction or limitation, which limitation implies, in its turn, some imperfection or potency ; from which it follows that an act which is complete and perfect in its own order, both as a substance and as a species, cannot be multiplied in that order ; and also that if any form or act is multiplicable, this cannot come about from the form or act itself ; since this in itself implies no limitation.  The multiplication must therefore come from potency or matter.

To prove their contention that the principle of individuation must be matter determined by quantity, the Thomists argue in the first place that no other principle can be discovered which will satisfy the necessary conditions, viz. to multiply substantial individuals within the species ; since in any material substance we can distinguish four, and only

---

[1] Cf. Salmanticenses, *Cursus Theol.*, Vol. I, Tract. I, Disp. I, Dub. 2, No. 45 f.
[2] *The Reactions between Dogma and Philosophy* (1926), p. 368.

four, elements : matter, form, subsistence (i.e. that by which the thing is put in the category of substance, and made self-supporting or existing *per se*, or on its own account), and existence. The last two cannot possibly be the principle of individuation, since they both belong to the existential order, and so presuppose, as a necessary condition of their own individuality, an individual nature already constituted. The reason of this is that existence being, in itself, all of a kind, must, if it is to be differentiated and made individual at all, be so differentiated by something other than itself, i.e. by nature. Moreover, we are, in fact, asking how we can have an individual nature, so that the question is concerned with the order of nature or essence, not existence. Neither can form be the principle we are looking for, since form differentiates things specifically, for the very conception of form implies that it is form which makes a thing to be of a determined species : so that when form varies, the species varies. Consequently, matter, as the only remaining element in the thing, must be the principle of individuation. Matter, however, does not seem to be capable of filling the rôle required of it, for it is, as we have seen, altogether potential and undetermined in itself, so that it could not determine, or differentiate, anything else. If, then, it is to do this, it must be in some way determined. Such determination as is required evidently cannot come to it from substantial form, since we are looking for numerical, not specific, determination : while the very word 'numerical' suggests that it does come from that accident, which is most closely united to it, and which is numbered, viz. quantity ; which is also, as we saw, individual of itself (cf. p. 65). In so far, then, as matter has a relation to this quantity rather than that, it can be, and is, the principle of individuation.

Again,[1] if we look at the question directly we see that two things are required for the principle of individuation ; first, that it should be an intrinsic substantial principle of incommunicability of form ; and, second, that it should be the principle whereby one body is made distinct from all others. Now, that matter is an intrinsic substantial principle is clear,

[1] For the following argument cf. *Summa Theol.*, Pars III, Q. 77, a. 2.

and moreover, being the basic and primary substratum of bodies it is unable to be received in anything else ; from which it follows that any form which is received in it will likewise be unable to be received over again, and so will be rendered incommunicable so far as reception in a subject is concerned. The principle of distinction from others, on the other hand, is not matter, since this is in itself undifferentiated ; while the source of differentiation and division is extended quantity, for a thing is rendered naturally incapable of existing in several things if it is undivided in itself, and divided from all others. It is clear, moreover, that it is extension which divides substance, and so is a kind of individuating principle, inasmuch as forms are numerically differentiated by being in different parts of matter. That quantity is indeed, in this way, a principle of individuation can be seen in the order of pure quantity, inasmuch as we can imagine several lines of the same species, differing only by their position in space : and the same is true of other geometrical figures. Such difference in position, however, belongs to quantity. Hence a double principle of individuation is required, matter and quantity, or matter determined by quantity. From this we can see the way in which the phrase ' *materia signata quantitate* ' ought to be understood : a much controverted question.

Sylvester of Ferrara held that *materia signata* is a compound of matter and the quantity which actually informs it. This idea is perfectly clear and acceptable if we consider an existing individual ; which, of course, has a particular quantity ; but it is not satisfactory if we consider the individual in the process of coming into existence, and attempt to determine how it came to be individualised ; since the matter could not be actually informed by a particular quantity until it had already received a substantial form. Now, it is precisely with the individuation of this form that our enquiry is concerned ; and so we cannot ascribe such individuation to actually informing quantity, since being posterior to form it cannot be, in the same order, prior to it, and so cannot make the matter to be this rather than that, and thus individuate form.

In order to meet this and other difficulties in the opinion of Ferrariensis, Cajetan and the majority of Thomists say that *materia signata* must be explained as first matter which has a radical requirement for this quantity rather than that : for first matter, being the potential principle of *bodies*, requires quantity.

First matter in general requires quantity in general, and so this or that determined matter requires this or that determined quantity.   Hence the radical requirement for a determined quantity is considered as prior to the coming of substantial form, and actual quantity, to the body.   This, perhaps, lessens the difficulty, but does not clear it up ; for how can matter which is altogether undetermined have a determinate requirement ?   To answer this an appeal is made to the Aristotelean principle of reciprocal priority of mutual causes.[1]   According to this principle, causes, which are causes of one another are in different genera of causality ; and in this case, quantity, being an accidental form, is posterior to substantial form in the genus of efficient causality, but, since it is at the same time a disposition which disposes matter to receive this form, it is prior to it in the genus of material disposing causality.   So the matter in which the new form is about to appear, being disposed to receive this form, is also disposed to receive the quantity which goes along with it.   This explanation, however, seems only to give us matter with a requirement for some quantity within the limits of the quantities which are suitable to the form in question, as e.g. the quantities suitable to elephants as opposed to those suitable to mice.   Such quantity, it is plain, cannot be said to be individually determinate ; in fact, the very idea of it is of that quantity outside whose limits we should not find a member of the species, and within whose limits we might find any individual of it, not a particular one.   Now, as we have seen, quantity essentially consists in a plurality of parts, and one quantity is differentiated from another, and is this quantity as opposed to that, by a different

[1] Cf. S. Thomas in V Metaph., Lect. 2 ; de Veritate, Q. 28, Arts. and 8.   John of S. Thomas, *Cursus Phil. Phil. Nat.*, P. II, Q. 1, A. 7 and Q. 9, A. 4.   *Salmanticenses Cursus Theologicus*, Tom. I.   De Principia Individuationis, Disp. I, Dubium 5, Sect. 3.

mination. The Scholastics express this by saying that it has a transcendental relation to ' this ' quantity, i.e. a relation which is not something added to it, but is its very self ; just as matter as such has a transcendental relation to material form as such. They are correlatives, one implying the other. The matter remains purely potential, but its capacity is limited ; as in the case of two vessels of different sizes, the smaller one's actual content would be less than that of the larger, and yet both may be equally empty ; so, in the case of our two ' matters,' both may be equally potential. The matter which has a transcendental relation to a definite quantity is no less potential than matter in general, but there is less potentiality.

Again, it might seem that our principle, though sufficient to account for the individual distinction of two bits of inanimate matter, such as two stones, is hardly sufficient when we come to things of a higher order, such as two dogs, and still more two men. This difficulty arises, partly, from the fact that we often confuse individuality with personality ; but we can hardly insist too much on the distinction between them, for they are, in fact, at the opposite ends of the scale. Quite apart from this theory of individuation, consideration shews, as we shall presently see, that personality is the highest and most perfect thing in nature, whereas individuality is almost the lowest.[1] Further, it is to be noticed that by individuality we mean something negative : this thing is *not* that, whereas, as we ascend in the scale of beings, we get, along with this negative character, a gradual increase of a positive character as the things become more and more masters of themselves. Such self-mastery is in proportion to the capacity for action on one's own account, by and for oneself ; in other words, in proportion to the capacity for immanent action. Now a plant has immanent activities which inanimate things have not, being able to nourish itself, grow, and reproduce its kind ; animals have still more of such immanent activity, for they direct themselves by sense, and men most of all, being able to determine their own

[1] Cf. Maritain, *Three Reformers*, pp. 19 ff., where this distinction is shown at length with many of its applications.

actions both by sense and reason.  Thus we have a growing centralisation and self-control, but the negative division from other bodies which is characteristic of individuality remains the same :  and we can legitimately attribute individuation to matter, while recognising a growing unification in the thing itself as we ascend the scale.[1]

As to the way in which we distinguish one individual from another, there is no doubt that we do so by remarking their different accidental characteristics, such as position, dimensions, shape, colour, etc. ;  but though individuality is known to us by means of these, it would be a confusion of thought to conclude that they are therefore its principle.

If, then, the principle of individuation be matter affected by a transcendental relation to a determined position, it follows that material substances are not individuated absolutely in themselves, but in relation to other individuals, from which they are separated ;  and consequently that the principle of individuation, though intrinsic, cannot be, as Suarez maintains, the entity of the thing considered absolutely.  For, if this were so, the matter of one thing, considered absolutely, would be different from the matter of another, and so would not be common matter.  This would lead us to conclude that any two substances differ essentially or specifically of themselves.  Such a conclusion, however, is definitely Nominalistic, since there could, in this case, be nothing universal in nature.  All things would be essentially different, and no essential concept could apply to several of them.  On the other hand, if, with Scotus, we make individuation something added to the nature of the thing, we equivalently assert that nature without such addition is universal ; and since such nature is found in individuals, the universal as such will be found in individuals.  This view, therefore, tends towards an extreme form of Realism.  In saying this our intention is only to point out the tendencies which seem to be implicit in the views of these two great thinkers, not to suggest that Suarez was a Nominalist, or Scotus an advocate of an extreme form of Realism.  In any case, the balance

[1] Cf. M. C. D'Arcy, S.J., *Thomas Aquinas*, pp. 148 ff., where this difficulty is discussed and the notion of immanence emphasised.

between an extreme Realism and Nominalism is undoubtedly preserved in the theory of S. Thomas, in which the individual neither absorbs the universal, nor is absorbed by it. Such a moderate realism avoids both scepticism, which is the outcome of Nominalism, and Monism, from which extreme Realism cannot escape. From this point of view, therefore, this thesis may be said to be a postulate of the Thomist theory of knowledge. Indeed, whether we look at the change and motion in the material world, or at the multiplication of individuals in it, or at our knowledge of it, the facts force us to say that the only intelligible explanation which can be given of them is that this world and all things in it are composed of two elements, one of which is actual and the other potential, and of which the latter limits the former.

# CHAPTER XIII

## SOME GENERAL CHARACTERISTICS OF THE INANIMATE WORLD

Physical Laws and Theories—The Formation of the Material Universe—The Infinity and Eternity of the Universe.

## I. *Physical Laws and Theories*.

To enquire into the ultimate cause of the universe and the method of its production, if it is not self-sufficient, does not come, strictly speaking, within the scope of natural philosophy, since this considers the material world in itself. At the present time, however, it is more than ever evident that it is subject to change, and has not always been in the state in which we now find it. Its changes, nevertheless, must be held to be regulated by determinate rules; for since the Thomistic theory of bodies recognises that they have determinate natures, they must also have determinate modes of action. Such modes of action are commonly called the laws of nature. It is clear that such laws have a certain necessity, since they are consequents of the natures of the bodies; but this necessity is said to be 'hypothetical'; i.e. dependent on the fulfilment of some condition; the condition in this case being that the circumstances remain the same, and that no disturbing influence comes into the system of inanimate nature from without. If this condition be fufilled, bodies will always act in a certain determinate fashion which follows from their nature. We may not, however, be able to formulate these laws adequately, and any formulation of them will naturally be bound up with the way in which the world is regarded by physical science at any particular epoch, and so with physical theories, the discussion of the character and value of which belongs properly to Epistemology, or the theory of knowledge. It may not, at the same time, be out of place to remark here that some writers now regard these theories as having only a phenomenal value, with little or no connection with the realities which may or may not underlie them : while others take them simply at their face value, and transport them bodily into natural philosophy. In this latter view, atoms, electrons, protons, waves, the ether, etc., are treated as substances on the same terms as bodies which fall under direct sensible observation. This view seems hardly tenable, and in any case is not necessitated by the notions of the physicists themselves, who certainly regard sub-atomic elements as being of a different character to gross matter. The other extreme seems also to be inadmissible, inasmuch as the theories are founded on quantitative examination of the material world, and therefore cannot be wholly unconnected with the material reality of which it is composed. From this it is clear that philosophy cannot ignore physical theory, nor yet regard it as expressed in the same language as that which it uses itself. To what extent physical theories are intended to, or in fact do, represent ontological realities, is one which must be left over for more detailed consideration at a later stage.

## II. *The Formation of the Material Universe.*

Since the changes which occur within the material universe come within the limits of the subject matter of natural philosophy, it is within its scope to examine them, and so to consider the whole system of such changes, or the world-process in general. In such an examination it will necessarily be directed by rational or metaphysical principles, such as the principle of finality, which, though it is only in metaphysics that they are demonstrated to be absolutely general ones, applying to all being, can yet be legitimately employed here, since natural philosophy has established their validity as applied to bodies, as in the case of the principle of finality, by showing that bodies have determined natures. Its function will consequently be rather negative than positive, in so far as it will endeavour to see whether the views put forward by natural science are consonant with reason or not.

The current theory with regard to the formation of the material universe is, as is well known, the following :

It is supposed that the material universe at first existed as a uniformly distributed gas, which, supposing the total amount of matter to have remained constant, and calculating on the basis of the amount of matter now existing, must have been extremely tenuous. The first stage in the growth of the universe would be the condensation of this gas into giant nebulæ, not stars, as Newton conjectured. Such condensations must have been started by some disturbance in the primeval gas, and unless this motion were directed exactly towards the centre of the condensation it would cause it to spin. As the gas is contracting this spin will increase in proportion as it does so, and the result of the process will be nebulæ rotating at different rates. This is, in fact, observed, viz. that the nebulæ are so rotating. A nebula which was not rotating would assume a spherical shape under the force of its own gravitation, but rotation will cause it to be flattened at the poles and broadened at the equator until it reaches the limit of such flattening, which is not a plane surface, but a figure of the shape of a double convex lens. After this point, since flattening cannot proceed any further, the nebula will begin to eject matter from its sharp equatorial edge, and a thin layer of gas will be formed in the equatorial plane. Any disturbance in this mass will cause condensations in it, of which the larger ones only survive. When the weights of the smallest condensations which could form and be permanent are calculated it is found that most of them are comparable with that of the sun. For this reason, and others, therefore, it is considered that this is the actual process by which the stars (of which, of course, our sun is one) were formed. Thus the sun and all the stars will have been born out of rotating nebulæ. The galactic system (the Milky Way) is supposed to have been a rotating nebula which has gradually condensed into the Galaxy which we now observe, and in which our solar system is situated.

Turning now to the formation of the Solar System, we see that according to the foregoing theory it will have begun with the sun as a condensation of the gas of the galactic nebula, which condensation will be in rotation since its parent was rotating. The first serious scientific attempt to account for the formation of the Solar System in its present form was that put forward by Laplace in 1796. He suggested the idea that the system was originally a nebula in rotation which would gradually shrink, and its shrinkage making it rotate more and more quickly, he showed that it would flatten out and emit matter in its equatorial plane in the way described above with regard to the formation of the stars. Thus the planets would be left behind by the main mass (the Sun) as this shrank continually. This view was accepted for nearly a century, but has now been abandoned, for, according to the theory the Sun broke up and produced the planets owing to its excessive rotation. This, however, could not have been the cause of their production, since it is now known that a star which rotates too fast does not form a system similar to the Solar System, but bursts into pieces of nearly equal size, a result which is observed in binary and multiple stellar systems. Moreover, on calculating the angular momentum of the primeval sun, it is found that it could not have been sufficient to make it break up at all ; and, lastly, the mathematics of condensations shows that though Laplace's nebular hypothesis would hold good with respect to vast masses, such as the giant nebulæ, it cannot account for the formation of small bodies such as planets, since the gas left behind by the rotatory motion of the Sun would be too tenuous to condense, it would simply be dissipated. Thus it appears that though, roughly speaking, Laplace's hypothesis is applicable to the birth of suns from the original nebula, it cannot account for the birth of planets from the Sun.

Since there is no known method by which a single star could give rise to a planetary system, the theory is put forward that the Solar System arose through the approach of another star to the Sun while the latter was still in a gaseous state. This is known as the tidal theory, which suggests that some two thousand million years ago a second star approached near enough to the Sun to raise in it an enormous tide of the nature of an arm of gas drawn out from the Sun's matter. This arm would be of sufficient density to allow condensations to form within it, the larger of which condensations became the planets. These will follow a somewhat irregular orbit round the Sun, in the course of which they may approach near enough to it for matter to be drawn out of them in the same way as they themselves were drawn from the Sun ; and in this way the production of their satellites is accounted for. This idea is confirmed by the fact that the orbital planes of the planets are different from the equatorial plane of the Sun, a fact which is unaccountable on Laplace's theory, but which fits in well with the notion that matter was drawn out of the Sun by a passing star, which was not in the plane of the Sun's equator.

Now, it is clearly not the business of philosophy to decide what degree of probability attaches to these theories from the scientific point of view : this is determined by the extent to which they cover the known facts, and the simplicity of the picture which they give. Philosophy can only say whether, if they are taken to represent what really occurred in the past, they involve any elements which are repugnant to reason. Now it is clear that they all presuppose that the evolution of the material universe came about, not at random, but in obedience to the natures of the bodies considered, which all have their peculiar properties and laws ; though some laws are common to them all—such as gravitation—and others to large classes—such as the laws governing the condensation of gases. No account is given of the origination of the primeval nebula, or of the first movements in it which caused rotation, etc. So, no objection can be taken to the theories on the ground that they violate the principle of causality ; and since they all recognise determinate characters and laws in natural bodies, they do not violate the principle of finality. Hence, from no point of view can it be said that they are irrational ; and it is clear that since the primeval gas is supposed to have had a definite constitution, it would contain virtually the developments and evolution which followed from it.

From a scientific point of view the general theory of the way in which the stars were produced enjoys, at least, a high degree of probability ; though it should be recognised that all we can affirm positively is that the observations show that the known phenomena are such as they would have been if the theory represents the actual events. The universe looks as if it had been formed in this way.

III. *Is the Universe Finite or Infinite in Extent, and in Duration ?*

(*a*) The first question has already been answered implicitly, since we have seen that an absolutely infinite quantity, whether discrete or continuous, is an impossibility. It is thus clear that since a universe which was actually infinite in extent would involve the actuality of both these infinities, it is therefore impossible.

(*b*) The second question does not admit of so definite an answer. It might be thought, at first sight, that we could rule out an infinite duration of the world on the same grounds as we do its infinite extent ; but it is clear that if we cannot exclude such a possibility we can then ask whether it is a fact that it has had an infinite duration.

Let us consider first the possibility of an infinite duration of the world. If the universe were unproduced by any cause it would clearly have such a duration, since it exists now, and a thing cannot bring itself into existence. Hence, we should have answered both our questions—as to possibility and fact—affirmatively ; saying that it is, and so obviously can be, eternal. If, however, the world has been brought into existence, does it follow that it had a beginning in time ? As is well known, S. Thomas startled his contemporaries by maintaining that reason was unable to prove the necessity of such a beginning in time, even though the world was acknowledged to have been created by God. This assertion depends on the statement that causal priority does not necessarily involve a priority of time ; and, in fact, in production from nothing no priority of time can be involved, since time only begins with the production of the world. There cannot be a moment before the first. The universe itself which is made is also not incompatible with infinite duration, since it is what it is by reason of its nature, which is quite independent of time ; and this holds good whether we consider a single static thing or a whole series of successive ones, for in the first case the single being, in the second the whole series, would endure from all eternity.[1]

If, then, we cannot exclude the possibility of the infinite duration of the world in the past, we can only weigh the probabilities for and against such an infinite duration having been the fact ; and all Scholastics, together with most theists, think that the weight of probability is on the side of a finite duration of the material world, both in the past and in the future. They argue that since everything of which we have any knowledge had a beginning, it is natural to conclude that the world as a whole also had a temporal beginning. They appeal, further, to the law of entropy, according to which the energy of the world is tending towards a state of equilibrium, and consequently since this state of equilibrium has not yet been reached, the process cannot have been going on for ever, since all that is required in order to reach it is that the process should go on long enough, a condition which would evidently be satisfied in an infinite time. Hence, in the past, there must have been a beginning of this process, when the available energy was at its maximum ; and in the future there must come a time when a state of energy equilibrium will be reached, and when the world will cease to be in the state in which it is now.

Further, on the supposition that energy is liberated and made available by the ' annihilation ' of matter, as is suggested by many scientists, it will follow that if the law of entropy holds good, and the material of the universe is finite, there will be a definite limit, however remote, to the process of the liberation of energy, and consequently there must come a time when all the matter in the universe will have been annihilated. Similarly, in the past, if we were to go back to infinity, we should have to suppose that the matter in the universe was infinite in weight, a supposition which is said to be impossible on physical grounds.[2]    In accordance

---

[1] Cf. *Summa Theologica*, Pars I, Q. 46, Arts. 1 and 2 ; *Contra Gentiles*, Lib. II, Cap. 31–38 ; *Opusculum De Eternitate Mundi*.
[2] Jeans, *The Universe Around Us*, Ch. VI.

with these ideas Sir James Jeans says : ' the present matter of the universe cannot have existed for ever : indeed, we can probably assign an upper limit to its age of, say, some such round number as 200 million million years.'[1]

It is clear that these arguments are not absolutely demonstrative, both because they do not show that there is a contradiction in the supposition that the world has had an infinite duration, and because they only possess the same degree of probability as attaches to the physical theories on which they are founded. From this point of view the argument which concludes from entropy that the world will not always remain in the state in which it now is, seems more certain than that which asserts that the matter of the present universe will come to an end. What their scientific value is can only be estimated by physicists, philosophy being able to point out only that, however highly they may be esteemed in this way, they are not demonstrative ; and that in itself the hypothesis of an eternally existing material universe does not involve any contradiction or absurdity.

It may be well to add, in conclusion, that to speak of the world beginning ' in time ' is clearly an inexact phrase, for it is impossible that there should have been any time before the world was, time being the measure of the motion of mutable being, which therefore began, if it began at all, with the first of mutable things. We can only speak of creation in time in the same way as we might speak of the source of a river being in it.

### Conclusion.

With these considerations as to the beginning and end of the material universe the Cosmological section of philosophy closes ; and we have next to examine a special class of beings which are found in it, viz. animate ones, the discussions with regard to which form the second part of Natural Philosophy, which is commonly called by the Scholastics Psychology.

[1] Op. cit., p. 327.

# THE PHILOSOPHY OF NATURE

## PART II.—THE PHILOSOPHY OF ANIMATE NATURE

### INTRODUCTION

THE investigation into the nature of living beings is held by the Scholastics to be a part of Natural Philosophy. This fact is of considerable importance, since to overlook it would result in a fatal confusion of this study with what is now generally known as Psychology. The latter is, in fact, an entirely different science ; but the name Psychology was originally applied to the philosophical examination of the animate world, and for the last two hundred years the Scholastics have used it in this sense, and so as the name of that part of philosophy which we are now beginning to con-sider. Philosophy, as we saw, deals with the very natures of things, and is concerned with their actions and behaviour, only in so far as these give us insight into their natures. The recently constituted science of Psychology, on the contrary, is interested to discover the way in which living things, and particularly human beings, act, and to establish, if it can, the laws which regulate their conduct and behaviour. The distinction, therefore, between Scholastic and modern Psychology is similar to that which we have already noticed between Cosmology and Physics. Cosmology tries to determine the inner nature of material things, while Physics is concerned with the laws of their action ; so that the former discusses the very essence and reality of motion, for example, while the latter lays down its laws, or the ways in which it is observed to occur. Modern psychology is therefore an experimental and natural science, while Scholastic psychology is a rational and philosophical one, dealing with the being of living things. If this distinction be borne in mind from the start it will prevent any false expectations being entertained as to the kind of truths which may be hoped to be discovered by means of Scholastic psychology, as it would be idle to look for explanations of particular human actions in a science which sets out to explain the nature of man in general, or to seek for a discussion of abnormalities in one which professedly deals with the normal.  So our study will deal with the nature of man and other living things and with their powers, but will not attempt to investigate in detail all their particular actions and behaviour, especially abnormal ones.  The distinction, moreover, takes the sting out of the objections made to rational psychology which assert that it deals exclusively with unobservable entities such as the intellect or senses ; for by ' unobservable ' is meant that these realities cannot be known experimentally in the laboratory, and rational psychology does not profess to be an experimental science.  At the back of such objections there is always, in fact, present the conviction or prejudice that nothing can be known which cannot be so experimentally observed ; but this is a prejudice which concerns the theory of knowledge in general (it is, in fact, what is known as Nominalism), and has no greater bearing on psychology than on any other philosophical study.  The discussion of it, therefore, would be evidently out of place here, and we must continue to trust to the common-sense belief that reason can give us knowledge which is additional to that which we can derive from sensible observation.  If anyone should feel any qualms about trusting to the powers of the reason before he has examined them, perhaps the consideration that the proposition, ' nothing can be known but that which can be observed experimentally,' is itself not open to experimental verification—and therefore on this hypothesis unknowable—may be sufficient to allay them, at least provisionally.

That rational and experimental psychology are specifically distinct sciences is undoubtedly genuine Thomistic doctrine, as can be seen, both in particular passages where S. Thomas distinguishes the experimental and speculative knowledge which we have of the ' soul,' asserting their difference,[1] and

---

[1] Cf. *De Veritate*, X, 8, III.*C.G.* 46 ;  and Barbado, *Actus Primi Congressus Thomistici*, p. 94.

from his general principles for the distinction of the sciences which will be discussed later.[1]

If, then, it be granted that there is a psychology which is a rational or philosophical science, we can pass to a consideration of its nature more in detail.

The word psychology seems to have been introduced by Melancthon, and means literally the science of the soul, i.e. the science of the life-principle ; and this may be taken to be a nominal definition of it ; which, though it tells us what is the field of its investigations, is yet too vague to enable us to distinguish psychology from other sciences dealing with life, such as biology.

Now we have already declared that the psychology which we are going to consider is to be a part of philosophy, so that we can add this to the definition, and assert that psychology, in our sense, is the philosophic science which treats of the intrinsic principle of life, i.e. of vital operations.  According to this view of it psychology will deal with life wherever it is found : in man, in animals, and in plants, and indeed if we wish to discover the nature of life in itself it would be absurd to exclude any of its manifestations from our scrutiny.  At the same time, both because of the greater facility for studying it, and because of its higher interest for us, no doubt the life of man will occupy the foremost place.  Hence we shall have to discuss the very nature of life in general, and in its various grades ; to do which we shall be bound to consider the nature of vital operations, since it is only by observing the actions of a thing that we can arrive at any knowledge of its nature.  In doing this we shall make use of our common knowledge of vital phenomena, and also of the facts which have been discovered by the investigations of experimental science in this field ; to which we are to apply those rational principles which will lead us to the further knowledge of the primary causes which produce these phenomena.

From these remarks can be seen the distinction and relation between this philosophic science and the experimental sciences which deal with living bodies, such as Biology, Physiology, Morphology, Anatomy, and so on ;

[1] Cf. *Epistemology*, in Vol. II.

for the first of these, though dealing with the whole range of living bodies, yet treats them only from the point of view of discovering how they function, not of what they are in themselves, while the others are concerned merely with some particular aspect of them.  But though distinct they are also complementary, for rational psychology takes into account the data which they supply, and they, in their turn, supplement it by giving us knowledge of the way in which living things function and behave.  This behaviour of living things in the various circumstances in which they are placed is more particularly the province of experimental psychology, which has been variously defined as the science of psychical states and processes, or knowledge of psychic phenomena.  So Professor Stout says : ' Psychology treats of psychical states and processes, their objects as such, and the conditions of their occurrence,'[1]  Woodworth says it is ' the science of the conscious and near-conscious activities of living individuals.'[2]  Ward asserts that ' it is the science of individual experience—understanding by experience, not merely, not primarily, cognition—but also and above all, conative activity or behaviour ' ;[3] while William James calls it ' the science of mental life, both of its phenomena, and of their conditions.'[4]  It is clear that all such definitions limit the province of psychology to the study of the observable manifestations of life, excluding that of the very nature of life itself and of the fundamental causes of the activities of living things.  The discussion of these would, by most modern writers, be considered to be metaphysical, and though Thomists would not agree to rational psychology being reckoned as a branch of metaphysics, since their formal objects are different, yet they are at one with the non-Scholastic writers in recognising that experimental psychology is a natural and not a philosophical science.

That rational psychology is of the greatest utility is evident if we consider that its aim is to understand our own real nature.  Its main problem is the relation between mind and

---

[1] Stout, *Groundwork of Psychology*, p. 1.
[2] Woodworth, *Psychology*, p. 17 (cf. p. 1).
[3] Ward, *Psychological Principles*, p. 28.
[4] James, *Principles of Psychology*, Vol. I, p. 1.

matter ; according to our solution of which will follow our view as to the intellectual, moral and religious capabilities of man.  So a recent writer says : ' If we knew just how mind affects body, and how body affects mind, we should have the clue to many a philosophical riddle, and a clue which would give us much needed guidance not only in philosophy but in many a region of practical, moral, and religious activity and experience in which our generation is groping rather blindly and is longing very eagerly for more light.'[1]

Our discussion will naturally fall into three parts dealing with the three great realms of living things : plants, animals, and man.  This must be prefaced by some account of what we mean by ' life ' in general, and completed by an investigation of the origin of, and connection between, living things.

[1] Pratt, *Matter and Spirit*, p. viii.

# DIVISION I.  LIFE IN GENERAL

## CHAPTER I

### VITAL OPERATIONS

Vital Operations in General—Their Distinctive Characteristics—
Different Kinds of Vital Operations—Vegetative, Sensitive,
Intellectual.

SINCE all living things have at least vegetative life, it will be
convenient to include under this head not only those general
philosophical conclusions which we can arrive at by a survey
of the animate world as a whole, but the more particular ones
which relate to the life of plants.

The nature of life in itself is naturally regarded by Aristotle and St. Thomas from the point of view of the motion
which it exhibits, since, as we saw, they regard ' mobile
being,' or things subject to motion, as the proper object of
the whole of Natural Philosophy, of which our present discussion forms part.

Now the word motion can be taken in three senses : (1) In
its strictest sense it signifies local motion ;[1] (2) it is applied
to any successive mutation, and is then defined as the act of
that which is in potency as such.[2]  This meaning, though
wider than the first, yet applies to motion properly so called.
(3) A still wider meaning is the application of the name to
any change, i.e. any transit from potency to act, even if the
change be instantaneous.  A last and very loose sense is
when the word motion is made to cover any kind of operation, even if there is no transit from potency to act, so long
as we conceive of the operation as if there were such a transit.

---

[1] Cf. *Aristotle*, VIII Physics, Ch. IX.
[2] Cf. *Cosmology*, Ch. VIII, p. 109.

This last meaning applies only to the divine operations. In speaking of motion in connection with life, we do not limit it to any one of these senses, but it is taken to include them all, though the second sense is more particularly applicable to vital motions.

SECTION I. *Vital Operations in General.*

Observing, then, the motions of living things of all kinds, Aristotle notes that their motion has a common characteristic and peculiarity, it is self-motion—they are automatic. Even the humblest of living things nourishes itself and grows, thus causing itself to change ; and this power is found nowhere in the inanimate world. Hence he defines a living thing as one whose natural property it is to be able to move itself ;[1] or rather this definition implicit in Aristotle is made explicit by S. Thomas.[2]

It should be noted that S. Thomas says the living thing is one which is *able* to move itself, not one which actually does so : for it is this capacity which properly constitutes the essence of a living thing. The Scholastics call this life *in actu primo*, and oppose it to actual self-movement, or vital action, which is called life *in actu secundo*.

We may notice in passing that since to move oneself is opposed to being moved by another, self-motion, properly speaking, consists in the production by the agent of an operation which remains in the agent, and so is immanent action. However, we cannot at this stage be quite certain that the action of living things is immanent, i.e. proceeding from an intrinsic principle to an intrinsic term, since it will only be so if they are essential unities, not two or more things accidentally joined together ; and this has not yet been proved.

It is clear from common observation that there are three kinds of living things with markedly different characteristics, viz. plants, animals, and man. If, as we shall see presently is the case, these three kinds are distinguished specifically or essentially, it is clear that the word life will apply to them in

[1] VIII Physics, 254[b]15. Cf. S. Thomas, *Summa Theol.*, I.18,1 and 2 ; IaIIae.3,2, ad 1.
[2] *De anima*, L. II, Lect. 1.

N

senses which are also specifically distinct ; in other words, it is an analogical concept, used of the things to which it is applied in senses which are simply speaking different, though from a certain point of view, viz. that of self-motion in general, the same.

If it be true, then, that the essential characteristic of living things is their capacity for self-motion, an important corollary follows, viz. that they are necessarily organic. For all motion, as we have seen, involves a transit from potency to act. Now it is clear that a thing cannot be both in potency and act in the same respect at the same time ; in other words, it cannot be capable of becoming something, and have, at the same time, become it ; and it necessarily follows that if we have a thing which moves itself and so makes itself pass from potency to act, there must be one part which moves and another which is moved ; it cannot, as a whole, both move and be moved.[1] The parts, then, of a living thing must have different functions and different activities, which will proceed from principles of action which differ, at least accidentally.[2] Though it is clear from this that if there are bodies which are altogether inorganic, not having qualitative differences in their different parts, they will be inanimate ; it does not follow that all inanimate bodies are inorganic in this sense, and in fact we have seen reason to believe that a rudimentary organism in this philosophical sense is to be found in the inanimate world as well as in the animate.[3] It was, nevertheless, the observed structural organisation of living things—both in the single cell, as well as in more complex bodies—which so struck the scientific imagination as to make the name organism coextensive in biology with animate bodies, while inanimate ones are known as inorganic. Though this distinction may not be an absolutely fundamental one, yet there is no doubt that it is one of the ways in which living bodies differ from inanimate ones ; which differences it will be convenient to enumerate at this stage.

---

[1] Cf. I.C.G., c. 13 (Tertio probat).
[2] Cf. 13th Thomist Thesis. *Revue Thomiste*, 1921, pp. 276, 280.
[3] Cf. *Cosmology*, Ch. XI, pp. 148 ff.

(a) *In the Physical Order :*

1. *In Internal Structure.* As we have just noticed, living things are composed of heterogeneous parts, either cells or combinations of cells, forming organs. The cell consists of two parts, the cell-body (protoplasm, or more properly cytoplasm) and a nucleus which consists of a modified protoplasm (karyoplasm). The nucleus is spherical and denser than the rest of the protoplasm. Such cells are found only in living bodies ; inanimate ones not presenting such differences of internal structure.

2. *In Shape.* Generally speaking, living things of different species have a determinate shape, the varieties of species and of shape being very numerous. The fixity of such shape increases as we ascend in the scale of life, the lowest forms being able to vary their shape considerably. Such determination in shape is not found in the inanimate world except in the case of crystalline formations, but here we do not get the immense variety of shape which is found in living things, there being six, and only six, types.

3. *In Chemical Composition.* Living things are composed of many and almost the same chemical elements, of which a number are not found in inanimate ones in nature ; whereas inanimate bodies have, individually, only a few chemical constituents, and differ from one another in the elements of which they are composed. Moreover, the elements found in living things are constantly changing, whereas those in inanimate ones are stable.

(b) *In their Mode of Being :*

1. In their way of coming into being, *their origin.* Living things always come to be by means of generation by another living thing : whereas chemical action, affinity, and valency, suffice for the production of inanimate ones.

2. *In Duration.* Living things need nourishment in order that they may endure as living things ; and even so, their powers fail and they die, no extrinsic cause being needed to destroy them ; whereas inanimate ones endure so long as they are not corrupted by an extrinsic cause.

*(c) In their Activities and Tendencies :*

It is here that we see the most marked, and from the philosophical point of view, the most significant distinction between the two orders.

1. *With Regard to Nutrition and Growth.* Living things all feed and nourish themselves, so preserving their life and repairing waste tissues ; while they also add to their own structure intrinsically, and grow. Inanimate bodies, on the contrary, if they increase at all do so by the mere juxtaposition of more matter to themselves from without. In this connection we may notice that all living protoplasm breathes, taking in oxygen and giving out carbon-dioxide ; it also secretes products useful to the organism and excretes those which are useless or injurious to it. Such activities are peculiar to living things.

2. *With Regard to Reproduction.* All living things increase by reproduction, giving rise to successors, similar to themselves and formed out of their own substance. The most primitive method of reproduction, as we shall see, is fission, by which the living thing splits up into two. No non-living things behave in this way.

3. *With Regard to the Regularity of their Actions.* The actions of the living thing are rhythmic, as breathing and the beating of the heart. Some vital rhythms are in tune with cosmic changes such as the action of the tides, or the changes of the seasons. This last is very obvious in plants. Though it is clear that such rhythm is not absent from the inorganic world, yet it is much more marked in the organic, where it is found in all individuals, and not merely in the mass : and like other vital actions has its source within the living thing itself.

These observations afford us strong grounds for thinking that living things differ essentially or specifically from inanimate ones. We shall have occasion to return to this question later, since it is evidently one of great importance for philosophy, being another example of the problem of the one and the many, which, as we saw,[1] is a leading issue in natural philosophy.

[1] Cf. *Cosmology*, p. 22.

Meanwhile, in our observations of the animate world we have noticed that there are, apparently, three different kinds of life in it, viz. that of plants, of animals, and of man. Can this distinction be justified philosophically ?

SECTION II. *The Different Kinds of Vital Operations.*

We examine these operations in order to discover what are the kinds, or grades, of life. Now the Scholastics are unanimous in asserting that there are three main grades of life which include all others, vegetative, sensitive, and intellectual. To establish this assertion they appeal to the following consideration,[1] among others :

Since it is the essential characteristic of vital motion, as we have seen, to be always from within, or intrinsic, it will be more perfect, or more fully vital, in proportion as this characteristic feature is more completely found in it. Now, in any motion we can consider three elements : the execution of the motion, its determining form or principle, and its object. Consequently, life will be more perfect, and so allow us to distinguish grades of perfection in it, in proportion as one, two, or all three of these elements are intrinsic to the living thing. Now, observation shows us that in plant life only the first of these elements is intrinsic, for though plants undoubtedly move themselves, and so execute their own motion in growth, and so on, yet, since they have no knowledge of the end to which their motion is directed, it is clear that both this end, or object, and the principle of their motion must be determined for them by nature, and cannot be due to any activity of their own. If we now turn to the animal world, we see that the animals, like the plants, execute their own motion, but they also do so with some knowledge of what it will bring them, and it is this knowledge which is the principle of their motion, making them move ; though they still are apparently not capable of determining the end to which they will move for themselves, but act according to the instincts or natural tendencies of their nature. Nevertheless, it is clear that both the execution of the motion and the principle which makes them move are

[1] Cf. *Summa Theologica*, I.18,3.

intrinsic to the animal itself, which, by knowledge, receives into itself, in a certain fashion, the object towards which it moves ; and thereby causes its own motion. When we come to man we observe that he, like other animals, moves himself and knows the object to which he moves, and that he further determines for himself what this object shall be, choosing any means he pleases for arriving at some end which he has in view. Hence the very object of his motion itself is constructed, as it were, by man, and his vital motion is wholly intrinsic and so in a high degree perfect.[1] Evidently the most perfect life of all would be one in which the vital motion was absolutely intrinsic, not seeking anything outside itself at all, nor receiving the form of its motion from without, a state of things which could only be found in the case of an infinite being, of God.

[1] Cf. also *Summa Theologica*, I.78,1.

# CHAPTER II

## THE PRINCIPLE OF LIFE

Is it One Only in Each Individual ?—A Difficulty—Opinions on the
Divisibility of the Life-principle—Answer to the Question.

THERE can be no doubt that such vital actions, as we have
just been examining, must proceed from some vital principle,
since they are clearly accidental, the living thing acting now
in one way, now in another. Aristotle and S. Thomas call
this principle of life the soul, and if what we have just said
about the three grades of life be true, it follows that there
must be three kinds of life-principle, or soul, to be found
among living things. It will be convenient to note here the
definition which Aristotle gives of the soul, though we cannot
at this stage claim that the definition has been fully verified.
According to him, then, the soul is ' the first act of a physical
organic body.'[1] Now first act is substantial form, and this
definition will be true if living things do indeed differ essentially from inanimate ones, since it is clear that such essential
difference must proceed from the principle of life in them,
which will therefore specify them, and be their substantial
form ; and, secondly, if they are essential unities, so that
they can be said to have one, and only one, form or first act.

It is necessary, then, for us to see whether in fact the soul
is one only in each individual living thing ; and we are
immediately confronted with a fact which seems incompatible with its being so. Just as when we were discussing the
unity of substantial form in chemical compounds, the chief
difficulty in the way of our asserting it was that the mixture
can always be resolved into its elements, so that it seemed

---

[1] ΠΕΡΙ ΨΤΧΗΣ. B.1.412.b.5. εἰ δή τι κοινὸν ἐπὶ πάσης ψυχῆς δεῖ λέγειν, εἴη ἂν
ἐντελέχεια ἡ πρώτη σώματος φυσικοῦ ὀργανικοῦ.

that the substantial forms of the elements remained as such in the mixture, so here we find that in the lower grades of life at least, and to a certain extent in the higher, a living thing can be divided into two or more parts without losing its life, and so without losing its substantial form.  It looks, therefore, on the face of it, as if there were many principles of life (or cyto-dynamic principles, as they are sometimes called) in such things.   Another solution is nevertheless possible, for it is conceivable that the life-principle, or the soul, might itself be divided on the division of the body.  But it will at once be objected that only such things as are quantitatively extended can be thought to be divisible, and quantitative extension belongs to matter, not to form.  A little consideration only is needed to show us that substantial form is, in spite of this, divisible ; for it is clear, if we take a bucketful of water out of a pond, we have the substantial form of the water in the bucket, and another remaining in the pond : the matter being divided, the form is divided along with it.  This consideration answers the objection, for though the substantial form is not of itself (*per se*) either extended or divisible, yet it is, or may be both, by reason of the extension and divisibility of the compound of which it forms part.  It is, as the Scholastics say, ' divisible *per accidens.*'  It is possible, then, that the substantial forms or souls of living things should be divisible.  Is this the case, or are we to adopt some other explanation of the fact mentioned above that in some cases living things can be multiplied simply by division ?  Before speaking of the opinions on this question, it will be useful to mention some instances of multiplication.  In the first place fission is a common and normal method of reproduction among plants, and occurs in most of them, a part of the original plant dividing off and forming a new one.  Gardeners make use of this property by taking cuttings of plants, and we all know that a flower or branch of a plant does not die immediately it is cut.  The same method of reproduction is found among the lower forms of animal life, as in the case of the amœba and of Hydra. The same is true of the sea-anemones and many aquatic worms.  If we turn to artificial division, we find that life

can be preserved in parts divided off from animals much
higher in the scale than these.  We are all familiar with the
fact that if an earth-worm be accidentally cut in two it will
regenerate the cut surfaces and form two worms.  Experiments have also been carried out which have resulted in the
preservation of life for a time in parts dissected from highly
organised animals, such as dogs.  Thus pieces of tissue have
been kept alive (nourishing themselves and growing) for
considerable periods : e.g. life was preserved for sixty-one
days by Carrel, and for eleven months by Ebeling.[1]

Again, parts have been transplanted from one animal to
another, e.g. a segment of the carotid artery of a dog was
transplanted on the aorta of a cat.  More spectacular, though
less important from a philosophical point of view, are the
successes obtained in the preservation of the functioning of
an organ or group of organs extracted from a living animal.
So, a frog's heart has been kept beating for thirty-three days
after extraction, and for this it is necessary that the muscles
of the heart should preserve their relations with the nerves.
Similarly, nearly the whole of the internal organs of a cat
were extracted and preserved alive for periods ranging up to
thirteen hours after the death of the animal whose organs
they were.[2]  Since, however, nearly the whole organism is
preserved alive, while the rest dies, no question as to the
division of life arises, and the rhythmic pulsation of the heart
may be ascribed not to life but to chemical action.  It does
not appear, moreover, that in any of the other experiments
we can say with certainty that the dissected tissues or parts
were truly living, since increase by means of assimilation of
nutriment is doubtful, and reproduction of the cells, i.e. the
production of really new cells by cellular division, almost
certainly absent.  There is purely dimensional growth, not
organic growth.  It does not appear, then, that in the higher
animals it is possible to preserve life, truly so called, with its
three marks of nutrition, growth, and reproduction, in parts
cut off from a living organism, though in the plants and little
organised animals we see that such a process is a normal and

[1] *Journal of Experimental Medicine*, Vol. XVII, n. 3, p. 273.
[2] Cf. Gemelli, *Religione e Scienza*, pp. 134 ff.

natural one.   Is, then, the life-principle, or soul, of such thing as these latter divisible ?

Four answers are given to the question : Is the soul divisible ?

1. The first is that all souls, including that of man, are divisible.   This is, in substance, the view of materialistic biologists, who, since they consider living things to be merely physico-chemical compounds, maintain that, like other compounds of this kind, such as water, they can be divided without changing their character.

2. On the other hand, some say that no soul is divisible. Some recent writers (as Hugon[1]) hold this view and explain it as follows : They think that the vital principle is actually one and potentially multiple.   When the body is divided the division must be such that sufficient organisation for life is preserved, which is an indication that the soul as such is not divided.   Hence in this view the consequence of the division is not the division of the soul, even *per accidens*, but the induction of a new soul, a soul which is new in act, though it was present before in potency, in the greatest propinquity to act.   Hence, such a process is more properly called genera-tion than division of the soul, being the origin of a new living thing from a previously existing one.

Mediating between these two extreme opinions there are two others :

3. Some, as Scotus and Nys,[2] think that all souls, with the exception of the human soul, are divisible.

4. Others, including S. Thomas and the majority of modern Scholastics, hold that while the souls of plants and the less complex animal organisms are divisible, those of man and the more complex animals are indivisible.

There is probably little difference between this opinion and the second one mentioned above, except in the mode of expression, and which mode is preferred will depend upon the view taken of the results of the experimental work which has been outlined ; for if it be held that life was really

---

[1] Hugon, *Cursus Philosophiæ Thomisticæ*, Vol. III, pp. 64 ff.   Cf. John of S. Thomas, *Phil. Nat.*, Pars III, Q. 2, A. 1 ; and *Revue Thomiste*, 1923, pp. 290 ff.

[2] Nys, *Cosmologie*, Vol. II, pp. 30 ff.

preserved in the excised tissues, we shall be led to express ourselves as do the exponents of the second view ; but if not, it will seem more reasonable to say that, as far as is known at present, the souls of the more highly organized animals are not divisible.  In the case of man, it would be impossible (since, as we shall see, his soul must be held to be simple) to maintain that his soul was divisible ; nevertheless, if it were proved that human tissues could be kept alive apart from the organism, such a fact could be explained by the second view, inasmuch as a vegetative soul could be generated in the excised part by the power of the rational soul which gives vegetative life to the whole organism, just as, in fact, vegetative souls are generated in those cells which naturally divide off from the body, viz. the reproductive cells.  While saying this, it should be borne in mind that, properly speaking, it is not such souls which are generated, but a new compound, and, what is even more essential, that the vital principle of this compound is not new in the sense that it in no way existed before, but only inasmuch as what was previously potential now becomes actual.[1]  This way of explaining the matter meets also the principal objection which is raised to the second view, viz. that we cannot say that a new soul is generated in each of the parts since this would involve the destruction of the original soul, which consequently could not generate ; nor yet that a new soul is generated in one only, since often the parts are exactly alike, so that there is no reason for asserting that one is, as it were, the ' mother ' of the other.  If, however, we maintain that the potential multiplicity of the soul is made actual in such fission, we can see that neither of these statements need be made, since neither soul will be wholly new, but we shall have two actual souls where before we had a single actual one which was potentially two.  And this is the very way in which S. Thomas speaks with regard to fissiparous generation ;[2] which is well set out by Père Sertillanges, who says : ' The degree of organisation of some living things is so restricted that no particular organ is essential for its life, or incapable

---

[1] Cf. Cajetan Comm. in I P., *Summ. Theol.*, Q. 76, A. 8, n. 10.
[2] *De Potentia*, III, a. 12, ad 5.

of being regenerated by the life left in the other organs. The vital " idea " being complete . . . in each of the divisible parts, to separate them will produce, not death, but multiplication. The soul, being simply the *immanent* " *idea* " of life, can therefore pass from unity to multiplicity, because from the start, by reason of the conditions of its support, it was multiple potentiality. The case is, *mutatis mutandis*, similar to that of the homogeneous continuum, where division multiplies the form numerically.'[1]

This, then, seems the most satisfactory answer to the question : Is the soul divisible ? Where life can be preserved after division, the soul may be said to be divisible *per accidens* : by which we mean that what was before actually one and potentially multiple becomes, on the division of the body, actually multiple.

As far, then, as the generic consideration of the soul is concerned, there seems to be nothing in the facts we have just discussed to cause us to assert that there are many souls in any individual living thing ; and to that extent the Aristotelean definition of it as the *first act* of a physical organic body is justified. We shall have to return later to the consideration of the specific difference of living and inanimate things, as well as to that of the positive reasons for asserting they are essential unities. The discussion of the first of these problems will naturally occur as part of that concerning the lowest grade of life, the vegetative, while that of essential unity will reappear in connection with each of the three grades of life in turn.

---

[1] Sertillanges, *S. Thomas D'Aquin.*, Vol. II, p. 88.

# CHAPTER III

Are they Distinct from the Soul ?—How are they to be Distinguished from One Another ?

So far, then, we have seen that there is, prima facie, much justification for the supposition that living and inanimate things differ in kind, and that the generic consideration of life does not provide any ground for saying that the life-principle in a single individual is multiple. We are thus justified in asserting provisionally that it is one only, but even so it is clear that vital activities are many, and it is natural to ask how these two statements are to be reconciled, and how these manifold activities come about. This is the question concerning the powers of the soul in general, and is suggested by the definition which asserts that the soul informs an organic body ; for the reason why the body is organic is that different organs are required for different vital operations.

Two questions can be asked about these vital powers :

1. Do they exist, or are they simply the soul itself ? ; and,

2. If they do, how are they to be distinguished from one another ?

QUESTION I. *Are the Powers of the Soul Really Distinct from it ?*

Aristotle, S. Thomas, and the Thomists consistently maintain such a distinction between the essence of the soul and its powers. There is, however, a widespread opposition to this doctrine, both on its own account, and also because, owing to a misapprehension, it has been confused with what is spoken of as ' faculty psychology ' by modern psychologists, and which is, as it seems rightly, regarded by them with contempt.

The objections to the distinction in itself proceed, in the main, from a Nominalist point of view, and we find it rejected by the Medieval Nominalists, like Ockham, as well as by modern Empiricists.

All these recognise nothing but individual vital actions and states, an attitude which clearly rules out any powers which underlie these states or any substantial principle of them. All such principles will, therefore, be regarded as metaphysical phantasms. Again, if it be supposed that the faculties are real agents, distinct and separable from the soul, the positing of such faculties would land us in absurdities, for it is clear that we can have no willing without a subject who wills, and so on. This objection was expressed by medieval writers by saying that the soul is simple, and therefore cannot be split up into faculties. Distinction, however, does not necessarily imply separability. Perhaps the most common objection to faculties nowadays is that they explain nothing. So Prof. Stout says :[1] ' To say that an individual mind possesses a certain faculty is merely to say that it is capable of certain states or processes. To assign the faculty as a cause . . . of the states or processes is evidently to explain in a circle ; or, in other words, it is a mere failure to explain at all.' No doubt in the decadence of Scholasticism, and later, it was supposed that the question ' why do I think ? ' could be answered by ' because I have a thinking faculty,' just as Molière's physician, in answer to the question ' why does opium produce sleep ? ' answers, ' opium produces sleep because it has a soporific tendency ' ; but this was not the intention either of Aristotle or S. Thomas in asserting the existence of faculties. They were not interested in them as explanations, but as facts. It would be no answer to the question ' why does a man see ? ' to say ' because he has eyes,' yet few people would on this account deny that he had eyes, or say that it would not be nice to mention the fact in polite society, which seems to be the attitude of the critics of the faculties. Prof. Ross[2] puts this well with regard to Aristotle. He says that Aristotle does not evade ' the task of genuine

---

[1] Stout, *Manual of Psychology*, Bk. I, Ch. III, p. 114.
[2] Ross, *Aristotle*, p. 133.

explanation of facts by referring to a mystical faculty of doing this or doing that. He is simply taking account of the fact that the soul does exhibit a variety of operations and that behind each of these intermittent operations we must suppose a permanent power of so operating.'

We ask, then, do these powers, as a matter of fact, exist, i.e. are there such powers really distinct from the soul itself ?

By power the Scholastics mean the proximate and immediate source (*principium quo*) of action as such.

In saying this they implicitly state with regard to vital powers that these are not the fundamental sources of action, either adequate, since this is the nature taken as a whole, or inadequate, since this is the soul ; and, moreover, that such powers are not to be considered as that which acts, which is the living thing, but only as that *by which* the living thing acts. Just as it is inaccurate to say ' my legs dance,' but true that ' I dance with my legs,' so, strictly speaking, it is inaccurate to say ' my intellect knows,' and true that ' I know with my intellect.'

That their contention is true can be seen if we consider that a living thing is a substance and cannot therefore be a power which is essentially directed towards the production of actions, which clearly are accidents, since they come and go in the course of life ; for it is evident that two things which are essentially related to one another in this way must be at least of the same generic kind, otherwise they would have no community of nature, and so would not be essentially related. Consequently these powers must be accidental, and so really distinct from the constitutive principle of the living thing, the soul, which is substantial.

S. Thomas also advances a second reason which applies in a special fashion to the soul as the substantial form of the living thing,[1] for substantial form not being an efficient cause cannot be directed to the production of any effect beyond the constitution of the compound of which it is the form, and so not to that of operations. As, however, we have not yet justified the statement that the soul is the substantial form, this reason can only be noted in passing. The first reason is

[1] *Summa Theologica*, I,77,1.

sufficient and we ought therefore to recognise the fact that the soul has powers which are accidents distinct from itself. The recognition of this fact does not, as we saw, afford any explanation of vital actions; but it is useful in helping us to classify them, as is generally recognised.[1]

QUESTION II.   *How are the Powers of the Soul to be Distinguished from One Another?*

This question, which is called by the Scholastics the question of the specification of the faculties, presents no special difficulty, if it be granted that the soul has faculties distinct, though inseparable, from itself. It must, however, be clearly understood that in looking for an essential distinction between the faculties, we are considering them precisely as faculties, or powers; by whose means the living thing attains certain ends, as, for example, knowledge of the colour or odour of an object. If, instead of this, we asked how the faculties of man, for example, were distinguished from those of some other animal, the answer would clearly be that they were distinguished by being human or not, i.e. by reason of the natures whose powers they are.[2] Considered, then, precisely as powers, they are directed towards the production of certain definite operations, as seeing, etc., and hence their natures must be such as will produce these operations; and will, therefore, be essentially different if the operations towards which they are directed are essentially different. Consequently, it will be by means of their operations that the powers of the soul will be specified. But we can go further, for these operations themselves are only intelligible and definable in so far as they are directed towards certain objects, since what makes an action to be of a particular kind is its being directed towards a particular end. The powers of the soul, therefore, will be immediately specified by their operations, which being, in their turn, specified by their objects, the powers will be mediately specified by these. If, then, we wish to distinguish one

[1] Cf. Stout, op. cit., p. 115; and McDougall, *Outline of Psychology*, p. 13.
[2] Cf. Cajetan, *Comm. in Primam Partem Summæ Theol.*, Q. 77, A. 3, No. 6.

power of the soul from another, we shall have to seek the source of this distinction in the objects towards which the soul's actions are directed. It is clear that since we are seeking a specific distinction, or distinction of nature, the objects which will cause such distinction are not those which differ merely materially, but those which differ specifically, i.e. in nature or formally. Where we have different formal objects, then, towards which the vital activities are directed, we shall also have different vital powers.

Distinct powers, therefore, are necessary for different classes of operations, as well as distinct organs, and it looks as if the unity of the living individual were seriously impaired. Would it not be simpler to say that a living individual is really a collection of differing living things ? This suggestion is confirmed by the fact, which is quite certain, that all living things are composed of cells, which are separated from one another by the cell-wall, and so are structurally discontinuous. We see, then, that we are constantly brought back to this question : Is the ‘ individual ’ living thing an essential unity, possessing one nature throughout, or should it rather be considered to be a collection of distinct entities ?

Though we must, no doubt, consider this question in detail later, in connection with the three great classes of living things, it is convenient, and even necessary to see whether we can come to any conclusion about it with regard to living things in general, since we find ourselves hampered at every turn through lack of an answer to it.

# CHAPTER IV

## THE UNITY OF THE LIVING INDIVIDUAL

### Opinions—The Thomist View—Definitions of Life.

THOSE who hold what is called the mechanistic conception of life, according to which a living thing, like a machine, is composed of many parts which have each their own work to do, and do it independently of the rest by means of energy given to them from outside, answer our question by saying without hesitation that the living individual is merely a ' colony ' of cells each living with its own life. The life of the individual is thus simply the sum total of the lives of its cells, and it has no essential unity ; and, moreover, they suppose that the cell-life is simply a chemical process, whose nature has not yet been discovered.

This opinion is based partly on the facts which we have noticed, but still more on a materialistic prejudice and the wish to bring all the facts known to us into a form in which they can be dealt with quantitatively according to mathematical methods.

Now the facts of cellular structure, and the differentiation of the organs are only a selection from those which are known to us with regard to living things, and a wider view will show that not only are we not compelled by them to accept the opinion that the ' individual ' is really a colony of cells, but that they fit in perfectly with that which is forced on us, if we consider the organism as a whole, viz. that it is an essential unity.

In order to understand this we are to observe that in order that there should be essential unity it is not necessary that there should also be material continuity in the strict sense, i.e. that the extremities of the parts should be the same.[1]

[1] Cf. *Cosmology*, p. 67, and Ch. XI.

In fact it is clear, quite apart from the results of microscopical investigation, that the living thing cannot be continuous in this sense, since, in order that one part should act on another, it is necessary that it should be divided from it, for otherwise it would act on itself, so that S. Thomas says[1] that 'in animals which move themselves, there is rather a kind of binding together of the parts than perfect continuation.' If, then, we consider the living individual philosophically, we see that all the operations of its different parts are related one to another and subordinated to one another in such a way that each and all are directed towards a single end which is the preservation and the well-being of the whole individual. Now this co-ordination and tendency shows that there must be in them some single unifying principle which directs and guides the various activities of the living thing, a principle which, in order to unify, must be one, and since it directs the activities from within must itself be internal and the principle of nature of the individual. In this the difference between a living individual and a machine is evident, for the latter is directed by some extrinsic principle, any adjustment either of the whole mechanism or of its parts having to be made from without, as is the original co-ordination of the working of the various parts so as to produce the effect for which the machine is intended. Such an internal determining principle of nature is, as we have seen, what the Scholastics call ' form ' ; and where the nature is substantial, as in the present case, ' substantial form.' So that we have good grounds for asserting that each living individual has a single substantial form, and is therefore an essential unity ; so long as we take all its activities into account, and do not confine ourselves to some arbitrary selection made from them, such as the mere conversion of the energy contained in foodstuffs into that of the body, or to some isolated fact, such as that the body is composed of cells. We shall see later that the mechanistic hypothesis, and with it the contention that the individual living thing is really a ' colony,' is even incapable of accounting for these

---

[1] S. Thomas in VIII Phys., Lect. 7, No. 8.

facts, since it is impossible to make sense of them unless the whole organism be taken into account. The differentiations of the parts, organs and powers of a living thing are so far from being incompatible with its essential unity that their very variety, inasmuch as they are all co-ordinated and harmonise with one another, makes the unity of nature in the whole much more apparent that it would be otherwise. Just as if we see a large body of men who all act in harmony with one another we are much more struck with their unity than if there were only a few ; and the more various are the types which a body comprises, the more remarkable will be their unity. Nations exemplify this to some extent, a union of races, such as is to be seen in America ; still more, the best example of it in any body of men being, no doubt, the Catholic Church, which includes men of all nations and types. We can, therefore, assert without hesitation, though we shall see as we go on much to confirm us in this view, that every living individual, i.e. every living thing which can preserve life in situal isolation from others of its kind, is an essential unity, and therefore that the Aristotelean definition of the soul as the first act (or substantial form) of a physical organic body is justified. It follows also, since they move themselves, that being such unities their action will be, strictly speaking, immanent as proceeding from an intrinsic principle and tending to an intrinsic term, and further that they will be specifically distinct, i.e. of a different nature from inanimate ones. The full discussion of this last point must be postponed to another chapter when we consider vegetative life more in detail. To close this one it will be useful to set out some of the definitions of life in general which have been suggested.

In contrast with the Thomistic definition that a living thing is a substance whose natural property is to be able to move itself, and to act immanently, the others are very vague and unsatisfactory. So the *Oxford English Dictionary* says it is ' the property which differentiates a living animal or plant, or a living portion of organic tissue, from dead or non-living matter,' which is to define life by itself. Bichat, the physiologist, has a similar circular definition ; for, according to him, it is ' the complexus of functions which resist death.'

Somewhat better is Herbert Spencer's statement that life is : ' the continuous adjustment of internal relations to external relations.'  This, however, merely describes certain vital phenomena without any attempt to penetrate to the reason of them, and is, therefore, incomplete both physiologically and philosophically.

Many similar vague descriptions of life might be quoted, whose inadequacy is so evident as to lead to the assertion that life is indefinable.[1]  That it is not so, however, we have already seen.

[1] Cf. Shipley, *Life*, ch. I.

# DIVISION II.  VEGETATIVE LIFE

We turn now to consider more particularly the various grades of life.  It goes without saying that we shall do this from the philosophical point of view, not from that of Natural Science.  For the results arrived at by the latter, the reader must be referred to books which deal professedly with biology and kindred sciences.[1]  Our aim will therefore be to discover, if possible, the natures of the three grades in general, i.e. to make plain their generic character and their specific differences.

[1] e.g. *Life*, Sir A. E. Shipley, C.U.P.  *Biology*, Geddes & Thompson. Home University Library.  *Life*, Geddes & Thompson, 2 vols.

# CHAPTER V

### THE NATURE OF VEGETATIVE LIFE

Opinions—Mechanism, Vitalism, Thomism—Reasons in Favour of
the Thomist View.

BEGINNING, then, with life at its lowest level, in the plants,
since this is the level at which living things exhibit differences
from other physico-chemical compounds, we are to ask
whether these differences are differences of kind or only of
degree, i.e. whether we are here dealing with a species of
material things—for plants are clearly material—which is
essentially different from that which comprises what are
generally called inorganic ones.

There are three opinions on this question. *The first* is that
of the Materialists, according to whom plants are merely
more complex physico-chemical compounds than are
inorganic bodies, but are not to be said to differ from them
in kind. This view is no new one, being found among the
Greeks ; Democritus, Leucippus, Empedocles and others all
maintaining that life is merely some form of matter in
motion.

Theories of this type were given a new vogue in modern
times by the speculations of Descartes, who thought that all
the actions of plants and animals could be accounted for
purely mechanically, and these views combined with the
growing prestige and success of experimental science led
eventually to the identification of life with its manifestations,
so that it was thought to be the mere sum of all vital phenomena. Such was the view expressed by the Empiricists, as
Hume, and in recent times seems to be that which was held
by the eminent psychologist, Wilhelm Wundt.[1] We may
notice that the mechanistic view of life is still regarded as
orthodox by biologists of the present day.

[1] Cf. his *Einleitung in die philosophie.*

Another view has, however, been widely held which is diametrically opposed to the preceding ; for according to many authors the life-principle or vital forces are to be thought of as being essentially immaterial, i.e. as in no way physico-chemical, but some added unknown entity. The first to make this view explicit was Stahl (1660–1734), in reaction against the mechanistic hypothesis of Descartes. He held that bodily processes are guided both consciously and unconsciously by the soul, and that it is because they are so guided that living things differ from inanimate ones. This theory with various modifications was the predominant one from the end of the seventeenth century till the middle of the nineteenth. Prominent among its adherents were anatomists like Bichat, chemists like Liebig, or medical men such as the members of the Montpellier school in the eighteenth century. The vital principle was regarded as in some way a source of bodily energy, and it was owing largely to the breakdown of this notion due to the new discoveries (by Mayer and Helmholtz) of the sources of muscular energy, that the vitalistic hypothesis came to be discredited in the middle of the nineteenth century.; though it is doubtful whether an even more potent cause of this was not the acceptance of mechanical explanations in science generally at this time. The whole intellectual atmosphere was indeed poisonous to vitalism. It is still not dead, though at present not popular among scientists. Indeed it seems to be an hypothesis with which science can have nothing to do, if indeed science does not deal with ultimate causes ; and as Prof. J. S. Haldane points out, it is one which is of no practical use in biology and physiology.[1]

If we do not adopt vitalism it might seem that we should be driven to a mechanical view of life. This, however, does not follow, since vitalism as put forward by the biologists is necessarily a scientific theory, not a philosophical one. In order that the vital principle may come within the scope of a scientific theory, it is necessary that it should produce some results which can be subjected to scientific tests, which will ideally be measuring tests, though in the present

---

[1] J. S. Haldane, *The Sciences and Philosophy*, Lect. 4, esp. p. 74.

state of the biological sciences this ideal cannot always be attained. In any case, in order to be acceptable it must be shown to produce observable effects which cannot be, and appear never likely to be, accounted for by the observed material elements. So it was thought to be the source of physical energy, a notion which was soon disproved, and no satisfactory material effect of the vital principle has since been substituted for this ; while experience shows that the progress of physical and chemical experiments constantly accounts for more and more of the hitherto unexplained phenomena on a physico-chemical basis. The abandonment, therefore, of vitalism as a scientific theory only leads to the conclusion that it was not a genuinely scientific one, and does not even entail the adoption of mechanism for scientific purposes, though unless some alternative to it is produced, no doubt scientists would work on that basis, in the absence of any other.

We, however, are not concerned to discover a theory which is most suitable for the advancement of natural science, but to point out what reason demands, if we wish to avoid contradictions. This brings us, then, to the strictly philosophical theory of the nature of life put forward by S. Thomas. With reference to plants, this theory maintains that these are not, in the last resort, the mere sum of the chemical elements of which they are compounded, and the forces of these elements ; secondly, that they possess an essential unity ; and, lastly, that this unity and the vital operations of the plants are due to a ' soul ' which is their substantial form.

The first part of this statement clearly negatives a merely materialistic and mechanistic conception of plant life. It cannot be proved, according to the Thomists, in isolation from the second part ; since their argument for it has always been based on the fact of immanent action in plants, which, as has been pointed out, can only be established when we know that the subject of the action is an essential unity. The nature of this argument marks the theory of a philosophical as opposed to a scientific one, since it investigates the ultimate nature of the thing in question, not those attributes which are amenable to sensible observation and experiment only. The Thomists argue, then, as follows :

Transeunt action differs in kind, or essentially, from immanent action, since in the former there need be no activity which is native to the thing which acts, the principle of action will not be within it, but its action will be caused by extrinsic influences acting upon it. So gunpowder will be exploded or set in action by a blow from outside, but will never blow up of itself if it be isolated. Moreover, it is clear that the term of such action is not within the thing itself, but in the launching of the bullet or other external effect ; and such is its primary effect, not merely a secondary one. In an immanent action, on the contrary, the initial source of action is in the agent itself and is not introduced into it from without. True, it may be stirred up or stimulated to act by extrinsic influences, but the action though initiated by such stimuli and using, in so far as it is expressed in physical movement, etc., energy received from without, is yet itself directed by, and derived from, the agent. The term of such action also must be primarily in the same agent if the action is to be truly immanent. This being so, we can see that these actions have nothing in common beyond the generic character of action, since the thing which acts immanently makes itself pass from potency to act, while that which acts transeuntly does not. If we now apply these considerations to the life of plants, it becomes plain that this life is manifested in actions which are, strictly speaking, immanent. In the first place there can be no doubt that the essential vegetative operations are produced by the plant and remain within the organism, since they are the operations of nutrition, growth, and generation. In nutrition the plant receives its nourishment within itself and assimilates it to itself ; in growth it is the plant which grows ; and in generation, though it is true that the remote term of the operation of reproduction is a new plant distinct from the old, yet the proximate term is the reproductive cell which is evolved inside the plant from the substance of the plant itself, and which remains a part of it, at least for a time. In the second place we can see from finality that plants are substantial unities, so that the apparent immanence of their actions which we have just noticed is a real immanence. The test of substantial unity is whether the being under consideration is such that all its parts act primarily and essentially for the good of the whole and only secondarily for their own benefit, for since action is to be attributed to that which acts, where there is an essentially unified action there will also be an essentially unified agent. This is a consequence of the general principle that a thing acts primarily and essentially for its own good and only secondarily for some other thing, since the source of every natural tendency is the inclination of the thing to that which is suitable to its nature, its own good. Consequently, if a thing were a collection of units accidentally joined together it could not act as a whole, for the good of the whole, primarily and essentially ; but each part would act for its own good. So if we observe such action taking place, we must conclude that the thing in question is an essential unity. Now this is precisely what we do observe in the plants since the actions of their parts are primarily directed to the preservation, building up and steady increase of the plant as a whole ; to making good any damage it may suffer, and finally to reproducing another plant of the same specific type.

We may confirm these considerations by noticing what takes place when life ceases, for during life the vital operations are directive, tending to a certain specified end, while the purely material operations in living things are directed by these things themselves. While a body lives, all its chemical, physical, and mechanical powers are directed towards the fulfilment of the purpose of the living body, but when life ceases, all these powers tend to fulfil their own purpose independently, with the result that the former co-ordination ceases and disintegration sets in in the body.

The vital principle, then, in bodies is the co-ordinating and unifying principle, by which the living thing is specifically constituted in its being and operation and distinguished from inanimate ones. This is, as we have seen, precisely what the Scholastics mean by the term substantial form, so that it is clear that the first principle of life is the substantial form of the living thing.

It is plain from this that no living thing can be a collection or colony of living beings, nor composed of a number of substances which remain actually and specifically distinct in it, since its substantial form or first principle of life constitutes it as a specifically distinct being.  If, then, it had more than one substantial form it would be constituted a being by one of them, and again so constituted by the others, thus being made over again what it was already, which is impossible. Hence the substantial form or first principle of life in any one living thing can be one only ;  and it itself must be an essential unity and not a ' colony.'

# CHAPTER VI

## THE TRANSMISSION OF VEGETATIVE LIFE

Reproductive Processes—Thomist View of Reproduction.

BEFORE proceeding to deal with animal life, there is one function which is common to both plants and animals, about which it will be convenient to speak here in a little more detail, viz. that of reproduction. All material living things ensure the continuance of the life of their species by means of generation or reproduction. There are two main modes by which this is brought about : fission, i.e. a division ; and conjugation, or joining together.

The first mode includes two reproductive processes. In some cases a plant will develop a little bulge on its outer surface, which grows gradually larger and eventually breaks off from the parent plant. These are spores, which develop into new plants. In other cases a part of the plant simply divides off and forms a new plant of the same species. This is called vegetative reproduction and is found very commonly even among the highest plants. It also occurs in the animal world, but does not reach very high up in the scale. It is found among the hydroids ; and even animals as high in the scale of development as sea-anemones will divide into two, many worms also reproducing in this way. Such vegetative reproduction by mere fission is evidently a very simple mode of propagating the species. The name fission is often confined to the second kind of reproduction just mentioned where the parts are of equal size, as in the amœba ; while that of gemmation is given to the process by which a small bud breaks off from the parent as in the yeast-cells. As we ascend the scale of life the process of reproduction becomes more complicated. First we have fission stimulated by conjugation, i.e. by the passing of protoplasm from one organism to another, as in the case of paramœcium. A further stage is reached when reproductive cells are formed in the body of the animal. These are of two kinds, ova or eggs, and minute swimming cells, called antherozoids in plants, and spermatozoa in animals. Roughly speaking, where this is the case we find in the plant or animal the two sexes—male and female—the female producing the eggs, the male the antherozoids or spermatozoa. These two, then, combine by the penetration of the spermatozoon into the ovum. That this may happen it is clear that the spermatozoon must be separated from the male parent, and live a life of its own ; and the same is true to a certain extent of the ovum. It is this fact which is of importance from our point of view. S. Thomas and the ancients thought that neither the male nor the female reproductive elements were living, but that both were produced from some superfluity in the nutriment of the plant or animal, and not from previously living parts. They thought, further, that the female element was merely passive, and the sperm alone active ; the latter acting as the instrument of the generator. These ideas are clearly untenable to-day : for it is now certain : (1) that the ova and the spermatozoa are true cells which are living before they are separated from the organism ; (2) that the ova are not merely passive in the process of generation, but active, though normally they require to be first acted upon by the spermatozoa before they can exercise their activity ; (3) that the fecundated ovum (i.e. after penetration by the spermatozoon) begins at once to exercise vegetative operations, i.e. to nourish itself and grow ; (4) that the germinal cells can, even without conjugation, evolve themselves into a new individual, at least in some cases and for a time. The most common instance of this is parthenogenesis (virgin-birth), when the ovum which is not fecundated can, if placed in suitable conditions, grow either naturally, as occurs in many plants and among the bees, where the males are born in this way, and in many other species ; or else growth may be induced by artificial means, as has been done in the case of sea-urchins' and frogs' eggs, among others. The first three facts require that we should admit from the first moment of fecundation a principle of life in the ovum as well as in the spermatozoa, and all four indicate that both male and female elements have vital principles of their own from the start. Hence, we have two living beings, the ovum and the spermatozoon, and it is necessary to admit that at the moment of fecundation, there must, in order that we may have true generation, be a corruption of the previous forms or vital principles, and a single new vital principle must be drawn from the potentiality of matter : otherwise we should have the union of two complete beings, which could not give a single complete being.

The most difficult case is obviously that of man, since here we cannot admit, as perhaps we might in other animals and plants, that the vital principle is itself divisible. The process seems to be as follows : at the moment when any part of the human individual is separated from this individual, this part, considered as properly a part of the human compound, is corrupted, i.e. loses its previous form which was the soul of the man or woman. This corruption must be, at the same time, a generation. What is it that is generated ? It may be a non-living body, as when a leg is amputated, or a living one. In the case of the germinal cells it will be seen from what has been said that it is a living one. The living spermatozoon now penetrates the ovum, and gradually the ovum changes its nature and becomes one with the spermatozoon. This is a second corruption and generation, the corruption of the previous forms of the spermatozoon and ovum, and the generation of the new form of the individual. This form will certainly be a vital principle, but these considerations afford no grounds for deciding whether it is properly speaking a human soul, i.e. a rational one, or some other form of life. The process is therefore much more complicated than S. Thomas thought, but the essential principles of his explanation by corruption and generation are still applicable to it.

In the case of plants and animals their souls, forms, or vital principles are universally recognised by Scholastics to be drawn out of the potentiality of matter, under the influence of the active principle of life in the parents. The reason of this statement is not far to seek, for we have seen that all the essential operations of plants are dependent on matter, and so their nature must also be of the material order and dependent on matter. Hence their life will disappear on the corruption of their bodies, and will also have its beginning in dependence on matter. The production of these forms, therefore, comes about in just the same way as that of the forms of inanimate compounds as outlined earlier in Cosmology.[1] What is true of the substantial forms of such living things will *a fortiori* be true of those of their generative elements and cells, so that the forms of the antherozoids, spermatozoa and ova will all be drawn out of the potentiality of matter, and these in turn will draw from matter the substantial forms or life-principles of the new plants or animals.

What is said here applies to plants and animals in general, but it is evident that if—as we shall see later is the case—man has a soul which is independent of matter or spiritual, such a soul cannot be drawn out of the potentiality of matter, so that in this, as in many other ways, he is an exception to those laws which govern the animal world in general. Nevertheless, since it is clear that the forms of the human spermatozoa and ova are not human souls, since they are corrupted when fecundation takes place, these can be brought out of matter under the influence of the life-principle of the parents, so that the first stages in human reproduction will follow the same lines as those which govern generation all through, in the lower animals and in plants.

Such generation, though belonging to the material order, is nevertheless not a mere resultant of physical and chemical forces, just as the life of plants and animals is something which is not purely physico-chemical ; as Balfour says : ' though mechanical laws can account for rearrangements, they cannot account for creation ; since, therefore, consciousness is more than rearrangement, its causes must be more than mechanical.'[2]

---

[1] See pp. 135 ff.
[2] A. J. Balfour, *Theism and Humanism*, p. 43.

# DIVISION III.  SENSITIVE LIFE

We can now take it as established that things possessed of
vegetative life, and therefore living things in general, differ
specifically or in kind from inanimate ones.  The interest of
the study of plant life from the philosophical point of view
lay largely in the fact that since plants are the lowest forms
of living beings, it is among them that we must look for the
line of demarcation between the animate and inanimate
realms ; and we have seen that though they possess much in
common with inanimate substances, yet they have one
power which is never found in the latter, viz. that of immanent action.  We are now to go on to consider whether we can
assert that in the world of living beings there are similar
lines of demarcation which separate them into classes which
are different in kind one from another.  If there are, no
doubt the first will be that which divides animals from
plants ; and we ask therefore whether these two classes of
things are in fact different in kind.  Now the distinguishing
characteristic of animals is that they are capable of knowing
things other than themselves by means of their senses ; and
we shall be justified in concluding that this characteristic is a
specific one if we can show (*a*) that they can, in fact, gain
such knowledge, and (*b*) that plants never can.

# CHAPTER VII

Nature of Cognition—S. Thomas' View—The Materialist and
Idealist Views—The Thomist View Further Explained.

## *What Do We Mean by Knowledge?*

BEFORE we can discuss the question of the distinction of
plant and animal, we must have a clear idea of what is
meant by the word ' knowledge ' in general, and sensation or
sensitive knowledge in particular.

S. Thomas' view of the nature of knowledge, while based
on observation of the facts, is worked out in close connection
with his metaphysical system, or his general view of the
nature of reality.

In all the main questions which we have so far investigated,
we have seen that S. Thomas finds his solution in the application of the distinction between potency and act. This is no
mere artifice, no ' abracadabra,' but something which is
forced upon him by the nature of the case ; as, for example,
' time ' becomes inexplicable without this distinction, as do
also the natures of material things. As we observe the
numerous instances in which this key unlocks the door, we
shall begin to feel sure that it is indeed a master key ; and
by the end of our enquiry we shall be quite certain of this.
The question as to the nature of knowledge is no exception
to our rule ; for if we consider what it is that occurs, at least
apparently, in knowledge, we shall say, no doubt, that it is
the union of the knowing subject with some object other than
itself. Now such union demands certain prerequisite conditions, both on the part of the knowing subject and on that
of the object. From the point of view of the object, the first
necessity is that it should be something, i.e. something
definite and fixed, at least to some extent ; for it is impossible

to have knowledge of a thing which is in a state of flux, or altogether undetermined. While we grasp it, it would have changed, and we could never know it. We should continually have to say : ' I thought I knew ' ; we could never say : ' I know.' Our lives would be like those of Lewis Carroll's Mad Gardener :

> ' He thought he saw a banker's clerk
>     Descending from a bus.
> He looked again, and found it was
>     A hippopotamus.'

So we say that gold is yellow, heavy, opaque, etc. If we remove all these, and every other determination from it, we can say nothing about it, for we can have no knowledge of it. In other words, the object can only be known by means of its determinations, its constant attributes, its forms. The underlying substance or potency or matter can only be spoken of and known in terms of the act which is proportionate to it. Thus only determinations, i.e. acts or forms, are intelligible. From this it follows that since knowledge is a kind of union between the knowing subject and the object of knowledge, and the object being a determination or form, the subject must in some way correspond with this form or act, for it must be capable of receiving into itself the forms of things other than itself. Further, it must receive these forms in a peculiar way. If it simply becomes the things which it knows, by the reception of their forms, as light becomes coloured when it passes through a coloured glass, we should not have what we mean by knowledge, since this implies the perceived union of the subject with something other than itself. Hence the knowing subject must receive the form of things other than itself, not as its own form, but as they are the forms of these other things, these known objects ; in contradistinction from a nescient subject, which can only have its own form, or if it receives those of others, receives them, not as they are the forms of things other than itself ; since in receiving them it makes them its own form. So a stone lying in the sun's rays receives one of the sun's forms, heat, and becomes hot ; but the heat once received is its own, not the sun's. So a cannibal who eats his enemy does not become his enemy ; his enemy becomes him. The knowing subject which receives the forms of other things as such is thereby made greater than before : it is enlarged. For form is that which makes a thing what it is ; if, therefore, the knowing subject receives the forms of other things which remain the forms of other things after reception, it becomes these other things in a certain way ; and if there are beings who are capable of knowing all things, these are also capable of becoming all things, and in so far as they do know, so is their very being developed and widened.

Apart from this view of the relation of subject and object in cognition, which is that of S. Thomas, there are two other general ways of conceiving this relation, which, though in some respects simpler and more obvious than his, yet in one way or another fall short of giving a complete account of it. On the face of it, it seems as if we must either say that the cognitive faculty is perfected by the object which in some way changes it intrinsically, so that the faculty is merely passive with regard to the object, after the fashion of a photographic film ; in which case cognition will not be a vital or immanent action, which it certainly is : or else if this last is to be maintained it seems that the object must be related to the faculty merely extrinsically ; and the faculty will be active only in the eliciting of its act, and will not, properly speaking, know the *object* at all, since this will be something extrinsic to its act. In other words, we seem to be faced with the dilemma of saying either that knowledge is entirely immanent, when the object will not be known, since it is outside thought (or sensation), which is the position taken up by idealists : or else that it is not immanent, but a transient action of the object which impresses itself on the subject, the latter being quite passive, and so not exercising any vital action, such as an act of knowing must be, at all. This last is the view of the Materialists, who wish to reduce cognition to a physical, as opposed to a psychological, impression on the organism. In either view, therefore, an essential element in our notion of knowledge is declared to be unattainable ; in the first, that the subject can be united in knowledge with something other than itself ; in the second, the vital character of the act of knowledge.

Now the Thomistic view, in asserting that those things which are capable of cognition differ from those that are not, in having a capacity for receiving the form of something other than themselves, resolves this dilemma ;  for in so far as it is the *form* which is received, it is clear that we are not dealing with a merely material impression, as the Materialists suppose, and in so far as this form is not that of the knowing subject, but of the thing known, the act of knowledge will, in a certain way, extend outside the subject ; which will not be prevented by the prison walls of its own self from grasping objects outside it.   That such a process may be possible it is necessary, as S. Thomas shows, that the subject should be to some extent immaterial ;  and this will be the very basis or root of cognition.

After what has been said as to the nature of knowledge, this further conclusion needs indeed but little elucidation, since to receive the forms of other things in so far as they are the forms of these things is clearly to receive them immaterially, and only that which is itself immaterial, to some extent, can do this.   So long as the forms of the known objects are restricted by the matter of these objects, they remain individual and are incapable of being shared by any other thing, for matter limits form as potency limits act. The forms, therefore, to be shared by other things or united to them must be dematerialised, and in such a state can evidently only be received by a subject which is itself immaterial to some extent.   So a dog knowing a cat does not know it in its material entity as a whole, its flesh and bones as we might say, but knows certain characteristics or forms of it, as its shape, smell, colour, etc.   It is true that it does not know such forms in general, but only as they characterise this particular object, and therefore the process of demateri-alisation is incomplete, but it could not know the object at all if it had to receive it into itself in its physical entity as a whole, it would merely absorb it into itself.   Since it does not do this, and yet is united to it, it is clear that it must be to some extent immaterial like the forms which it receives, since to receive others as others is quite evidently not the same as receiving them as oneself, nor yet the same as receiving them as a compound with oneself, the resultant being some third thing differing from both recipient and the thing received, e.g. a whitewashed wall. This last kind of reception is that by which a capacity or potency receives an act ; so that if this be ruled out, the only kind of reception which remains is that by which an act receives a further act, by which form receives form ; and this will be cognitive union. Thus we see that the necessary basis of knowledge is that the subject should be actual, formal, i.e. not merely potential or material. If this be true, and it seems to be an inescapable conclusion from the analysis of the act of knowing, it is evident that the materialistic view of this process is peculiarly superficial, for in conceiving of it as material they render it impossible. Probably the thorough-going materialists, such as the Behaviourists, would admit this conclusion ; but, of course, in doing so they stultify themselves since neither this conclusion nor any other thing can in this case be known. The Idealist solution, though at first sight much more subtle and profound, is, on examination, seen to be an incomplete analysis of cognition ; for while they are right in insisting that it must be a vital and immanent action, they cannot rid themselves of the notion that such action must be contained in the subject in a material and quantitative fashion ; and so consider the idea, not as something which opens up on the object, and by whose means we see it, but rather as if it were a photograph of, or substitute for, the object enclosed within the camera of our minds. Cognition, then, cannot be mere reception of some form, a purely passive reception, since this occurs in that imperfect reception of it which is distinct from knowledge, as when the air or water receives warmth from the sun. It always involves some efficient causality on the part of the subject, which will be continuous so long as the knowledge lasts. Hence the undoubted importance of attention and concentration ; the subject must not only be one which is in itself capable of knowing, but in order to know actually must make the effort to know. The bee in gathering honey does not flit aimlessly from flower to flower, as the butterfly does, but sucks each one dry. It is impossible to pour knowledge into a man as we pour water into a jug. So, though the cognitive faculty is called passive, inasmuch as it does not change its object, but is changed and fertilised by it, yet it is indeed operative and active. So Dr. Ross points out that, in Aristotle's view, sensation is an alteration which is ' the advance of something towards itself and towards actuality,'[1] and he adds that ' it is only if reception of form means awareness of form that it is a true description of perception.' Such activity is a necessary condition of cognition even in its simplest forms, since apart from it the subject would remain involved in itself—as indeed the Idealists think it does—and there would be no distinction between it and the world outside.[2] That such ' autonomy ' of the intelligence, along with its dependence on, and heteronomy with regard to, the object, is an integral part of the Thomistic view of this matter has been ably and lucidly brought out by M. Maritain for, as he says, the intelligence ' only knows the object by becoming it, and this of itself and actively, in the final perfection of operative activity.'[3]

Another consequence of great interest follows from this position, namely, that this cognitive union is the closest of all unions. For it is closer than that which joins form and matter, since in the latter case the matter does not become the form, but is intimately united with it to compose some third thing, whereas in the former case the subject becomes the form in a certain way, receiving it immaterially.[4]

[1] Ross, *Aristotle*, p. 136.
[2] Cf. Selbie, *The Psychology of Religion* (1924), p. 54.
[3] Cf. Maritain, *Réflexions sur l'intelligence* (1924), p. 55.
[4] For a full discussion of this point see ' Gredt. De Unione omnium maxima inter subjectum cognoscens et objectum cognitum ' in *Xenia Thomistica*, Vol. I, pp. 303–318.

# CHAPTER VIII

## THE PROCESS OF KNOWLEDGE

Necessary Conditions for Union of Subject and Object—Their
Assimilation Involves Change in Both—The Intentional
Species—Why they are Necessary—And Universally Necessary
—The Two Kinds of Species: Impressed and Expressed—Their
Nature and Mode of Production—Their Precise Function—
Are Expressed Species Present in Every Cognitive Act?

In order to complete our notion of the nature of knowledge
it is necessary to see how knowledge, the peculiar kind of
union between subject and object which we have just been
considering, is brought about. What is the process employed
in knowing; or, to use a metaphor, which must not be
understood too literally, what is the mechanism of
knowledge?

Broadly speaking, two kinds of answer are possible, viz.
that the union is effected either by the action of the cognitive
faculty itself, or by that of something other than the cognitive faculty, i.e. by the external object. The first view is
that taken by all the transcendental and objective Idealists,
as Kant, Fichte, Schelling, and Hegel, while the second is
held by all who maintain that our knowledge takes its rise
with things external to us, or, as we commonly say, by
Realists; among whom are to be reckoned the Materialists.
The view of these last may be at once dismissed, since it
neglects an essential element of the problem, maintaining
that the object is present in the cognitive faculty in its
physical entity, which is obviously untrue, since it is clear
that the object is in the knowing subject in a different way
from that in which it exists in nature. That the view of the
idealists solves the question of the union of the subject and
object is patent, since the object is thought to be evolved
from the very fabric of the cognitive faculty, and thus, being

the faculty, is evidently united to it. The very simplicity of this solution, nevertheless, indicates that it is rather a denial of the problem than an answer to it. It is, in fact, contrary to the notion of cognition as being an expansion of the knowing subject, by means of which it enlarges its boundaries to become other than itself ; this view making knowledge to consist in the mere evolution of the knowing subject itself. Our conception of the nature of this process of knowing will evidently be determined by the view which we take of the nature of the cognitive union, and we shall therefore try to explain what this process must be if we accept that idea of its nature which is set out above.

As we have already remarked, the cognitive faculty, considered simply in itself, is passive, and, consequently, if it is to become active, it must be acted upon by the object. The question therefore is as to the way in which the object acts on the faculty and determines it.

In the first place it is clear that in order that the object may be joined to the cognitive faculty, these two things must be in some way assimilated to one another, since a thing cannot be made one with another which is altogether different from it. Animals of different species, such as dogs and cats, do not interbreed ; and we are here, in speaking of a sense and the object, dealing with two things which differ much more radically from one another than do animals such as these. If, then, they are to be united, either one or both of them must undergo a change. That there is a change in the sense *organs* is clear, and is universally admitted. For example, in the sense of sight, the eye is affected by the light waves ; in hearing, the ear is affected by the vibrations of the air, and so on. Moreover, the nervous system connected with any sense-organ is affected by the changes which occur in that organ, and a ' stimulus ' is thereby carried to the brain. This being so, it can hardly be doubted that a change occurs also in the sense itself, since this must be affected by these modifications of its instrument, the organ of sense. In the abstract it might seem that such a change in the sense was sufficient to assimilate it to the object, and that it is not necessary to assert that the latter is also changed, but the

Scholastics, and particularly the Thomists, have always maintained that such a change in the object is essential in order that it may be known. The object, according to them, is not known as it is in itself outside the mind, but by means of what they call an ' intentional species.' The object, of course, as it exists outside the mind, remains unchanged, but it produces a likeness or representation of itself, by whose means it exists in a new way in the animal or man who knows, and consequently *as known* it is changed. This likeness of the object is the intentional species ;[1] of which the Scholastics recognise two kinds, the impressed and the expressed species ; the first being the form of the object which is transferred to the cognitive faculty, making it actively to know the object, while the second is, as it were, a sensible (in the case of the imagination) or intellectual reproduction of the object held up before the mind, in such a way that the object is known by its means. It is to be noticed, and we shall later have occasion to emphasise this, that in no case is the species something which, being known first, leads to knowledge of the subject, but always a pure means by, or in which the object itself is known.

We are here concerned, however, with intentional species in general, without going into this distinction between the impressed and expressed species ; and it is with reference to the species so generally considered that S. Thomas says that it is ' the likeness of the very essence of the thing ; and is, in a certain way, the very essence and nature of the thing with regard to its intentional (i.e. mental) existence :' not with

---

[1] The reason why the means whereby the object is present in the cognitive faculty are called intentional species is as follows. By species generally is understood the definite complete nature of a class of things ; e.g. the species ' man ' is the nature of rational animal which is found in all men. Now, as we know, the nature of a thing is determined by its form ; so that intentional species are sometimes also called intentional forms. They are called intentional to distinguish them from those forms which fix things in their physical entities : substantial and accidental forms ; and to indicate that they are not something absolute, but essentially relative, determining the knowing subject in his ' stretching out towards ' (*intendere*) the object. The fact that they are called species or forms, on the other hand, makes it clear that they are thought to be the determining elements of the objects known, though inasmuch as they are in the knowing subject, they are in a different state from that in which they are when in the object itself ; as will shortly be explained.

regard to its natural existence, as it exists in things.[1]  The words ' in a certain way ' relate to the different states in which this nature is found within, and outside, the mind ; to its different modes of existence.

' Such a form,' as S. Thomas observes,[2] ' can be considered in two ways ; first, as it is in the knowing subject ; and, secondly, with respect to the relation which it has to the thing whose likeness it is.  Considered in the first way it makes the subject actually know, and considered in the second, it determines this knowledge to be knowledge of some determinate object.'

It is two-faced and two-voiced, with one it wakes up the subject, and with the other it introduces it to the object. Considered in the first way it must be assimilated to the nature of the cognitive faculty, and so be in some way immaterial ; while considered in the second way, it has the nature of the known object, and is simply the intentional reproduction or representation of it.

That the contention as to the necessity of intentional species, in order that there may be knowledge, is justified, is seen if we consider the ways in which union between subject and object (which is the very essence of cognition) could be brought about.  In the first place they might be identical, and if this is not so the union might be effected by the object being communicated to the subject from without, either in itself, i.e. immediately, or by some medium.  These exhaust all the possible modes of effecting the union.

The first supposition is in fact an impossible one, since it would imply that the cognitive faculty was identical with all things that it either does or can know.  So Empedocles thought that the ' sensitive soul is in a certain way compounded of all sensible things ' ;[3] an opinion which, as S. Thomas points out, would lead to two unacceptable consequences, namely, that the senses could themselves be sensed, being composed of actual sensibles, and that they could sense without exterior sensibles being present, since they themselves would be actual sensibles.  It follows, then,

---

[1] *Quodlibet*, VIII, A. 4.    [2] *De Veritate*, X, 4.
[3] S. Thomas in II de Anima, Lect. 10.

that they are only potentially able to perceive the sense objects ; and in order actually to perceive them they must be actuated by these objects, i.e. informed by them, not identified with them. This information cannot, however, be immediate, both because the sensible objects acts primarily by a material impression on the sense organ, and only by means of this impression on the sense itself ; and also, since the sense object is a finite entity, its form is limited to that entity, and so cannot be also the form of another, viz. the sense. If, then, the sense is not united to the sense object either by identity or immediate information, it must, if it is to be united to it at all, be so united by mediate information, i.e. by the mediation of a form received from the sense object ; a form which differs from that which informs the sensible, not in its nature, but only in its mode of existence ; being to a certain extent dematerialised, and so made capable of informing an entity other than itself ; which form is what we call the intentional species. Since, then, union between subject and object is brought about in cognition, this result can only be achieved by means of intentional species ; which must therefore exist.

This conclusion holds good for finite knowledge of whatever kind, though we have here spoken chiefly of sense-knowledge. For it is clear that in the case of intellectual knowledge, since the object of the intellect, as we shall see, is the whole of being, it would be necessary, in order that the intellect should be identified with every being, that it should actually possess the forms of all beings or be infinite. Similarly, the intellect cannot be immediately informed by the forms of its objects, since, as we have seen, these forms, being those of finite things, are limited to the things which they inform. Hence intellectual knowledge must come about by means of mediate forms, or intentional species.

This conception of the process of knowledge applies universally to every form of cognition, and we cannot make any exception even in those cases, such as sensations of touch, where the object is in immediate contact with the sense organ. In fact the species are not required in order to transfer the object through some intermediate physical medium, but in order to render it capable of being known. For this purpose a mere material presence is not sufficient, otherwise knowledge would be indistinguishable from a purely mechanical impression, and therefore in all cases this material thing, the object, must be in some way raised to a state in which it is to a certain extent immaterial, a function which can only be performed by the intentional species.

As is implied in all that has so far been said, the species are required for two purposes ; first, that the object may be made present to the faculty ; and, secondly, that it may be raised to a condition consonant with that of the faculty itself, since like is known by like. It is clear that the intentional species are required for the second purpose at least, in all cases, since the cognitive faculty being a vital one, is more or less immaterial, while the object of the senses is wholly material.

So far we have spoken of the intentional species in globo, but something must be added on the role of the two kinds of species, impressed and expressed, which are recognised by the Scholastics. Without the impressed species no know ledge of finite things is possible, since it is the function of these to unite subject and object by assimilating the object to the subject, dematerialising it to a certain extent. The use of the expressed species, on the other hand, is altogether different, for these, as we have said, are likenesses or representations of the object, and are therefore only required when the object itself is not present. From the point of view of knowledge, the object is absent not only when it is absent from the physical point of view, not being presented to the faculty at that particular moment, as occurs in the case of the imagination, and in intellectual cognition of objects of which knowledge has been acquired in the past ; but also when the object, though present physically, is yet not proportionate to the faculty, as is the case in all intellectual cognition, where the object in itself is an individual and concrete nature, while the object as known is a universal and abstract one. The expressed species thus terminates cognition, not as if, being first known itself, it should lead to knowledge of the object, but as a term in which the object is

simultaneously known.  Cognition must evidently, being an
action, have such a term ;  so that where it is not already
given, as it is in the case of the knowledge of the external
senses, it must be produced ;  or, in other words, the expressed
species must be formed.  This expressed species is called by
the Scholastics the image or phantasm, in the case of the
imagination ;  the mental word or formal concept, in the
case of the intellect.

Much ridicule has been poured on the notion of impressed
species on the supposition that these are some sort of
effluvia or material particles, thrown off by the objects,
which fly across to the sentient subject.  Though this may
have been the opinion of Democritus, it certainly is not the
view which the Scholastics take of these species, since they
hold that the mode of existence which the species or forms
have in the object and sentient subject is different, being
physical in the one case and pyschical or intentional in the
other ;  not physical in both, as would be the case if the
supposition as to their being effluvia were correct.  Are we,
then, to suppose that the species are entirely spiritual and
not material at all ?  This cannot be held either, since in this
case no cause could be assigned of their production, both the
object and the percipient being material things, and so
incapable of producing something purely spiritual.  If, then,
they are neither wholly material nor wholly spiritual, they
must be something intermediate, and are to be called material
in so far as they belong to the material order, but not material
in the sense in which physical and chemical forces are.  Their
nature, in fact, must exactly correspond with that of the
sentient organism which receives them, and this is itself
something belonging to the material world ;  though its
forces, since it is living, are not purely chemical and physical
ones.

In order to obtain a thorough grasp of the Thomistic
theory of intentional species, it is important to understand
the way in which it envisages their production.  In the first
place, it should be noted that what an agent communicates
is not its matter but its form, as S. Thomas explains,[1] point-

[1] II de Anima, Lect. 24.

ing out that though every thing which is acted on receives from the agent a form which is to some extent without matter, yet there is a difference between the way in which a merely physical subject receives forms, and that in which a knowing or percipient subject does so. The physical thing receives the form with the same material disposition to the form as is present in the agent, so that it cannot be said to receive the form wholly without matter, even though it does not receive the very same matter as is in the agent. He exemplifies this by the case of air warmed by the fire, which in the process receives the same material disposition to the form of heat which was present in the fire, even though it does not receive the wood or coal. It is materially changed, and not formally only. This holds good of the action of all merely physical subjects of action, but in the case of percipient or cognitive subjects it is not true, since these receive the form from the agent or object, without receiving the same material dispositions to that form as were present in the object, and, in fact, they remain unchanged with regard to their physical being after the reception of the form. Consequently the similarity between the subject and object is one, not of nature, but of representation. The species, therefore, are produced by the objects, but their mode of being in the subject depends on the nature of that subject, which, being a cognitive one, receives them without their material dispositions. They are, as it were, filtered by the subject which receives them ; so that their partially immaterial character is accounted for. We can understand the reception by the subject of these intentional forms more clearly if we consider that every form makes its subject to be of a particular kind, as the form of heat (an accidental one) makes the subject hot, and the form of life (a substantial one) makes the subject living. Now these intentional forms make the subject actually knowing ; leaving it, however, physically unchanged ; and simply determining it to pass from the capacity or potentiality for knowledge to the act of cognition. Hence the intentional form does not make the subject physically of a particular kind, but simply makes it an actually knowing subject ; so that it gives it no other fresh being than that by which it is constituted as formally a knowing subject. The species, then, though resembling other forms in making the subject to be of a particular kind, yet differ markedly from these others in not being the source of the operations which follow on them ; since the operation which follows on intentional species, viz. the act of cognition, is generated by the cognitive faculty. This is clear, since the impressed species simply determines the faculty to know, while the expressed species follows on cognition, and is that in which the subject formally has knowledge.

So Cajetan[1] explains the difference between cognitive and nescient things by pointing out that the latter receive their forms by the operation of some extrinsic agent, which acts efficiently on them ; while the former do not receive their forms from the external object, which is known, but are made formally or actually knowing by means of the exercise of their own operation, when they are actuated or specified by a certain object, i.e. when their attention is caught by it ; so that the efficient principle which makes them actually knowing is the cognitive faculty itself, and not something external.

We can thus understand the statement which S. Thomas often makes : ' The sense in act is the sensible in act, and the intellect in act is the thing understood in act ' ; for the form of the known object, the intentional species, does not combine with the faculty to compose some third thing, as is the case in nescient subjects, when matter and form combine, but simply actuates, or calls out, the operation of sensing or understanding. In this way the form of the object becomes the form of faculty, which so informed or actuated, therefore becomes the object in the psychic order, though, of course, remaining unchanged as regards its own nature in the physical order. Further, it is clear how the species con- tributes to cognition, for if it be considered in relation to the object by which it is produced, it must be said to be the instrument which the object uses to determine the faculty, so that both it and the object contribute to the production of knowledge. Since, however, it is the active force by which

---

[1] *Comm. in S. Theol.*, I.14,1.

the object produces its effect, it is correct to say that the object is an immediate contributory principle of knowledge, for the active force of a substance is to be attributed to the substance itself, as Cajetan says : ' *Accidentalis vis non sua, sed substantiæ est virtus.*' If, on the other hand, the species be considered in relation to the cognitive faculty, we must, as we have seen, say that it is the faculty which is the active cause of cognition, though it is only so active under the actuation and determination of the species, which can therefore be called, to this extent, an active principle ; inasmuch as it, in union with the knowing subject, constitutes a single principle of cognition.[1]

If it be true, as is said above, that the function of the expressed species is to be the term of the act of cognition when the object is either not present or not proportionate to the cognitive faculty, it is easy to see what answer must be given to the question whether such species are present in every cognitive act ; a question which has been hotly disputed among Scholastics. The question may be put in other forms besides the one just mentioned, for if it be maintained, as is done by some recent Scholastics, that the expressed species is only logically distinct from the act of knowledge, it is clear that it will be present in all such acts, so that to ask whether this distinction is real, or logical only, is a second form of the question. Again, an action which is always directed towards the production of a term is called a predicamental action, while one which is not so directed, and produces nothing but the reality of the action itself, is called a metaphysical one. So the question can also be put in the form of asking whether the cognitive act is a predicamental or metaphysical one, since in the former case it will always be directed towards the production of the expressed species. The Thomists, as against Suarez, unanimously teach that no expressed species is produced in the acts of external sense knowledge ; and this for several reasons. First, because such species would be useless, since the object is itself sufficient to terminate the act ; and, secondly, it would be positively harmful, since it

---

[1] Cf. S. Thomas, *De Veritate*, Q. 8, A. 5 and 6 in corp. and A. 7 resp., d 2um (of the last series).

Q

would prevent the sense from grasping its object immediately, so that we should have experience, not of the object, but of the species. Thirdly, the view that the expressed species is really identical with the cognitive act is untenable, since the species is that *in* which the object is known ; whereas the cognitive act cannot be said to be that *in* which the object is known ; but only that *by* which we know it, without abandoning the Thomistic theory completely, and adopting a purely conceptualist one ; since the *act* of knowing must be something entirely our own or subjective. Hence we are not obliged to posit an expressed species in all cognition on the ground that it is identical with the cognitive act. Lastly, it seems clear that cognition is not designed for the production of a term, since, even when a term is produced, as in intellectual knowledge, the cognition continues after its production, and is, in fact, perfected and completed by the contemplation of the term produced, whereas in a predicamental action, the action ceases once the term has been produced. The fact then, that the perfection of cognition comes about after the term has been produced, shows that this production is achieved for the sake of cognition and not vice versa, as would be the case if cognition were a predicamental action instead of being, as it is, a metaphysical one ; and so, a disposition or quality of the subject.

This doctrine brings out the true immanence of knowledge inasmuch as the act of knowledge is something perfect, and complete in itself, and not designed to produce something other than itself, while at the same time it gives no support to Idealist theories of knowledge according to which we only know our own mental acts ; since it maintains that the object is known, either in itself, or in a representation which is really distinct from the act of knowing. Cognition, consequently, is rightly defined as metaphysical action, by means of which possession is taken of a form immaterially, i.e. without the potentiality of matter. So cognition, as such, has nothing to say to matter, to potentiality, to imperfection and consequently is what the Scholastics call ‘ a simply simple perfection,’ i.e. one which in itself involves no imperfection.

# CHAPTER IX

The Senses are Organic—Their Distinction and Number—Where
Sensation Takes Place—The Objects of the Senses—Immediate
and Mediate Sense Objects—Can we be said to Sense the
Externality of an Object?—The Inversion of the Retinal
Image—Internal Sensibility—The Sensitive Appetite.

AFTER this consideration of the nature and process of
knowledge in general, we can now pass to that of the knowledge of the senses, of sensation. In doing so we shall first
investigate the nature of the senses in general, and then the
different kinds of sense.

We ask, then, in the first place, whether the senses are
organic or inorganic faculties, i.e. whether they are dependent on the organism or not.

That sensation is a vital action, by which the sentient subject knows corporeal objects, which act on the sense organs, is
hardly open to dispute ; and it follows that three things are
required for sensation : (1) an object, (2) an impression made
by that object, and (3) that the sense which is thus affected
should really know the object, i.e. sensation is a kind of
cognition.

By a sensitive faculty we mean a proximate and immediate
principle of cognition by means of which the sentient subject
is united to material things.

In asking whether such faculties are organic or not we mean
to enquire whether they are dependent, for their existence
and action, on the whole organic compound, on the material
organism itself ; and we presuppose that sensation cannot be
explained merely mechanically, since it is a kind of cognition,
which, as we have seen, in our discussion of cognition in
general, cannot be a merely mechanical process. Are we,
then, to adopt the opinion which is at the opposite extreme

to this materialistic one and say that the senses depend intrinsically only on the vital principle or soul; a view maintained, at least with regard to human sensations, by the Cartesians.

This question is of considerable importance, since it deals with the relations of soul and body, and if sensation be allowed to be an act of the soul alone, then, first, we shall have to prove in some other way, than by its intrinsic dependence on the body, that the soul is its substantial form ; or else concede that an animal is not an essential unity, but a duality, composed of two complete and heterogeneous substances. The opinion of the Cartesians was, in fact, due to their taking this latter view of the nature of man. Moreover, whatever we say about this question of essential union. it would be difficult to deny that the sensitive soul is, of its own nature, and consequently in the lower animals as well as in man, spiritual and immortal. If, however, we establish that the senses are organic it will naturally follow that the animal is an essential unity, since it operates as a whole, and consequently that its soul is its substantial form, and also that it is not spiritual. Further, we shall have prepared the way for showing that the intellectual soul in man is the form of the body, even though it may be spiritual ; since in man the principle of sensation and intelligence is the same.

Actually the proposition that the senses are organic is one which is not likely to meet with much opposition at the present day, when the tendency is to take a materialistic rather than an immaterialist view of vital processes ; and S. Thomas gives us a simple, but convincing, reason for granting that it is true. For, as he points out,[1] if the operations of the senses are intrinsically dependent on the organism the senses themselves must also be intrinsically dependent. Now it is clear that sensation does depend intrinsically on the organism, since experience shows : first, that the objects of the senses are always singular and concrete things, which could only affect the sensitive faculty by a physical impression on something material, viz. the organ of sense ; secondly, that the sense itself is affected and

[1] *Summa Theologica*, I.77.5.

weakened by the physical forces of the object, as sight is by too much light, or light of an unsuitable kind, touch by too much pressure, and so on, and that it is sometimes destroyed by the corruption of the organ of sense ; and, thirdly, that the sense perceives all things as extended, i.e. material. For all these reasons, then, we are justified in asserting that the sense operations are intrinsically dependent on the matter of the organism ; and consequently that the senses themselves are organic.

We can now turn to a more detailed consideration of the particular senses. It is at once obvious that the sensations of which we are aware are of very different kinds. So, e.g. the sensation of seeing an object is quite different from that of hearing a sound ; and consequently in trying to classify sensations we shall soon pick out what are commonly called the five senses of sight, hearing, smell, taste, and touch. Common observation had always distinguished these five senses, but from a philosophical point of view the division is arrived at by considering the objects from which the sensations are derived, viz. colour, sound, odour, savour, and tangible quality. It is clear that to say that the object of touch is what can be sensed by touch is to say nothing ; and, in fact, this sense has a very indefinite outline, and is really a genus of sensation covering both sensations of pressure, or resistance, as well as those of temperature—of heat and cold. What are called nowadays ' organic sensations,' viz. those connected with internal feeling of the organism, as sensations in the stomach, bowels, etc., as well as muscular sensations, and so on, all come under this head. Sensations of touch, moreover, are generally present along with the sensations of the other four senses, particularly in tasting and smelling, though they are also present to some extent, generally without our being aware of it, in seeing and hearing.

Nevertheless, since in the last-named sensations we do not know, by pure sensation, that the objects of sight and hearing are acting causally on our organs, but regard them as being things not in contact with our bodies, these two senses are often named by the Scholastics the superior senses, while those senses in whose action we are aware of causal action of the objects on the organism, in the sensation itself, are called the inferior ones, viz. smell, taste, and touch.

Some remarks may be made about particular aspects of the sensations of these inferior senses. With regard to the sense of touch, touch-sensations include, as we said, those of heat and cold. There are spots on the skin, known as heat and cold spots, and also areas covering a system of nerve-endings, at which sensations of heat and cold are aroused on contact with points or surfaces. Pain sensations are also included under the sensations of touch ; but, of course, such sensations are not to be confused with feelings of pain, which belong to the affections or emotions. With regard to the sense of taste, there seem to be only four or five savours properly so-called : sweet, sour, bitter, salt, and alkaline. The variety of savours which we usually suppose ourselves to recognise are a combination of taste and smell. Odours, lastly, are almost impossible to classify, owing to their variety and composite character.

Each of the sense organs is connected with areas in the brain by means of the nervous system, of which the auditory, visual, and olfactory areas have been most definitely located.

In view of this fact many modern psychologists consider that sensation takes place in these sensory areas, i.e. that we actually sense, not in the sense organs, but in the brain. This opinion seems to have been too hastily arrived at ; for it is based on the fact, or supposed fact, that if the sensory area in the brain is destroyed, the corresponding sensation does not take place. This fact would only show that the brain plays an essential part in sensation ; and does not warrant the conclusion that it is the brain alone which senses. On the other hand, we have positive reasons for adhering to the opinion that sensation takes place in the sense-organs, and is thence carried by way of the nervous system to the brain, so that we, as subjects, become fully conscious of it, only on the completion of this process. This view is in accord with the strong testimony of experience, in so far as we always localise our sensations in a particular part of the body : e.g. in the leg or arm, and the fact that a man may ' feel ' sensations in an amputated limb only shows how strong is habitual imagination, which, when the nerves, before connected with that limb, are affected, still persists in localising the sensation in the absent limb ; not that when the limb is present the man really had no sensation in it. The testimony of common experience, then, ought not to be reckoned erroneous, unless there be some certain reason which renders it untenable. Such a reason was thought to be the fact that impressions of light and sound could be engendered by direct excitation of the visual and auditory centres ; but it should be noticed that it does not seem possible to do this in subjects which have never possessed the sense in question ; and, moreover, the impressions so produced are not of any determinate object, but indefinite ones of illumination or noise, etc., in which, again, imagination would have a part to play. The opinion we are opposing seems to rest on an inveterate prejudice that the organism is really a mere mechanism, like a photographic camera, so that the organs and nerves could only be mere media to transmit a physico-chemical impulse to a purely material receptacle, and so could not be said to receive the impressions themselves. If, however, we reject this view as being a merely *a priori* one, as it is, and founding ourselves on experience, maintain that the organism acts as a vital whole, there seems to be no reason for abandoning the doctrine that sensation takes place, i.e. the object is sensed primarily, in the organs on the body's surface, and is completed, and made fully conscious, when their impressions affect the sensory areas in the brain ; and so the general sensitivity, and the whole sensitive subject.

*The Objects of the Senses.*

The Scholastics distinguish two kinds of sense objects, essential and accidental ones. The first class is again divided into proper and common sense objects. By an essential sense object they mean one which is in fact presented to, and grasped by, the sense or senses in question, as distinguished from an accidental object which is not in fact grasped by a sense, but being known by some other faculty, an accompanying the essential sense object, is known by the subject along with it. Thus bodily substance is an accidental sense object; for, though it is not known by any of the senses—it cannot be seen, or heard, or touched, and so on—but only by the intellect; yet, since it goes along with what is sensed in itself or essentially, viz. bodily accidents, it is said to be accidentally sensible. The class of essential sensibles called proper are those which are the immediate objects of any sense, which specify it, and so are grasped only by that sense and no other, while common sense objects are those which are mediate objects of any sense, and are often grasped by more than one sense.

Such mediate sensibles are, however, of two kinds: those which are known in themselves through some medium, and those which are not known in themselves, but in some representation or image of themselves. To make clear what is meant by this we might use the example of the telescope. In the usual form of telescope the star is seen directly, and in itself, though only by the medium of the instrument; whereas in the reflecting telescope, what is seen is an image or reflection of the star, not the star itself, the medium of seeing this image being the instrument; and that of seeing the star its reflection in the mirror of the telescope. The first class of immediate sensibles, viz. those which are mediately sensed in themselves, are quantity and things connected with it, viz. motion, rest, shape, and position. These are presented to the sense by means of something else, e.g. colour, but nevertheless they are presented as they are in themselves. Shape cannot be seen without colour, but nevertheless the shape of a coloured object is *seen*, is grasped by the sense of sight.

The second class of mediate sensibles are very different from these, for what is grasped by the sense here is not any sense object, as it is in itself, but as it is in some image or reflection of itself. This reflection which represents the object as it is in itself, more or less accurately, is to be found in all sense perceptions, since there is always one essential sense object which is immediately sensed, and is within the organ of sense, in immediate contact with the nerve endings, as e.g. the retinal image, or rather the extended coloured surface which is in immediate contact with the retina ; and another mediate essential sense object, viz. the object from which this extended coloured surface is transmitted, i.e. the external object. This last is known only by the mediation of the internal object.

Simple sensation does not distinguish between the object as it is outside the subject, and the object as it is within it. Both are known by it, but confusedly, the internal object not being known as internal, nor the external as external. This is clear, since we do not see an object as being in our eye, nor hear a sound as the vibration of that part of the air which is in immediate contact with the basilar membrane of the ear, though scientific investigation shows that these internal objects are present, and that it is only by their means that we see or hear the external ones. Consequently the external object is not known to be external by means of sensation alone ; it is not an essential sensible, but only an accidental one. We conclude that it is external by repeated observations and comparison of different sense experiences, and so may be said to *perceive* its externality, though we cannot *sense* that it is external. The external object, then, considered from different points of view, can be said to be either an essential sensible, or not an essential sensible, but an accidental one. In itself, simply as coloured, round, etc., it is an essential sensible, though a mediate one known in its intra-organic representation ; but in so far as it is *external* it is not an essential sensible at all. Consequently, as it is, if considered absolutely in itself, without relation to the internal sense impressions which it produces, or even considered precisely as the source of the whole complex of such impressions, the external object is an accidental sense object which comes to be known gradually by putting together and comparing a large number of sense experiences. In this process imagination and, in the case of man, intellect play a large part ; and thus the way is laid open to numerous mistakes and illusions.[1]

From what we have said it will be clear that what any sense

---

[1] The theory here sketched with regard to mediate sensibles is derived from Fr. Jos. Gredt, O.S.B. See his *De Cognitione Sensuum Externorum*, Edio 2ª Romae, 1924. This essay can also be usefully consulted for the analysis of the objects of each of the senses in particular.

perceives immediately, and essentially, is the proper sense object which is internal to the organ of the sense in question. Thus the sight, e.g. senses the coloration of the ether which is in immediate contact with the retina : it does not sense essentially, and in itself, the object from which this impression is derived, nor yet the retinal image produced by the 'internal' object. This explains why it is that though the retinal image is inverted the object is not seen as inverted, a fact which is generally explained by saying that custom enables us to 'rectify' the inversion of the retinal image, interpreting it, by the imagination, as direct. But if what is seen is not the physical (or photo-chemical) impression on the retina, which is certainly inverted, but the interior object which represents the external one, this object will *represent* not the position of the rays of light as they are about to fall on the retina, which are already refracted, but the position from which the rays come, and so their direction ; so that the eye will see, as coming from above, what does indeed come from above, and from below, what comes from below. This explanation will only hold good if the sensation of sight takes place in the eye , whereas if it be held that the sensation takes place in the brain this difficulty with regard to the inverted image seems almost insoluble, since the brain can only register what is given it, viz. the inverted image ; and cannot perceive from what direction the light-rays come to fall on the retina, in which case the deliverances of the senses of touch and sight ought to be discordant, which is not the case. This affords then, a confirmation of the view that sensation takes place in the sense organs and not in the brain.

*Internal Sensibility*.

The Scholastics usually partition the functions which are performed by the internal sensibility among four 'internal senses' ; the common sense, imagination, estimative faculty and memory ; though Suarez considers these four to be but different functions of one sense.

The functions of the common sense would be those of sensitive consciousness, by which man and the animal would be conscious of their sensations, and that of discrimination and comparison between various sensations, e.g of sight and touch, by which the subject is at the moment affected.

Though traditionally the common sense has been considered by the Scholastics to be a separate faculty with a special organ, it does not seem clear that Aristotle thought it to be other than the general sensitivity.[1] In fact, this view, as Cardinal Mercier points out,[2] is consonant with the teaching of S. Thomas, and avoids the considerable difficulties which arise if we regard the common sense as a distinct faculty. Since the subject is itself a unity it will be able to unify and compare its own sensations, by means of the sensitivity which is distributed through the whole organism, and especially through the nervous system and brain. Another function which is exercised by the internal sensibility is that of imagining. We know as a fact of our own experience that sense perceptions of objects are often followed by our making representations of them to ourselves, picturing them, and forming images of them. This is the work of the imagination which, by means of the formation of such pictures or images, thereby enables the animal to retain the knowledge of sensible objects, to know them when absent, and to reproduce and associate them.

The third function of the internal sensibility is what S. Thomas called the ' estimative force ' or power, a function which is included under what now goes by the rather vague name of ' instinct.' By its means an animal is able to appreciate the beneficial or noxious character of the objects of sense, and so try to get them, or avoid them. This power arises from natural predispositions which are doubtless educated by experience. The animal being by nature of a certain kind finds some things useful to it and some harmful, so that its very nature moves it to acquire the first and reject the second. No really satisfactory explanation is, however, forthcoming to show how it is that a quite inexperienced animal is able to make such discriminations, as, e.g., to avoid

---

[1] Cf. Ross, *Aristotle*, p. 140.
[2] Mercier, *Psychologie*, Tom. I, paragraphs 100 ff.

eating poisonous or harmful herbs. It seems certain that any satisfactory explanation will have to allow that the animal has certain innate natural tendencies to definite ends. If such tendencies be ruled out, as they must be by any mechanistic account of animal behaviour, the fact of instinctive discrimination becomes inexplicable.[1]

The last function of the internal sensibility is sensitive memory by means of which the animal recognises past experiences as past ; the memory, thus differing from the imagination, which merely reproduces them without putting them in their setting as things experienced in the past. Such recognition of past experiences is clear in ourselves, when we recognise a face or a place which we have seen before, and is not to be denied to the lower animals, who also recognise persons and places from which they have been separated, sometimes for a long time.

### The Sensitive Appetite.

To complete our consideration of the activities of sensitive nature we must add something with regard to its conative capacities, or, as the Scholastics call it, ' sensitive appetite.' Though the word ' appetite ' is used by the Scholastics to signify any natural tendency which may be found in any thing, covering such tendencies as that of heavy bodies to move towards one another ; in this connection its signification is narrower and, excluding such innate or natural tendencies as those just mentioned, is confined to tendencies which follow on cognition. The tendencies which are brought into play by cognition may be purely natural ones, the instinctive tendencies of the animal ; or intelligence may combine with instinct, so that the resulting action is spontaneous, and not dictated merely by the nature of the subject : and, in the case of man, it is at least theoretically possible that he should desire what he knows by his intellect to be good quite apart from any impulse of his nature driving him to do so.

This notion of purposive tendencies in man, and *a fortior*

[1] For a full discussion of instinct see McDougall, *Outline of Psychology* Esp. Ch. IV.

in the lower animals, is altogether repudiated and excluded by modern psychologists of the materialistic and Behaviouristic schools, because it is not observable by the methods of natural science, which can know nothing of final causes, of the ' why ' of an action. The success of both biologists and psychologists in their attempt to bring vital phenomena within the bounds imposed by itself on physical science has been, however, very incomplete ; so that in both sciences there are many authorities who wish to retain the notion of purpose when dealing with animal or human behaviour, and even to make it central, and the ruling principle of such behaviour ; as does McDougall, and those associated with him in the Hormic school.

It is, in fact, extraordinarily difficult to deny the fact of purpose in human behaviour, and even those psychologists who do not allow its existence devote all their energies to a definite purpose : the exclusion of purpose. A detailed examination of the behaviour of animals, in order to determine whether their actions can be said to be purposive, would require a volume ; and, what is more important, is outside the scope of a philosophical investigation ; but both common and scientific observation of their actions shows that it is at least much the simplest explanation of them, and in fact the only one, at present in the field, which is reconcilable with all the known facts. From a strictly philosophical point of view, moreover, it is certain that where we have cognition we must also have appetition or conation ; so that on the supposition that the animals have the former, they must also have the latter. The reason of this statement is that every action must have a definite efficient principle and be directed towards some definite object or end. For if there were no definite efficient principle of action there could be no action, and if the action had no definite direction the agent would not do one thing rather than another, and so would not act at all. The actions, moreover, of things are governed by their natures or forms, i.e. they will act in accordance with their natures. Now the forms which are found in things are, as we have seen, of two kinds, their innate physical forms, and those which they acquire through cognition ; and each of these will direct their actions towards a definite object or end, so that in both cases there will be an inclination or tendency which accompanies the possession of these forms. In the case of physical forms we shall have a uniform, constant, and determined tendency towards a given end ; and in the case of forms acquired by cognition a tendency towards, or away from, an end, according as this is known as suitable or unsuitable to the agent in question.

We see, then, that if we acknowledge that animals have sense cognition we are also obliged to grant that they have a conative tendency which follows on it, and is determined by it, i.e. that they have a sense appetite. Whether, in fact, they have such cognition is the question which must now be discussed.

# CHAPTER X

## THE NATURE OF THE LIFE-PRINCIPLE IN ANIMALS

What We Mean by 'Animal'—Have they Sensation?—Opinions:
Descartes, Loeb—The Thomist View—Is Sensation Peculiar to
Animals?—The Life-principle in Animals Essentially Sensitive,
and their Substantial Form: so One Only—Belonging to the
Material Order, yet Specifically Distinct from that of Plants—
Summary.

As a result of our discussion of cognition we can now see that
sensation is a cognitive action, whose formal object is the
individual material thing which is presented to the sense,
and that cognitive action itself is a metaphysical one, by
which immaterial possession is taken of a form ; the form in
the case of sensation being, however, that of an individual
material thing, and so conveniently called a material form,
in contrast to those which are altogether denuded of matter,
either owing to their nature, as spiritual beings would be, or
through the operation of mind which takes away all materiality, and consequently all individuality from them.

If we are to ask whether animals are capable of sensation,
and if so whether they differ from the plants in this respect,
we must have a clear idea of what we mean by an animal as
distinguished from a plant. Though everyone has a vague
notion of what constitutes an animal, it would often be
found, on examination, to be that an animal is a living being
which has senses, as opposed to a plant, which has none.
Such a notion, if it were employed here, would evidently lead
us in a vicious circle, for this is precisely the question we are
enquiring into : whether animals do indeed possess this
peculiar power which is not shared by beings lower in the
vital scale. It is obvious that this preliminary notion which
we may have of an animal cannot be its essential definition—
its real definition—since if we return an affirmative answer

to this question it will be equivalent to saying that the specific difference of animal nature is sensibility, so that we must be content, at this stage, with a nominal and descriptive definition which may leave a certain amount of doubt as to whether some particular organisms are to be considered as animals or plants. The difficulty is paralleled by that which we experience when we ask whether rationality is the prerogative of man ; for here again we must take such outward characteristics as taillessness, erect walk, articulation of limbs, brain-structure, and so on, to indicate what we mean by man, and so find it difficult to decide whether certain fossil remains are human or not. We must notice that two questions are included in the one stated above, viz. (I) whether animals are capable of sensation, i.e. whether any of those beings which we agree to call animals are capable of it, and here the difficulty just mentioned does not arise, and (2) whether all animals, and they alone, are capable of it, where the lack of precision in our descriptive definition of ' animal ' is bound to result in a certain amount of doubtfulness and obscurity. We can say, for certain, that capacity for sensation constitutes a specific difference or difference in kind between those beings which have it and those which do not, though we may find it difficult to determine precisely where the line of demarcation is to be drawn.

Let us first see what sort of nominal, or descriptive definition we can give of ' animal.' From a physico-chemical point of view, animals may be said to be distinguished from green plants by the tendency of the processes of energy-transformation which go on in them. The tendency of the green plant is to accumulate energy in the form of high potential compounds, such as carbo-hydrates, proteid, fat and oil, while in the animal body the tendency is to break down these compounds into water, carbonic acid, urea and other nitrogenous substances. Thus the metabolic action in the animal is destructive, in the plant constructive.

A more obvious, as well as a more essential, characteristic which is to be observed in animals, as contrasted with green plants, is mobility, and mobility which is, at least in appearance, purposive. Not only is the mobility of animals much more extensive than that of plants, but the typical animal moves as a whole, while the typical plant only moves its parts, such as leaves, roots or tendrils, and these merely by reflex motions responding to some external stimulus. The variety of animal movements is also much greater than that of the plant. This capacity for movement is due to the structure of the animal as contrasted with the plant, for the former possesses a sensori-motor system which the latter does not. This system is the skeleton and muscles whereby the animal is enabled to move from place to place, to seize its food, and so on, and to masticate it, as well as the peripheral sensory and motor nerves, and the central nervous system and brain. No doubt the plain man would say of a creature that was observed to move itself from place to place that it was an animal and not a plant ; and though this characteristic, by itself, is not for us a sufficient indication of the nature of an organism, it occupies, no doubt, an important place in the characteristic behaviour of the typical animal. As animal life progresses the sensori-motor system becomes more developed and the animal grows more and more mobile. According to these indications, then, it will be sufficient for our present purpose to describe an animal as a living being whose characteristic metabolic tendency is analytic, and which is mobile, its mobility being due to the possession of a sensori-motor system.

We can now ask whether those beings which possess a combination of these characteristics are capable of sensation, while those which do not possess it, are not. We remarked that the capacity for sensation must constitute a specific difference, and the truth of this statement appears if we consider that sensation implies a degree of immateriality in its possessor which is not found in an insensitive being.

Such a surplus of immateriality is a positive addition to the being of a thing, and so is an element of being, found in it over and above that which is found in other entities. Evidently nothing more than additional being can be required to constitute specific difference, since there is nothing more than being, so that where we find a positive addition of being,

R

as in this case, we can affirm that we are in the presence of a specific difference.

Our first question, whether any animals, using the word animal in the sense indicated above, are capable of sensation, is one to which common sense readily gives an affirmative answer ; nevertheless, a negative one has often been given by philosophers. It must, of course, be denied that animals sense, by the materialists and those who deny that there is any distinction, except that of the degree of its complexity, between organic and inorganic matter. Their view on this point is clearly but a corollary of their general position, and we have already seen that it is impossible to maintain that living things are a mere compound of matter and its forces.

There are, however, others who while not denying the distinction between animate and inanimate things, nevertheless, will not allow that the animals sense. Of these the first is Descartes, who divided beings into two classes, those which are constituted by geometrical extension, and those which are endowed with thought. Since he held that the animals are not capable of thought, as a consequence he had to include them in his first class, and say that they are purely material constructions, inanimate and insensible. So he says : ' The animals act naturally by springs, like a watch.' He imagined that the more rarefied parts of the blood ascended to the brain, and there, in the ventricles, became what he called ' the animal spirits ' ; a kind of fluid contained in them, whose flow was regulated by valves in the nerves, which he thought of as fine tubes. On the stimulation of the surface of the body, threads in the nerves were pulled by it opening the valves, and allowing the animal spirits to flow along them, thus causing contraction, etc., of the muscles, motion, and the other phenomena of what we call life. Though this theory, with the growth of physiological knowledge, had to be abandoned altogether, the underlying notion that the motions of animals are to be explained merely mechanically has survived, and has been embodied in theories such as that of Loeb. This is known as the theory of ' tropisms ' ; which in its generalised form ascribes all the motions of animals to physico-chemical responses or reactions to external stimuli, such as light. So, for example, the motions of a caterpillar which moves up a plant and eats the green shoots at the top are explained by saying that, if at the beginning of the movement, the body of the caterpillar is at an angle to the direction of the light rays (in this case the sun's rays), one side of its body will be more illuminated than the other. This will cause the muscles on that side to contract, and so the caterpillar will be turned round towards the rays, and when its body is in line with their direction, both sides of it will be equally stimulated, and contracting equally, will cause it to move towards the light. This position will clearly be one of stable equilibrium, since on any divergence from it the unequal stimulation of the sides of its body will cause it to resume it. Such an organism is said to be positively heliotropic, or positively phototropic. Movements away from a source of light are explained in a similar way. Though, in fact, the hypothesis was only successful in explaining some parts of the movements of some of the lowest organisms, it was hoped that with increased knowledge it might be made to cover all movements of all organisms ; a pious hope whose realisation is becoming continually less probable, as new facts become known which cannot be forced within the limits of the theory.[1] Though, then, it may be true that tropism plays a part in directing the motions of animals, it cannot be considered to be an all-sufficient explanation of them. According to Professor J. S. Haldane, the mechanistic theory of life is now ' bankrupt,' and physiologists have lost interest in it ;[2] but whatever be the prevailing opinion of scientists with regard to it, the following considerations are sufficient to show it to be untrue in its application to the animals. For, in the first place, the variety of the motions of animals shows that they do not move merely in response to physico-chemical stimuli, since they change their motions and cease from action even though the stimuli remain constant. Further, they do not always respond in the same way to the same stimuli ; and

[1] Cf. McDougall, *Outline of Psychology*, pp. 62 ff. Johnstone, *The Philosophy of Biology*, pp. 148 ff.

[2] J. S. Haldane, *The Sciences and Philosophy*, p. 57, and the whole of Lect. 3.

very different stimuli often produce the same response. Moreover, they adapt themselves to the situation in which they are placed in a way which mechanisms cannot do, as Professor Haldane shows with respect to breathing in a progressively rarefied atmosphere.[1] Add to this, that if we grant, as we can hardly refuse to do in the face of our own experience, that we have sensible cognition, we cannot deny it to the animals, since they display signs of emotion similar to those which we observe in ourselves, exhibiting in various ways marks of pleasure, affection, anger, fear, and so on. It is also difficult to deny that they desire and go in search of food, drink, and other bodily gratifications if we allow that men do, since their mode of behaviour is precisely similar to our own. No one can refuse to admit that many animals have all the sense-organs which we ourselves possess, and all of them at least some of these organs. If, then, we admit that we have sense cognition by means of these organs, we can hardly deny such cognition to the other animals, especially in view of their behaviour and use of these organs. All these considerations, at any rate if taken together, ought to be sufficient to convince us that the animals are indeed capable of sense-knowledge, and are not to be considered as mere automata or machines. Are we, however, to regard this capacity as the peculiar prerogative of animals, or should it be extended to all living organisms ? Those who think that it should are chiefly influenced by the fact that we find no absolutely sharp line of demarcation either in structure or behaviour between the lowest forms of animal life and the highest forms of what are recognised as plants. Thus it is stated that ' some lower organisms, the Peridinians and the Algal spores, exhibit all the characters which we utilise in separating animals from plants.'[2] Apart from the fact that this statement seems somewhat exaggerated, since it is acknowledged that they possess but the rudiments of a sensori-motor system, if it be regarded as such at all, and other animal characteristics, if at all, only in a very elementary form ; it is surely a fallacious method of argument. What is shown by the facts is merely that there are some

[1] Haldane, op. cit., p. 94.    [2] Johnstone, op. cit., p. 201.

organisms about which we cannot be certain whether they are to be reckoned as plants or animals ; not, as is assumed, that we must attribute to some plants, and then, by an added assumption, to all plants, the essential characteristics which are found in acknowledged animals. From the point of view of philosophy it is of no consequence to decide what particular organisms are to be reckoned as plants and what as animals, the only question is whether some organisms must be held to be capable of cognition, while others cannot be said to be capable of it : for this, if it is the case, will establish the fact that there is a specific difference among organisms. No doubt the gradual fading, as it were, of the animal world into the vegetable, makes us suspect that plants differ only in degree, and not in kind, from the animals ; but we ought to base our theories on facts, not our facts on theories. We ought to say that since we see clear indications of sensation in almost all the organisms we class as animal, and no such indications in almost all those we class as vegetable, it is present in the one class and not in the other ; and not that since we think it may be present in a few examples of plant life, it must be present in all, even though observation lends no support to such a view. Probably the chief ground for making such an assertion is an unacknowledged prejudice, or belief, that in fact all living things have been evolved from simple protoplasm and therefore life must be essentially the same whether it be that of a man or an acorn. Such a falla-cious *a priori* way of arguing might be excusable in a philo-sopher during the decadence of Scholasticism ; but is much less so in the scientist in an age of positivism and enlighten-ment. Further, it is not by any means clear that the facts which are supposed to lend their support to this theory really do so. It is true that in what we may call ' boundary-forms ' we may find, on what is reckoned as the animal side, some energy-transformations which are of the same kind as those typical of plants, viz. synthetic ones, while analytic transformations are found among organisms reckoned as vegetables ; yet the main tendency in the first is analytic, and in the second synthetic. Again, though motility is found in some plants, as we have noticed, yet it is so

undirected and random, so lacking in any appearance of
spontaneity or purpose, that it looks much more like a tropism
than a sensitive reaction to felt stimuli, whereas the motions
of even the unicellular animalcule, such as Paramœcium,
exhibit fairly clear signs of conscious and spontaneous action.
So, on coming in contact with a solid object, it usually
reverses its motion and backs away from it, then turning
slightly swims towards it again, and lastly remains quiescent;
all without any change in the external stimuli ; so that the
changes in its movements must be ascribed to something
within the animalcule, viz. its consciousness or sensitivity.
So it does not seem possible to explain all its movements in
terms of reflexes or tropisms,[1] as apparently can be done in
the case of Algal Zoospores.  If all this is even approximately
true, it seems that the nature of these organisms is too
obscure to justify us in using our view of it as a basis for
asserting that all plant and animal life is of the same kind,
in face of the clear evidences of sensitivity which are manifested by the majority of animals, and the absence of any
such evidences in the majority of plants.

We can conclude, then, with a fair degree of confidence,
that animals are possessed of sensitive life, which is their
own peculiar prerogative, so that cognition being found in
the animal world and not in the vegetable, these two differ
specifically, or in kind.

Two corollaries follow from this : first, that the animals
are animated by a principle of life which is sensitive, since
there must be a source of their sensitive operations which is
of the same kind as these ; and, secondly, that this life-
principle is their substantial form, since, their specific
difference being sensitivity, that which makes them sensitive
beings will be that which constitutes their nature specifically:
that is to say, their substantial form ; and it is clear that it
is their sensitive life-principle which makes them sensitive
beings, and is therefore their substantial form.

It is hardly necessary to emphasise again, what has been

---

[1] H. S. Jennings, *The Behaviour of the Lower Organisms*, pp. 23 ff., who
concludes, from his observations, that ' the behaviour of Amœba is
directly adaptive,' and that its ' behaviour is not purely reflex.'

said so often already, that substantial form can be one only ; but applying this truth to the case in question, we see that the animals cannot have two life-principles, one vegetative and the other sensitive, but only one, which is formally sensitive and virtually vegetative, i.e. one which can cause those effects which would proceed from a vegetative one were it present. Further, since it is formally sensitive, it is of its nature occupied only with material objects and material operations ; in other words, its operations are essentially dependent on matter, and it itself is not spiritual, but belongs to the material order ; for we are bound to judge of the nature of a thing from the consideration of its essential operations. If, then, it is dependent on matter both for its operation and its very being, it will be generated from matter, and, on the corruption of the compound of which it is the form, will cease to be actually ; and so is not immortal.

Such, then, are the general conclusions which we can come to as to the nature of animals. Just as even the lowliest of living things in the realm of plants are superior to, and specifically distinct from, all inanimate things, being capable of immanent action, and so having an actuality and immateriality which is not found in the inorganic realm ; so also the animals are superior to, and differ in kind from, the plants ; being possessed of that immateriality which is implied by cognition ; and so of a positive perfection over and above those found in the lower realm. At the same time, their life is still altogether dependent on matter ; and they cannot be called spiritual, but must be reckoned as belonging to the material order. We are now to ascend one step further in the scale of living beings, and consider those which seem to bridge the gap, as it were, between the material and the spiritual, viz. men.

Before doing so, it may be well to pause, and look back over our account of the life of plant and animal ; and to synthetise our notions of the life-principle in these realms, since the Thomistic idea of the ‘ souls ’ of plants and animals has been so often misconceived. We are unable to agree either with the materialistic and mechanistic view of life, which represents it as simply the sum total of the physico-chemical forces of which the body is made up, or with that of the vitalists, such as Stahl, who imagined that there was in the living body some energy-producing force, or forces, over and above, and independent of, the physico-chemical ones which are present in it. The ' soul,' in S. Thomas' view, is not a thing or entity on its own account, but the directing, co-ordinating, unifying principle of the whole organism, whereby this organism acts immanently and as a whole. The action of this principle in no way affects the total energy of the organism, but merely directs it in a particular way. Just as a workman with a pile of bricks expends the same amount of physical energy whether he piles them in a disorderly heap, or builds a house with them, so the energy of an organic system remains the same whether the physical forces in it act independently, and at random, or are directed in a definite fashion, and co-ordinated by this vital principle. Further, though this ' soul ' belongs to the material order, as contrasted with the spiritual one ; being dependent for its very existence on the matter which it informs, it is, nevertheless, not in itself endowed with the properties of matter, not being in itself spatially extended, though it acts in space ; and not being a source of physico-chemical energy, though it directs it.

# DIVISION IV. INTELLECTUAL LIFE

We are now to investigate the third and highest grade of life, namely, human life. The most striking difference between man and the other animals is, no doubt, the possession by the former of intellectual powers ; so that our primary business will be to enquire into the nature of these powers ; first, with regard to their generic nature : to determine whether they are organic or not ; secondly, with regard to their specific nature, which is the question concerning the object of the intellect ; and, lastly, to ask how the intellect comes to know its objects ; the question of the process of intellectual knowledge, or of the origin of ideas.

In treating of these questions here, in the philosophy of nature, we shall use the same methods as those employed in dealing with the ones which we have already discussed ; that is to say, direct methods of observation, both of other men, and more especially, since we ourselves are men, of our own mental processes, by introspection. The question whether the results of such observations are valid, or whether we are led astray by deceptive appearances, is one which is outside the limits of our present enquiry ; since it can only be answered, if at all, by means of a reflective analysis of our knowledge ; and so is dealt with in Epistemology, whose aim is to investigate the nature of our knowledge by means of reflection. Thus questions as to the nature of universal concepts, and so on, are left over to a later stage. This being understood, we can now proceed to ask what the nature of intellectual life appears to be.

# CHAPTER XI

## THE NATURE OF THE INTELLECT

Views as to its Immateriality—S. Thomas' Primary Reason for
   Holding it to be So—Its Objects : Common Formal Object,
   and Proper Formal Object—Further Reasons for Regarding
   the Intellect as Immaterial—The Question of Its Activity—
   Our Knowledge of Individuals.

WE have seen that the root of cognition is immateriality, so
that a thing which is wholly and purely material can have
no knowledge ;  and since it is undisputed that the intellect is
a cognitive faculty, it follows that it must be to some extent
immaterial.  What, then, is the extent of its immateriality ?
Is it like the senses, which are organic, being dependent on
the organism both for their existence and their action, or, if
not, is it entirely independent of the organism ?  To be so it
would have to be independent of it both subjectively and
objectively, that is to say, it would have to be capable of
existing independently of the organism, and also able to
acquire its knowledge of objects without its aid.

The question whether it can do this last, or not, can only
be answered when it is known what these objects are, a
subject which is to be discussed later, so that here we are
only concerned to discover whether it is subjectively independent of the organism or not.  If this were the case, it would
neither contain matter as a part of itself, nor be dependent
on it for its existence and action ;  but having an existence
of its own, and not as an element of a compound which
receives existence only as a whole, would be strictly speaking
immaterial or spiritual.

It is obvious that materialism must deny any immateriality to the intellect, and, *a fortiori*, that it is subjectively
independent of the organism : a denial which is expressed
plainly, though crudely, in the assertion that ' the brain

secretes thought as the liver secretes bile.' A more subtle form of the same notion is to be found in the view of the Behaviourists that thought actually consists of minute movements of the larynx in forming sub-vocal speech. This theory as to the nature of thought was, of course, devised to bring it within the general scheme as to the character of all vital action, viz. that it is essentially a physico chemical reaction to stimuli of the same kind. Since we have already tried to show that vital action cannot be of this sort, we must omit any special criticism of this theory of thought, and resist the temptation to point out its inconsistencies. The English Empiricists, as Hume and the Associationists, carrying to its logical conclusion the movement begun by Locke, considered that intellectual thought is a combination of particular sense-images, and so implies no more spirituality in its possession than sensation does.

Those philosophers who have been in the main stream of philosophic thought since philosophy first emerged from its sources, beginning with Socrates, Plato, and Aristotle, or even earlier thinkers, have always consistently maintained the essentially immaterial character of the intellect. This tenet is common to those whose views in other respects differ widely : as S. Thomas, Descartes, Leibniz, Kant, Hegel, and their successors, as well as the modern representatives of this tradition, as Bradley, Croce, or Bergson. This conviction, so constant among philosophers, if not easily arrived at, yet is one which grows gradually in strength as each aspect of our experience successively confirms it. That reality is essentially immaterial, and that the human mind, as the nearest approach to absolute reality of which we have immediate experience, is so also, are assertions which become increasingly clear and certain as philosophic reflection continues. Some of the main roads by which we are led to this conviction must now be mapped out ; and it will first be well to trace that one which S. Thomas seems to have regarded as leading most plainly and directly to this conclusion.[1]

[1] *Summa Theologica*, I.75,2 ; Q. disp. de Anima, A. 14 ; *Comm. in de Anima*, Lib. III, Lect. 7.

This argument is derived from the unlimited scope of intellectual operations. It should be clear from all that has been said as to the nature of knowledge that it is a kind of union between its subject and object, whereby the knowing subject becomes, in a certain way, the things which it knows, while retaining its own nature. It must therefore be capable of becoming any of these, but not be actually any of them, since, if it were, it is clear that it could not become them. Thus, that the sense of sight may know various colours it must be *capable* of receiving or becoming all of them, but cannot *be* any of them. As a man looking through blue glasses sees everything blue, so the sense of sight, if it were itself of any determinate colour, could not know a variety of colours. If we now apply this principle to the intellect, we observe that there is no corporeal nature which is incapable of being known by it ; for, of whatever sort it is, we certainly can know it as a thing or a being of a definite kind ; and it therefore follows, from our principle, that the nature of the intellect cannot be that of any one of the bodies which it can know. Since, then, these are all the bodies there are, its nature cannot be corporeal or bodily at all, but must be incorporeal or spiritual. In saying that the intellect can know the nature of any body, since it can always know it as a being or thing of a determinate kind, we do not mean to imply that it can necessarily grasp that ultimate specific difference whereby it is, in the last resort, differentiated from all other bodies ; but that it can grasp it as a thing which is at least superficially or accidentally differentiated from all others. Moreover, since, as we have seen, it can know the essential difference between inorganic and organic bodies ; and, again, within the latter class, the essential differences between plant and animal ; and, as we shall see shortly, between animal and man ; it can grasp the determinate nature of all these bodies, and consequently, cannot be either inorganic or organic body : either brute matter, plant, animal, or man. These classes, however, cover all bodies ; so that it cannot be any body. Notice, further : it is said that it *can* know all bodies, not that it actually does so ; for since its knowledge is derived from experience, and it has no intuition of the natures of things, the process of acquiring knowledge of these is a long and arduous one ; but it can, nevertheless, absolutely speaking, penetrate beneath the superficial appearances to know what is essential to them, as, e.g., that they are animals or plants. It has been objected that the principle : ' that which knows any nature cannot have that nature intrinsically and physically in itself ' cannot be maintained at the same time as the proposition that the intellect can know being, since, in this case, the intellect would not have the nature of being intrinsically and physically in itself, and so would not be being, i.e. would be nothing, which is absurd. Such an objection shows that the point of S. Thomas' argument has been missed, since the nature of being is not a determinate nature which excludes others, but, on the contrary, an indeterminate one which includes all. The whole point of the argument is that the possession of a particular *determinate* corporeal nature by the intellect would render it unable to know things as of a different nature to its own ; as the sight knows all things as coloured, never as odoriferous or resonant—its own nature preventing it from knowing these other attributes—and knows only a certain very limited range of colours, the visible spectrum, all others being excluded from the range of its knowledge owing to the fact that the organ on which it is essentially dependent possesses a determinate bodily nature.

This argument, then, gives us a solid ground for thinking that the intellect is a strictly incorporeal and spiritual faculty, and, moreover, that it cannot act by means of any bodily organ, since, if it did it could only know that determinate class of bodies which have affinity with this organ, and not *all* bodies, just as the sight can know only a determinate class of colours.

Our conclusion that the intellect is thus incorporeal will be strengthened after an examination of its objects, which will at the same time tell us what its specific nature is, since faculties are specified by their objects,[1] and to this we now pass.

By ' object ' in this context we mean the formal object,[2]

---

[1] Cf. Part II, Ch. III, Q. 2, p. 194.      [2] Cf. p. 195.

and if we wish to discover the nature of the human intellect, as distinguished from any other, we shall have to find out what its proper, as distinct from its common, formal object is ; for the common formal object of the intellect is that which the intellect, as such, and not some particular kind of intellect, formally grasps ; while the proper formal object of the human intellect is that which is formally known by it alone. These two are also sometimes known as the adequate and proportionate objects of the human intellect. If, then, we ask what is the adequate or common object of the human intellect, as intellect, we see it must be that object outside of, and apart from, which nothing can be known, and which includes all the particular intelligible objects. This object must be being, for, in the first place, nothing is intelligible unless it is being of some kind ; for what is not being is nothing, and so not knowable ; since, to say I know nothing is equivalent to saying I do not know. Secondly, the only object which includes all particular objects of the intellect is being in general ; for every addition to being limits it ; and so, by such addition, being in general is transformed into a particular kind of being. So, for instance, spiritual being, human being, and corporeal being, are classes formed by the addition of some quality to being in general. From this it follows that since the intellect knows, or can know, things which are included in all such classes ; all its objects will not be included in any one of them ; some being found in one class and some in another. These classes of beings, moreover, agree in the notion of being, and in nothing else. Hence the objects of the intellect also, included in these classes, agree in the notion of being only ; which notion, therefore, includes all intelligible objects. So every notion must ultimately be resolved into the primary notion of being.[1] If, e.g., we were to ask : What is man ? the answer would be rational animal. What, then, is an animal ? We answer ; sensitive living substance ; and what is substance ? a thing or *being* to whose nature is due existence in itself. Similarly, with all other notions, analysis always leads us eventually to the notion of being. In the same way every judgement has as

[1] Cf. S. Thomas, *De Veritate*, I,1.

its formal element the word ' is,' whereby identity of being between the subject and predicate is affirmed ; and every argument assigns from the premisses the reason of being of the conclusion, so that in the three operations of the mind nothing is intelligible except as it is resolved into the notion of being. It is thus absolutely clear that if the adequate formal object of the intellect were not being, the intellect would not have an adequate formal object at all ; since nothing is intelligible except in so far as it is being ; and all those things which are intelligible agree in this common formal notion of being.

We can also look at this question from a purely metaphysical point of view, and observe that since the root of cognition is immateriality, a thing is intelligible in so far as it is immaterial. Now it is clear that the more immaterial a thing is, the more actual it is ; since actuality is opposed to potentiality, which includes materiality, so that lack of materiality implies greater actuality. Greater actuality, in its turn, implies more perfection, i.e. more positive being, and it follows that a thing is more perfect, more actual, more immaterial, more intelligible, in proportion as it is more positively ' being.'

The statement that the adequate object of the intellect is ' being as such ' is not, of course, to be taken to mean that the intellect does not know anything but ' being as such,' but that it bears on things precisely as they are beings ; and, as a consequence, knows also the differences and determinations of being : just as the sight which bears on things as they are coloured, knows also the differences of colour.[1]

We have now to ask what is the *proper* formal object of the human intellect ; that object, namely, which is naturally known by this particular kind of intellect, an intellect which is found in intimate union with a bodily organism. The answer which S. Thomas gives to this question is that this object is the natures of sensible things in so far as they are universalised, or abstracted from individuating conditions. By the word ' natures ' we understand all natures whether substantial or accidental ; but this statement is not to be

[1] Cf. *Summa Theol.*, I.5,2,0 ; and I.79,7,0.

thought to mean that the intellect immediately, specifically, and perfectly understands the natures of material things ; it comes to the knowledge of them gradually, at first perceiving its object under the general forms of being, substance, etc. Nor do we mean to assert that the intellect knows nothing but corporeal things, but that it perceives these natures first, and because of its own natural constitution, perceiving other things indirectly, and by means of this proper object. This idea is opposed to the notions of all those who grant man some intuitive knowledge, whether by way of what are called innate ideas, as did Plato and Descartes, or by an immediate intuition of God, as did the Ontologists. We can approach the question either *a posteriori* or *a priori*—using these expressions in the Scholastic sense—for we may consider either the way in which the intellect understands, as we experience it actually at work, and so arrive at a knowledge of its proper objects ; or we may consider the nature of the intellect in itself, and deduce what must be its object.

If we adopt the first way, we see that there are three classes of things which are known by the intellect : (1) sensible singular things, (2) supersensible things, and (3) the natures of sensible things. Now experience shows that purely super-sensible things cannot be the primary object of the intellect, since we always come to know them by way of sensible things. The fact that we cannot express our thoughts of spiritual entities except by means of words and phrases derived from our knowledge of material ones, shows this also. So the names, God, angel, spirit, are derived from roots meaning to invoke, send, and breathe, respectively, and this fact is true in all languages. Nor can singular things be the primary object of the human intellect, for we always understand first that a thing is a being, and after-wards that it is this or that being ; for example, we cannot understand the individual man unless we have first under-stood what human nature is. Hence it must be the natures of sensible things which the intellect understands first, and of its very nature.[1]

If, again, we consider the nature of the intellect itself, we

[1] Cf. *Summa Theol.*, I.84,3,6,7 ; 85,3 ; 87,1–4 ; 88.

arrive at the same conclusion, since the object of the intellect must be proportionate to it ; for, in knowing, it receives and unites itself to the known object, which therefore must be assimilated or made proportionate to it. . Now the intellect is an immaterial form joined to matter, and it follows that the known object must be of the same kind, viz. the dematerialised nature of material things.[1]

The process of cognition shows also that this is so ; since, when dealing with material things, the intellect abstracts from individuating conditions, and leaving them on one side, grasps the natures of the things, a fact which would be inexplicable if its objects were purely material, as the Empiricists maintain.   On the other hand, while dealing with immaterial or supersensible things, though it understands them, it does so by reconverting them into the sensible, by way of the imagination ; which could not be explained on the hypothesis that its proper object is the purely supersensible, since in this case we should not understand spiritual things after the manner of material ones, as we do, but material ones as spiritual.

Intellectual knowledge, then, consists in the reception by the intellect of the forms or essences abstracted from material things.   We see that this is so, apart from the consideration that the intellect is a spiritual faculty united to a material body ;  and we can therefore use this result to strengthen our conviction that it is indeed spiritual ; for it is clear that if intellectual operations are immaterial, the intellect must also be immaterial.   There can be no doubt that it is impossible for an organic, or material, faculty to know any object without its individuating conditions, since such a faculty depends in its action on an extended organ, so that its action and the result of its action cannot be independent of extension ; i.e. both of them are affected by a determined quantity.   Thus, an organic faculty will only know things which have such quantity, or concrete beings with their individuating conditions.   The intellect, on the contrary, has as its object, as we have seen, natures abstracted from their individuating conditions, and it therefore cannot

[1] Cf. *Summa Theol.*, I.12,4 ;  I.55,2 ;  I.84,7.

S

be an organic faculty, but must be immaterial. Further, its way of grasping these unextended objects is itself unextended or immaterial ; since it grasps the whole of its objects, and all their parts, simultaneously, in contradistinction to an extended faculty which grasps its object partially, and the parts separately. So the intellect sees the nature of a thing as a whole, whereas the sense sees, e.g., particular patches of colour.

Again, one of the most striking characteristics of intellectual action is the power of reflection, by which the intellect, as a whole, considers itself as a whole, reflecting on its own being and nature. Such a process is clearly beyond the powers of an extended or material faculty, which cannot reflect wholly on itself ; since, if it has parts outside parts of its very nature, these parts cannot all be together without destroying its nature. So a piece of paper cannot be completely folded on itself, so that the whole of it covers the whole of it ; but only so that one part covers another.[1] The intellect, then, is immaterial.

The cumulative force of all these considerations is very great ; for from whatever point of view we regard the intellect and its operations, we find ourselves led to the conclusion which we previously arrived at, from the widest view of its nature (when we considered it as being unrestricted in its range ; and so being, in a certain way, all things), viz. that it is spiritual or immaterial.

If, then, we grant that it is so, it might seem natural to conclude that it is essentially active, since a spiritual thing is, as such, not hampered by material restrictions ; and should be able to act without being, as it were, set in motion by anything material. Nevertheless, all that has been said so far as to the nature of intellectual knowledge suggests that the intellect receives quite passively the dematerialised forms of material things, having them imprinted, as it were, upon it ; and not stretching out to grasp its object. Which of these, then, is the true view of the intellect ? Is it active or passive ? This question cannot be answered by a simple affirmation that it is active and a denial that it is passive, or

[1] Cf. S. Thomas, II *Contra Gentiles*, c. 66

vice versa ; though such solutions have been attempted. Thus, the Transcendentalists, who consider the principle of immanence—that we can know only our own thoughts—as axiomatic, deny the passivity of the intellect altogether ; as do also the Cartesians, in consequence of their belief that the mind is always actually thinking ; and this view is, generally speaking, held to by all the advocates of innate ideas, who think that the intellect is complete in itself, through the ideas which are naturally inborn in it.  On the other hand, some Scholastics speak as if the intellect were wholly passive, and not active at all, a point of view which is suggested by the phrase ' *tabula rasa*,' the blank sheet of paper : and which may, without unfairness, probably be attributed to Locke, who, as Mr. Morris says : ' rejected the view that the mind is active as being evidently inadmissible.'[1]

Though S. Thomas certainly recognises a certain passivity in the intellect, such passivity is not in any way that of inanimate things, such as that of a sheet of paper, nor is it even of the same kind as the passivity of vital operations in general, such as nutrition, where the nutriment is simply received and absorbed. For knowledge is, as we have seen, an immanent action whereby the subject becomes, in a certain way, the object, and not vice versa ; and is, moreover, one which enables it to receive the object, in accordance with its own nature, but without changing the object. If, then, the intellect is called passive, this is only in relation to the object inasmuch as it is actuated by it, not in the sense that it is itself devoid of activity. Consequently, when S. Thomas says that the intellect is a passive power,[2] he is careful to explain that it is only passive in relation to the object or species which actuates it, because it stands to this in the relation of potency to act. It is therefore perfected by the reception of the species, and becomes actively understanding. So if we consider the intellect in relation to the act of understanding we shall say that it is active, since it produces this act. What was said as to the

---

[1] Cf. C. R. Morris, *Locke, Berkeley, Hume*, p. 26.  (Clarendon Press, 1931.)

[2] Cf. *Summa Theol.*, I.79,2.

activity of cognition in general,[1] finds its application here ; since, though the intellect in no sense makes the reality, but has to be actuated by it (here is its passivity), yet, at the same time, it actively apprehends it, and by its own action is simultaneously conscious of itself. So ' the intellect in act and the thing understood in act are one and the same,' being unified in the identity of one and the same act.

The intellect which actually understands, in this way, is called by the Scholastics the passive intellect, or the *intellectus possibilis* (since it *can* become all things) ; in conformity with their general rule as to the way in which the faculties should be discriminated, viz. with reference to their objects ; and this intellect is, as we have seen, in potency with respect to the objects which actuate it.

That such passivity as this must be ascribed to the intellect, if we wish to maintain that it is a faculty which discovers, and does not create, its object, is undeniable, when we consider that since the intellect in act and the intelligible in act are one, an intellect which was not potential to its objects would be those objects actually, and so actually universal being ; since the object of the intellect is, as we have seen, universal being. Intelligence of this kind is evidently not to be found among finite beings which come to know a limited number of objects gradually, and so are potential or passive with respect to them. To deny this would be to identify the human intellect with the divine, making it the intelligible forms of all things simultaneously and actually, knowing itself, and so all things, perfectly and at once ; a claim so incredibly arrogant as to be intolerable, apart from its obvious falsity in the light of experience.

A corollary as to our knowledge of singular things follows from the Thomistic teaching on the proper object of the human intellect ; for if this object be the natures of material things, which are universal, it is clear that the intellect is not primarily and essentially directed to the material things as singular, but only as universal. If, then, we know singular things at all, as we certainly do, since we judge and reason about them, and distinguish them from the universal, such

[1] Cf. pp. 216 f,

knowledge can only be indirect and secondary, and obtained by comparing their universal nature with the concrete image which we have of them as pictured in the imagination. Moreover, since the source of singularity or individuality is matter, and matter is not intelligible in itself, for the root of knowledge is immateriality, it is impossible to maintain that the individual *quâ* individual is intelligible in itself, and directly. It can only become so in so far as the universal form is seen to belong to this particular concrete imaged object. Suarez, in holding the contradictory view, that the intellect knows singular things directly, recognises that it is opposed to that of S. Thomas and all the Thomists ; but seems to have been led to adopt it for fear of falling into the opinion held by Cajetan that we know singulars confusedly only, and not distinctly, i.e. as distinct one from another. This consequence, however, in no way follows from the Thomistic position, and is indeed excluded by it ; and if the view of Cajetan is an exaggeration in the direction of intellectualism, that of Suarez undoubtedly tends to confuse sensible and intellectual knowledge ; which is, at least, an equally dangerous deviation in the direction of empiricism.

We have now a general notion of the nature of the intellect which we have seen to be an immaterial power by which man knows abstract universal natures primarily, and singular things secondarily ; in order to do which his intellect has to be acted on by the objects, and so is said to be passive, though considered from other points of view it is active.

From this general view of its nature it is natural to pass to an enquiry into its way of working.

# CHAPTER XII

## THE ORIGIN OF IDEAS

The Empiricists—Innate Ideas—The Transcendentalists and Hegel
—The Difficulty of the Question—The Thomist Solution—The
Active Intellect—Its Necessity and Function—Summary of the
Intellectual Process.

THE question ' how do we know ? ' naturally follows the discussion of the question ' what do we know ? ' ; and is
generally called by modern writers the problem of the
origin of ideas.

As our purpose is to explain the Thomistic view of mental
action, it will be unnecessary to subject to detailed criticism
the many divergent opinions which, particularly in recent
times, have been put forward on this subject. At the same
time it is useful to enumerate them shortly, since they throw
light on the real nature and difficulty of this question. These
views, generally speaking, are based on conclusions previously reached by their exponents on the relation between
body and mind, and the nature of their union. Thus, those
who deny the immateriality of the mind, making it something
bodily, will necessarily say that ideas arise entirely from the
senses and sensible things, while those who, at the opposite
extreme, regard the mind as wholly spiritual, and an accidental adjunct only of the body, naturally conclude that
ideas originate independently of material objects and the
senses ; while finally, if it be maintained that both mind
and body are essential elements of human nature, the origin
of ideas will be attributed to the senses and intellect in
conjunction.

Thus we find three general classes of opinion :

1. That of the Empiricists, according to whom sensible
experience is the adequate cause, not merely of sensible

knowledge, but also of intellectual. The movement which eventually resulted in the distinct formulation of this view was begun by John Locke, who recognised two processes in the acquisition of ideas,—sensation and reflection. He thus maintained, in a fashion, the distinction between the senses and the intellect. But it is to be observed, that since he accorded to sensation the acquisition of simple ideas which represent the primary qualities of bodies, such as solidity, extension, etc., which ideas, according to him, really resemble these qualities, while by reflection we only come to know the internal operations of our own minds ; and, further, that by putting together the simple ideas, already acquired by sensation, we form compound ones, he, in fact, equivalently asserts that reflection adds nothing new to the fabric of science, and the whole weight of the production of ideas rests on sensation. It does not seem as if Locke realised all the implications of his own doctrine, but they were quickly brought out by Condillac, in France ; and by Hume, the two Mills, and Bain, in our own country. These all got rid of the power of reflection as being useless, and substituted for it the alleged laws of the association of ideas, so that all ideas are but transformed sensations. From this theory their doctrine came to be known as Associationism.[1]

2. The second class of opinion maintains that ideas essentially originate independently of sensation. This view is found, in an undiluted form, in the doctrine of innate ideas professed by Plato, Descartes, Rosmini, and others. Plato emphasised the distinction between opinion and science, of which the first only is derivable from sense experience. Science, then, must come to the mind independently of such experience, so that the ideas which constitute it will be native to the intellect, which is supposed to have known them in a previous existence. Knowledge, therefore, in this view, would be reminiscence ; though perhaps this phrase is not to be taken too literally. According to Descartes, it is essential to the soul to think. Now thought is impossible without ideas, so that the soul must from the beginning

[1] For a short account of the details of this theory cf. e.g. McDougall, *Outline of Psychology*, pp. 237 ff. Stout, *Manual of Psychology*, pp. 117 ff.

possess at least some congenital or innate ideas, though Descartes did not deny altogether the possibility of acquiring ideas. Such acquired ideas fall, in his view, into two classes ; viz. : (a) those which are, properly speaking, acquired by way of the senses and which he calls ' adventitious ' ; and (b) those which are evolved by the mind itself, through the association of sensible images, which he calls ' fictitious ' ideas. Rosmini, lastly, held that the idea of being in general is innate, for he considered that it is impossible to think until this idea is present.

This general class of opinion is also represented, in a modified form, by the Transcendental Idealists, who consider that intelligible objects altogether transcend sense experience, so that the origin of our intellectual ideas must be sought in an analysis of thought alone. It is put forward in various forms by Kant, Fichte, Schelling, and Hegel. In his first period, Kant accepted the theory of innate ideas derived from Leibniz and Wolff ; but later, under the pressure of Empiricist and Sceptical objections, abandoned it, and felt obliged to recognise that there is, in our thinking, a universal and necessary element, as well as the fact that it is, at least partially, derived from the external world. The necessary element, which is formal, comes from our own minds ; the material element, from without. The formal elements he calls ' categories,' of which the intellect possesses twelve, into which all the objects of our knowledge are fitted. From this it appears that we do not know external things as they are in themselves, but as they are moulded by these forms or categories ; and there is, therefore, no guarantee that our intellectual knowledge will correspond with external reality. Fichte and Schelling carried the ideas of Kant to their logical conclusion, by abolishing the ' thing-in-itself,' and with it the individual ; leaving nothing but mind-in-general, or the Absolute. The development of this line of thought is completed by Hegel, who taught that the absolute and universal principle of cognition is the Idea of Being in its most abstract form, that is, ' Pure Thought.' In the first moment the Idea of Pure Being is pure indetermination, for determination implies an opposite, and in the beginning there can be no opposite.  Now pure indetermination is pure not-being, and therefore Pure-Being is Pure Not-Being ; so that the Idea and Reality of Being is itself its contradictory, and the reconciliation of contradictories.  Thus the Idea of Being contains that of Not-Being, which is therefore deduced from it.  Moreover, Being which is not-Being, and not-Being which is Being is Becoming, which is neither Being nor not-Being.  So that the third Idea of Becoming is deduced from the first two.  This process can be continued indefinitely till all the Ideas are deduced, and it is this which Hegel attempts to do in his Logic.  The origin of our ideas, then, in his view, is to be found in this first Idea of Pure Being ; and our whole knowledge is merely the development of this Idea, by means of the Dialectic method.

We may notice, in passing, that when it is said : ' in the beginning there can be no opposite,' this is equivalent to saying : ' in the beginning nothing can be an opposite,' and, in this case, there *is* an opposite of Being, viz. nothing. Being therefore *can* be determined, not it is true by anything external, nor yet as a genus or species, since it is transcendent, but in its positive entity as opposed to Not-Being, and consequently none of the conclusions follow.  They can only hold good if the phrase ' pure indetermination ' be taken equivocally, signifying the entire lack of determination of Being to genus and species, in the first place ; and an absolute void without determination of any sort, in the second.[1]

The foregoing theories bring out clearly the difficulty of this question of the origin of ideas, for, on the one hand, those who hold that all knowledge is sense knowledge can urge that if this be not true it is impossible to explain the fact that all our actions, even the most abstract, are only intelligible in terms of sense and sensible images ; while, on the other hand, those who think that ideas originate independently of sensation have strong grounds for asserting that the opposing theory cannot be true, inasmuch as the objects of the intellect, which are universal and necessary,

[1] For a full explanation of Hegel's theory *vide* Stace, *The Philosophy of Hegel*, esp. pp. 90 ff. ; and, for its criticism, Garigou-Lagrange, *De Revelatione*, Vol. I, pp. 244–272, esp. p. 271.

and the objects of sense, which are singular and contingent, are of different kinds, so that one cannot be derived from the other. Thus we seem to be on the horns of a dilemma : unless we accept Empiricism we cannot explain the facts of experience ; and if we do accept it, we cannot account for the necessary and universal character of our ideas.

3. The theory of S. Thomas resolves this apparent contradiction by combining both the elements of the situation in a higher synthesis, and is indicated by the phrase : ' Knowledge begins in the senses and is perfected in the intellect.' According to this view we are not in possession of ready-made ideas ; nor are they infused into us by God, or any separated Form ; nor do we gain them by intuition of God and the Divine Ideas ; while, on the other hand, the senses are not the proper cause of the ideas of the intellect ; and the mind therefore has to acquire them. As we saw, it is at first potential to knowledge, not actually knowing, and so is passive ; but, in order that it may be in possession of its ideas, it needs to be actuated and determined. Are we, then, to say that it actuates and determines itself, or that it is actuated by something other than itself ? Both suppositions seem impossible, for a thing cannot actuate itself, since to do so it would already have to possess that perfection which it is supposed to bestow on itself, nothing being able to give what it does not possess : nor yet can it be actuated by something other than itself, for the only thing other than the intellect which is present in this situation is the material objects of the senses which, being material, are not proportionate to the immaterial intellect, and so cannot perfect or actuate it. In this impasse, if we re-examine the statement just made, we see that though there can be no possible doubt that the intellect cannot actuate itself, since the hypothesis that it did so would involve a contradiction, yet the same is not true of the assertion that the only elements in the situation are the intellect and the material objects, for no contradiction is involved in the supposition that there is some active agent which concurs in the process of understanding, by dematerialising the objects of sense, and so bringing them to a state in which they are fit to be perfections, or actuations, of the

immaterial intellect. We are, therefore, driven by the logic of the facts to assert the existence of such an active agent, as the only means of extricating ourselves from an impossible situation. What is the nature of this agent ? Absolutely speaking, it might be something extrinsic both to us and the material objects. The whole of our experience of the process of knowledge, as well as the requirement that we should be sure of its truth, renders, however, such a supposition untenable. For the whole intellectual process exhibits itself as a gradual one, by which we come into possession of knowledge of things, slowly and with much effort, passing progressively from confused notions to distinct ones, and from the widest ideas, such as that of being, to specific ones, such as that of man. It is easy to see, that if ideas were implanted in our minds by some agent outside ourselves, this laborious process becomes inexplicable, for we should pass in a flash from nescience to full knowledge, as soon as the ideas were imparted to us. Moreover, if the ideas are given to us in this extrinsic fashion, how could we know that they correspond to the reality ? Evidently, this would only be possible if we knew what the reality was, independently of them, in which case they become quite useless. If, on the other hand, we do not know their correspondence with reality we cannot have any assurance of their truth, and so are left a prey to Scepticism.

If, then, we dismiss the hypothesis of an external agent which implants the ideas in us, and further observe, what is also clear, that the material objects themselves cannot be the formative cause of our ideas, for the very reason that they are material, the only conceivable cause of them will be some agent within us. In other words, the mind of man must possess some active power by which he is enabled to dematerialise the objects, and make them fit objects of the intellect. It is precisely the existence of such a power which S. Thomas asserts, since without it we can give no satisfactory account of the origin of our ideas. As it must evidently be an intellectual power he calls it the ' active intellect ' or ' *intellectus agens.*'[1]

---

[1] For a summary of this argument cf. Cajetan Comm. in I.79,3.

The function, then, of this mental power is to demateri-alise the objects, as offered by the imagination, in such a way as to make them able to be dealt with by the intellect which is to understand them. It will, therefore, abstract the formal element in them, leaving aside the material elements, and seize the universal, neglecting those characters which make the objects individuals. These objects are those offered by the imagination, as we have just said, so that the imagination has a necessary part to play in the intellectual process, by offering the material on which the mind is to work. This necessary condition of human knowledge—necessary, because man is partly material, partly spiritual—has very obvious dangers, since it is quite easy for us to mistake the imagined picture of a thing for its real nature. Such an error will always be made when the conclusions of one science are imported bodily, and as they stand, into another, as, for example, if a man were to argue from the determinism which physical science recognises in nature to the impossibility of freedom in human life. The image, then, presented to the intellect needs to be changed and made abstract, or as St. Thomas often says, 'illuminated'; the active intellect being a sort of mental X-ray which pierces through the flesh or matter of the image to reveal its internal nature. But just as such rays do not perceive the internal structure themselves, but only reveal it, so the active intellect does not itself know the universal form or nature which it reveals in the image, this being the function of the passive intellect, of which we have already spoken at length.

To complete this account of the way in which ideas originate we must recall what was said earlier.[1] Since, in intellectual knowledge, the object itself is not cognitively present to the mind, the intellect has to form for itself a representation of it to be the term of cognition, i.e. it forms an expressed species of the object, a formal concept, or 'mental word' or expression of what it has already understood by means of the impressed species. This concept, then, is not the thing which is understood; what we know is not our own ideas, but the object, in and along with these ideas.

[1] Cf. Part II, Ch. viii.

So the whole process of intellectual cognition may be summarised as follows : though it is not to be supposed that the elements which we find, by analysis, in the act have a temporal sequence, or work on one another like the wheels of a watch.   The intelligible object is in the intellect in a twofold fashion, first, as impressed and the principle of knowledge, secondly, as expressed and its term.   Now the impressed object is an habitual representation, which is called the intelligible species, and is abstracted from the images in the imagination by the active intellect whose instruments these images are.[1]   This impressed form of the object is the principle which determines the passive intellect and co-operates with it efficiently in the act of understanding, and so makes the intellect, when acting, one with the object. Lastly, the expressed species is the actual representation of this object, in which the passive intellect, now in act, as it were, says, or expresses, the object to itself, and actually assimilates it to itself.   This mental word or concept is not the act of understanding itself, but the intrinsic term of this act, giving satisfaction and completion to it, just as in the process of generation or reproduction satisfaction and completion is found in the conception and birth of offspring.

[1] John of S. Thomas, *Phil. Nat.*, P. III, Q. 10, A. 2.

# CHAPTER XIII

## THE INTELLECTUAL APPETITE ; THE WILL

Its Existence—Nature—What Necessity is—Freedom of the Will—
History of the Problem—Summary of Opinions—Arguments in
Favour of Liberty—The Limits of Liberty—Views on the Nature
of Liberty—The Answer to Indeterminism—The Answer to
Psychological Determinism—Summary of results arrived at.

In the preceding chapters we have dealt with the nature and
work of the mind in knowing. Another aspect of intellectual
life must now be investigated in order to complete our view
of its activities, viz. its volitional aspect, for it is universally
recognised that it exhibits itself not only in cognition, but
also in conation. No doubt is possible with respect to the
fact that some conative activity, or striving in general, is to
be found in man, for experience speaks too plainly. Moreover,
we have already noticed that action must be in some determinate direction, or towards some end, otherwise it would
have no direction, and so would not exist. It follows, then,
that to every species of activity will be attached a certain
striving to attain the end to which it is directed, though in
the case of inanimate agents, or those without knowledge or
consciousness, we cannot call such striving ' willing,' in any
proper sense. In things which know the end to which their
actions are directed we shall first begin to have desire for it,
for in their knowing of it, they will perceive it as something
which is either suitable, or unsuitable, to them. Desire, or
appetite, will therefore accompany, or rather follow, all
kinds of cognitive action, whether sensible or intellectual ;
so that if we grant the existence of an intellectual power in
man we shall be unable to deny him an intellectual appetite,
or will, also. As was pointed out, in dealing with the
faculties in general, such a power is not to be supposed to be
a thing in its own right, but is merely the means which a man

uses in striving to attain a desired end, just as the intellect
is the means he uses to unite the object to himself in cognition. Hence it is not the intellect which knows, properly
speaking, but the man, by its means ; and not the will which
desires, but man, by means of it.

## The Nature of the Will.

What, then, is the nature of this intellectual appetite ?
Clearly it is distinguished from the blind direction to particular ends which characterises the actions of inanimate
things, and also that conscious desire of sensible objects
which is to be observed in the actions of animals, since it
follows neither on the intrinsic tendency of man's nature as
a material being, nor on knowledge which is purely sensible ;
though it is true that he has tendencies which follow on both
of these. We observe that such tendencies in beings other
than man are characterised by necessity ; for a stone
necessarily falls to the ground, and a hungry animal necessarily desires suitable food. This suggests that the same
may be the case with the will. Even though it follows on
intellectual knowledge, not on sense perception, it may
necessarily desire what it thus knows.

Before discussing the thorny question whether the will is
necessitated, it will be useful to notice some points both
about the will, and about necessity, in order to have a
clearer idea of each of them.

In the first place, the will, being the appetite which follows
the intellect, will have as its objects those things which are
the objects of the intellect ; now, however, regarded as
things which are desirable, or good, and not merely knowable. Since the object of the intellect is being as such, that
of the will will be being in general, regarded as desirable, or
suitable, and this we call the good in general. Similarly, the
object proportionate and proper to the human will is the
good in material things, just as the human intellect is directed
to the being of material things.

With regard to the acts of the will there is clearly a distinction between those which proceed immediately from the
will itself, such as a particular desire or wish, as was that

of Browning when he says : ' Oh, to be in England, now that April's there ' ; and those which proceed from some other faculty, though under the influence and direction of the will, as are, for example, acts of walking and speaking. The first class are called elicited, and the second sanctioned acts.

### Necessity.

Secondly, with regard to necessity, we notice that it may arise either from an intrinsic, or an extrinsic, cause ; and an intrinsic cause, being the nature of the thing, such necessity is called natural necessity ; whereby a thing is obliged to act, if it acts at all, in accordance with its nature. There are two extrinsic causes from either of which necessity may arise, viz. efficient and final causes. If some external agent forces a thing to act in a certain way, such necessity is called compelling necessity ; while if the thing is obliged to act in a particular way in order to attain a given end, we have what is known as hypothetical necessity, since it must so act on the hypothesis that it wishes to gain this end.

If we now apply these notions to the will, we see that though the will can be bound both by natural and hypothetical necessity, it cannot be under the dominion of compelling necessity. The reason for the last part of this statement is, that since compelling necessity, by definition, acts on the will from without, it cannot affect the initiation, but only the execution of an act of the will, since the former proceeds from within. Such necessity, then, does not affect the act at its source, but at most prevents the will from setting in motion the faculty on which force is exerted. Thus compulsion may prevent a man from walking, but not from willing to walk ; so that external force, or ' violence,' as S. Thomas calls it, cannot dominate the will's elicited acts, but only its sanctioned ones. But if such compulsion as this is impossible, the will is, nevertheless, necessitated from within, because whenever it is desirous of some object, it cannot help also desiring the means which are necessary for its attainment ; as a man who wishes to be in some place, at a distance, must also wish to be transported over the distance, and so desire some means of transport. In this way the will is hypothetically necessitated. But it is also naturally necessitated, for it has its own definite nature, and must, therefore, of necessity, tend towards that nature's end, and obey that nature's laws. The end to which the will is thus naturally, and so necessarily, directed is good in general, so that it is bound to wish for complete goodness, or that which is suitable to man in every respect, perfecting him in every way and so giving him complete happiness. To suppose it could will otherwise than this is evidently an hypothesis which is contradictory in itself, since then it would will something which does not suit it, and so, is not desirable, and cannot be willed.

The will as nature is, no doubt, influenced by the life-history of the human race, and by inherited tendencies; though it should be noticed that such tendencies cannot alter the very nature, or essence, of the will in itself, since to do this would be to destroy it altogether; but can only modify its actions. Moreover, they cannot modify it to the extent of never allowing it to act in accordance with its nature, since this, again, would be equivalent to destroying that nature.

Though the will be necessitated in the ways we have mentioned, yet such necessity cannot reach to determining it to exercise the act of willing either what is entirely good for the whole man, or those means which are necessarily connected with some willed end; since the intellect may not put these before the will; in which case it will not exercise the act of desiring them. If, however, they are put before it, it must desire them of necessity.

*Freedom of the Will.*

We see, then, that our wills are necessitated, at least to some extent; and this leads us to ask whether such necessitation extends to all our volitions, a question which has given rise to interminable disputes. Dr. Johnson cut short this discussion in characteristic fashion, by saying: ' All theory is against freedom of the will, all experience for it.'

Whether this summary of the state of the case is true we shall soon see, but it is not difficult to understand why this

T

question has so continually engaged the attention of philosophers, for it is one which has a very definite bearing on our
everyday life ; and, in particular, it seems very difficult, if
not impossible, to attach any meaning to the word ' morality,'
if human liberty be denied. How can a man be said to act
rightly or wrongly, to do good or evil, if he is incapable of
acting in any other way, or of refraining from action ? Can
we say that a machine which works accurately is virtuous, or
one which does not, vicious, and so worthy of punishment or
reward ? So, it has always been felt, that unless liberty can
be defended, morality and the essential dignity of man would
be destroyed.

These may, perhaps, be thought to be but sentimental
considerations ; and we ought, then, to view the subject
impartially in itself, and not merely in the consequences
which a denial of freedom would entail.

Whether freewill exist or not, there can be little doubt
that we conceive of it as a ' power of choice ' ;[1] and since no
choice is possible with regard to that which presents itself
to us as an end absolutely speaking, it must be a power of
choice of means which are adapted to attain the end in view.
Now such liberty, or immunity from necessity, may be considered either as it affects action itself, or as it affects the
object of action. So we can conceive of two cases : first, if
the will is not determined to action, rather than the absence
of action, or vice versa—such a state being called by the
Scholastics liberty of exercise, or contradiction—and,
secondly, if the will can desire one or other object of action
indifferently, a state known as liberty of specification—or if
the objects are contraries, of contrariety. An example of
the first is that of a man who is free to walk or not to walk ;
of the second, of one who is free to walk to one place or
another.

*History of the Problem.*

Such are the preliminary notions which are necessary if we
are to deal with this problem with any lucidity ; for to state
a question clearly is often to go a long way in providing the

[1] Cf. *Summa Theol.*, I, 83, a. 4.

solution of it. That it has not been found easy to make such a statement will be seen if we glance at the attempts which philosophers have made to deal with it. The first to treat it professedly was Socrates, who pointed out that man desires only the good, from which he concluded that if he wills what is evil, this must arise from ignorance. Such evil desires will therefore not be truly voluntary, so that in a sense he is not free, being determined by knowledge. Though Plato, by saying that only true science is invincible, while opinion is a kind of ignorance which leaves the will free to follow it or not, modifies the Socratic doctrine considerably, this consideration does not really come to grips with the problem, but only makes it less difficult to continue to believe in freedom.

Aristotle, though 'he did not examine the problem very thoroughly,'[1] is, nevertheless, a decided opponent of both the Socratic and Platonic point of view, since, as he points out, a man must be held morally responsible for his opinions, 'for what appears good to him,' since he is responsible for his moral state ; for if he is not, virtue is no more voluntary than vice.[2] So he cannot agree with the saying of Socrates, 'No man is willingly bad ' ; even if his badness be attributed to his having an opinion, and not science, with regard to the point in question.

Though none of these theories go very deep into the question, yet they were of great importance as pointing out that the centre of the problem is to be found in the nature of the judgements which precede choice ; and in this way, contributing to an exact statement of the problem.

The Christian Doctors, generally speaking, assumed the existence of freewill in man, but as they tried to investigate its nature they gradually led up to a clear understanding of the meaning of the question : ' Is man endowed with free-will ? ' which is formally put by S. Thomas Aquinas.[3] The preoccupation of S. Augustine, and many of these thinkers,

---

[1] Cf. Ross, *Aristotle*, p. 201.
[2] Cf. *Ethica Nic.*, Bk. III, Ch. V, 1113b3–1115a3.
[3] *Summa Theol.*, I, Q. 83, a. 1. For the history of the problem in the preceding centuries cf. Lottin, *La théorie du libre arbitre depuis S. Anselme usqu'à S. Thomas D'Aquin*. (Publications de la Revue Thomiste.)

was rather with the difficulty of reconciling freewill with grace, and Divine prescience, than with the strictly philosophical question as to the nature and existence of liberty.

Passing to modern times, we are faced in the seventeenth century with an intellectualist determinism, or denial of freedom, whose first representative is Spinoza. Applying to philosophy the methods of mathematics, which takes no account of efficient and final causes, he consequently eliminates these from philosophy, and holds that the same necessity rules in the realm of being as in that of quantity, and that all things exist by reason of the mathematical necessity of the Divine nature, no choice being possible to God. The seventeenth century also gave birth to another form of determinism, that of Leibniz, which is known as Psychological Determinism. In his view, the last practical judgement, which ends a deliberation, is indifferent in the sense that it is contingent, i.e. that the contrary, or at least the contradictory, judgement is possible, inasmuch as it does not imply a contradiction ; but not in the sense that a man, in such-and-such circumstances, and being mentally disposed in a particular way, could form the contrary or contradictory judgement. To admit this would be, in Leibniz's opinion, to deny the principle of sufficient reason. Hence this last practical judgement is not, as Spinoza would have it, necessary as a conclusion of geometry is, but is necessary with a moral necessity.

This intellectualism and determinism was followed by a voluntarist, and indeterminist, reaction initiated by Kant, who, in the realm of Ethics, to which metaphysics is to be subordinate, introduced the supremacy of the will over reason ; an idea which was carried much further by subsequent thinkers.

### Summary of Opinions.

Thus we see that two extreme opinions confront one another : absolute determinism, which holds that the will is always necessitated by something extrinsic to itself, and absolute indeterminism, which considers that it is entirely autonomous, its determination not arising from determinate rational judgements, but incalculably, from its own hidden depths. The reasons, in obedience to which it appears to act, are thus not the true determining causes of its actions, but only ' excuses,' put forward to make it appear rational ; the real determination coming entirely from the will itself. Such a view as this last, even in a modified form, seems, however, to destroy that liberty which it is intended to safeguard ; since, if the reason is not guiding and dominant we shall really be acting on blind impulse, either by instinct, or under the influence of urges which are perhaps inherited from our ancestors, and, at any rate, are not under our own individual control ; since the only thing we can even profess to control is what is known to us, i.e. our rational judgements. Moreover, if our analysis of the nature of will is correct, it is essentially a rational appetite ; dependent, therefore, on reason, and, through it, on the senses ; the reason itself being dependent on these. So everything which influences the reason will also influence the will as, e.g., suggestion, training, circumstances and so on. This view is entirely consonant with our experience of free acts, since we do, in fact, determine such actions in accordance with the motives which are put before us. It agrees also with our conception of freedom of the will ; for we call a man obstinate or pig-headed, rather than strong-willed, who sticks to a course of action which is clearly shown to be unreasonable ; while the strong-willed man is one who does not falter in carrying out a resolution, formed after due deliberation, but who is ' open to reason,' as we say. Such a man will modify his action if good reason for doing so be shown him.

It would be desirable, though it is not possible in a short summary such as this, to review the development of the intellectualist and anti-intellectualist points of view, up to the time when they meet in an identification of liberty and necessity ; the first maintaining that whatever is right, is ; and the second that whatever is, is right.[1]

But, perhaps, enough has been said to suggest that both eliminate freedom, intellectualism denying it outright ; and

[1] Cf. Garigou-Lagrange, *Dieu*, 5e ed., pp. 595–601. Sorley, *Moral Values and the Idea of God*, pp. 394–423. (C.U.P., 1924.)

anti-intellectualism by implication, since it is not we, by the use of reason, but the facts, the push of nature, the ' élan vital,' or what not, which are the masters of the situation.

### Arguments in Favour of Liberty.

Let us then pass on to see what positive grounds there may be for asserting that we have the power of choice, being necessitated, neither by some external force of circumstance, nor yet by some internal force, whether of nature, making us subject to natural necessity, or of motive, necessitating us psychologically.

We have already seen that the will cannot be subject to compulsion ; and it only remains to enquire whether it is necessitated from within.[1] At this stage, with the object of making clear the Thomistic argument for liberty, we shall take it for granted that the will is, as we have already asserted it to be, the rational appetite, thus subordinated to the intelligence : ' Voluntas consequitur intellectum.'[2] We shall have occasion later to discuss this more fully. Proceeding on this basis, then, S. Thomas following the lead given by Plato and Aristotle looks for the source of liberty, or immunity from necessity, in that faculty which guides and directs the will, viz. the reason. Liberty will indeed be impossible if the judgement of the reason which immediately precedes the definite act of willing is determined of itself, without the intervention of the will ; whereas, if, at this moment, it is of itself indifferent or contingent, it will leave the will free to follow it or not. Obviously, that judgement which is, in fact, acted upon must be a determinate one ; but, as we shall see, this determination comes to it, not from the reason as such but from the will, or rather the whole man.

Freedom, then, must be conceded to us in the degree in which the judgement which precedes and guides our choice is, considered in itself, indifferent ; for, in this case, since it is in essence indifferent, its final determination, removing this indifference, will come to it, not from itself, but from something else ; otherwise it would give itself a perfection, a

---

[1] Cf. Summa Theol., I.19,3 ; 59,3 ; 83,1 ; De Malo, Q. 6, A. 1.
[2] Summa Theol., I.19,1.

determination, which it did not itself possess. That this judgement, so considered, is indeed indifferent, is seen if we consider that man, being in possession of the idea of good in general, i.e. of that which perfects him, is able to compare the particular goods presented for his acceptance with this general idea. So the state of affairs, just before the moment of coming to a decision, is as if he said to himself : ' What I desire, since it is that which perfects me, is good, total good ; whereas this object which is put before me, e.g. a sum of money, is good and not good, according to the aspect in which I consider it ; and consequently I am not bound to desire it, but I desire it from one point of view, though not from another.' This form of reasoning (which no doubt is rarely, if ever, explicit) represents truly the state of mind of a man immediately before his determinate decision and shows that the foundation of liberty is in the intellect, which knows the nature of good, and whose judgement is, consequently, indifferent when confronted with any object, or any act, which is not devoid of all evil or imperfection. This judge-ment, being in itself undetermined, cannot therefore determine the will ; and if it be true that what guides the will is the intellect, it remains undetermined by anything outside itself, and so has mastery over its own act, or is free. Clearly, this derivation of the freedom of the will from the indifference of the intellect only holds good for those who admit that the intelligence is of a different nature to the senses. The Empiricist, who reduces all ideas to sensible images, and so denies the possibility of forming a universal judgement, containing under itself many particulars, must also neces-sarily deny liberty to man. As S. Thomas says : ' *Pro tanto necesse est quod homo sit liberi arbitrii ex hoc ipso quod rationalis est.*'[1] He is guided, not by natural law, as a stone is in falling, nor by instinct, like the animals, but, in virtue of the universal range of his intellect, he can compare the particular good presented, with universal good, so that he is not determined by the object but by himself. Thus, we see that the immediate source of liberty is the universality of the will, resting on the universality of the intellect in

[1] Cf. *Summa Theol.*, I,83,1.

action, which is a consequence of its universal nature, of its spirituality. So that, in the last resort, it is the fact that man is a spiritual being which causes him to be a free one.

Before we turn to the consideration of the way in which man so determines himself, we may mention some other reasons which confirm our conclusion that he does so. In the first place, it is clear that to deny freedom is to run counter to an absolutely universal opinion, for even those who, in their speculations, deny it, nevertheless always leave these behind when they go out into the world, and behave as if they were free. The idea of moral responsibility is universal also, but how can a man be held morally responsible, and worthy of praise or blame, who, in fact, is bound to follow a certain course of action, who is a prisoner in chains which bind his very soul ?

What purpose, again, could advice serve if we were unable to revise a judgement we had formed, and so act in a different way to that which we at first intended ? Moreover, by introspection we see that we do indeed ' make up our minds,' as we say, how to act ; at the very moment of action we can change our decision, and even while action is in progress we can cease from acting, or even begin to act in a contrary way.

### The Limits of Liberty.

If, then, we have such freedom, what are its limits ? First, in order to have freedom at all, we must have liberty, both from compulsion by an extrinsic cause, and from necessity or determination arising from our intrinsic nature, since actions which proceed from our nature as men are not under our power. What nature bids us will we cannot but will, whereas it is essential to a free act that we should have power over it. Such unloosing of bonds as this is evidently a minimum requirement for freedom, but, in fact, it is not enough, if we are really to have mastery over our acts. We must here introduce a distinction which we shall find useful more than once, that between active and passive indifference. By active indifference we mean the power to produce or not to produce certain acts, while by passive indifference we mean merely the capacity for receiving various determinations. Bearing this in mind, we see at once that freedom implies active, and not merely passive indifference, for a passive capacity cannot exert mastery, being potentially at least, under the dominion of that which determines it. Active indifference must then be added to the minimum requirement for freedom. Nor is this all, for we have seen that the object towards which the will is directed must be such as does not determine its action, and the subject which wills must be such that it can will or not will an object. So, again, in our minimum requirement we must include both objective and subjective indifference, of which the first will, of course, be present if the object is not wholly desirable, but contains good and bad elements, and the second, where the subject has the power of choice.

Such being the minimum of indifference which is required if there is to be freedom at all, we may naturally ask also what is the maximum of liberty which is possible. It appears from the analysis we have made of freedom that there can be no liberty of specification except with regard to particular goods which have not, at the moment of willing, an evidently necessary condition with the acquisition of total good, since it is clear that total good, or entire happiness, must be preferred to all else ; there being no aspect of it which can appear displeasing to us. Hence when it is presented to us, if we will at all, we must will this, and cannot will anything else ; so that here we retain liberty of exercise[1] only. Even this liberty is very limited, for though it is true we can judge that it is better, at any given moment, not to consider our complete happiness, or to consider it, yet, at the same time, we cannot will anything whatsoever without virtually desiring to be happy. Thus, on the one hand, there must be active indifference in the will in order that there may be liberty at all ; but, on the other, liberty of specification is by no means always to be found in free acts, often we have liberty of exercise only. Such freedom as this, however, is sufficient to ensure that the will should be free, and never

[1] *Vide* p. 276.

disappears entirely, except in the case of intuitive knowledge of absolute good.

Within these limits, then, we may take it as established that we have freedom, in so far as we are not determined either by our own nature or by the object itself, since the final judgement of a deliberation is, considered in itself, indifferent, inasmuch as it presents the object to the will as partially desirable and partially undesirable.

### Views on the Nature of Liberty.

Is anything more than this indeterminate judgement required in order that we may actually choose ? This question brings us to the discussion of the views which are taken as to the nature of liberty. These are, in fact, of two opposing kinds, for, on the one hand, we have those who say that human liberty consists in this, that since the final practical judgement relates to a partial good the will is in no way necessitated by it, and so, where the intellect judges that two objects are equally good, or even that one is less good than the other, the will can, without further direction by the intellect, choose either of the two equally good objects ; or even, in the other case, that which is judged to be less good. This view of liberty, known as liberty of indifference or equilibrium, has been held by many eminent Catholic thinkers, notably by the Molinists and Suarez, as well as by Scotus. On the other hand, in resolute opposition to this opinion, that, in the last resort, the election made by the will is not dependent on the motives put before it by the reason, we find the adherents of Psychological Determinism who say that it is impossible to explain how an absolutely undetermined cause, such as the will is, in the Molinist view, can produce a determination. As Leibniz himself says : ' They ' (i.e. the Molinists) ' were asked not only how it would be possible to know to what an absolutely undetermined cause would determine itself, but also how it would be possible that there should not finally emerge from it a determination of which there would be no cause.'[1] Nevertheless, Leibniz, and his followers, maintain that human action is

[1] Leibniz, *Essays on Theodicy*, I, Sect. 48.

still free, inasmuch as it deals with objects which are in themselves contingent, so that it is possible to conceive without contradiction of a man acting in a way different to that in which he does, in fact, act ; though, at the same time, he cannot, at any given moment, choose to act in either one or other of two contrary ways, since he is predetermined to act in one only by ' an infinity of great and small internal and external movements, which for the most part pass unnoticed.'[1] The conception of liberty presented thus by Leibniz is that of a purely theoretical liberty : in fact, all the actions of our lives from the cradle to the grave could not be otherwise than they are, being predetermined in the states which immediately precede them, and so follow necessarily from them ; though they are not themselves necessary events, but contingent ones. That this is Leibniz's meaning is seen from the fact that in dealing with divine foreknowledge he is able to dispense both with the ' *scienta media* ' of the Molinists, and the divine decrees of the Thomists, and maintain that God foreknows free acts, solely in the causes which will produce them. They must, then, be predetermined in these causes.

If we now turn to the opinion of the Thomists on this question, we find them in partial agreement and partial disagreement with both parties ; for they agree with the Molinists that freedom is destroyed if the will, at the moment of choice, is determined either to act, or not to act, by causes outside its control, whether these be rational considerations or internal dispositions ; while they agree with Leibniz that it is impossible that the will, faced by two equal goods should choose one rather than the other, unless some new motive intervenes. They maintain, therefore, that nothing is willed unless it is first known as suitable to the subject, that an uncaused determination of the will is impossible ; and along with this, that the last practical judgement of the reason is not determined in itself, so that the will must intervene in order to determine it. Thus they wish to uphold, as against Scotus, the principle of intellectualism, the subordination of the will to the reason ; and, as against

[1] *Ibid.*, Sect. 46.

Leibniz, the determination of the reason by the will. They think, moreover, that adherence to both these propositions is forced upon us by the analysis of the act of choice, and not by any consideration of expediency.

Nevertheless, at first sight, it seems as if this position were an impossible one. Thus Suarez contends that these two propositions are mutually incompatible, since the act of the will which determines the practico-practical judgement must itself be determined by another judgement, in virtue of our principle : ' *Nil volitum nisi precognitum ut conveniens*,' and one which is determined in itself, since we cannot have an infinite series of these subordinated acts of the will and the intellect. Thus, since we maintain liberty to be a fact, we must abandon our assertion that the will follows the lead of the intellect always, and assent to his theory of liberty of equilibrium. So he does not hesitate to write : ' *Si voluntas in omnibus sequatur ductum intellectus destruitur libertas*.'[1]

He therefore considers that if we cling to the principle of intellectualism, we are driven to determinism, while if we allow that the will itself determines the judgement of the intellect, we must accept the theory of liberty which he favours, and abandon intellectualism. The Leibnizians would agree with this view that there is no middle road between the indeterminism of the liberty of equilibrium and their own psychological determinism.

### The Answer to Indeterminism. Liberty of Equilibrium Excluded.

Eminently logical though this verdict appears to be, the answer to it will be found in the very principles of intellectualism itself, of which the first, viz. that all the acts of the will are formally determined, or specified, by the intellect, seems almost too clear to need justification. For how can the will, which is of its essence not cognitive, know any good and so be attracted to it, unless the good is first put before it by a faculty which does know. The will cannot judge what is practically preferable, since it has no knowledge at all, of itself : it must depend on the *intellect* for knowledge of the

---

[1] Cf. Suarez, *Disputationes Metaphysicæ*, Disp. XIX, Sec. 6.

characteristics of the objects presented, and for judgement that one is practically preferable to another. This judgement cannot be given in favour of the less good of two objects, nor yet for one, or other, of two which the intellect judges to be equally good. If, then, it must be given for the better, it is the intellect which formally determines or specifies the will which, as has been well said, is like a blind man who uses the eyes of a paralytic in order that he himself may walk,[1] as he might do by pushing him in a Bath-chair. Though we may use such a simile as this, it is worth while reiterating the warning, already given, against succumbing to the tendency to which we are so prone—the tendency to substantialise, or even personify, our faculties. For the truth of the matter is that man by his intellect moves himself to will, and by his will moves himself to understand. Unless this essential unity of the subject be always borne in mind, we cannot hope to understand the interplay of the faculties. The will, then, being non-cognitive or blind cannot see for itself which of two actions is better, but must have its object put, as it were, into its mouth, when it will find it desirable and be attracted to it. But, it will be urged, this is plain determinism, for, in this case, it is not the will itself which chooses, but its choice is already determined for it by the intellect, independently of it. If it were true that the intellect comes to its determination independently of the will, the conclusion would certainly follow ; but it is not true, for we are here dealing with a judgement concerning what is desirable, here and now, for a particular man, not what is theoretically desirable in the abstract ; and it follows that no decision can be come to as to this, without taking into account the whole concrete state of the man by whom the particular object is to be desired. So S. Thomas, and the Thomists, constantly assert that this practico-practical judgement, unlike speculative ones, derives its truth, not from conformity with the thing, but from conformity with the sane or healthy appetite. Now man is a being whose will is, of its very nature, directed towards the plenitude of goodness, towards absolute good, and so no extraneous influence,

[1] Sertillanges, *S. Thomas d'Aquin*, Vol. II, p. 231.

whether of reason, passion, or habit can force it to desire any particular good. These influences will incline it in one direction rather than another, but can never necessitate it. Thus the very constitution of human nature dictates that the intellect should specify, and formally determine, the will, since this latter is blind; and that the will itself should determine the judgement of the intellect with respect to what it desires here and now; the intellect by itself being able to judge only in the abstract, and so to form an interdeterminate judgement; so that the man can only say: ' This in the abstract appears preferable '; not, ' This is to be desired by me here and now,' which can only be settled by the will which desires.

We are not, however, at the end of our difficulties, for if the intellect must determine the act of the will and the act of the will must determine the judgement of the intellect, we seem to be involved in a vicious circle. This is not so, nevertheless, for it is one and the same act of the will which determines the practical judgement, and is itself determined by it, though in different respects. This all happens instantaneously, so that it is not the will which first determines the intellect, and then the intellect the will, nor vice versa. There is no priority of time of one determination to the other, but both occur simultaneously. It is a case of the mutual causality so often spoken of by Aristotle, and the axiom : ' causes which are causes of one another belong to different genera of causality,' finds its application here. So we have seen, in Cosmology, that matter determines form by limiting it and making it individual, while at the same time form determines matter, limiting it and making it specific. Similarly, the soul moves and determines the body, giving direction to its actions ; and the body, at the same time, moves the soul, determining, by its physical constitution, i.e. here and now in the concrete, how these actions are to be carried out. In the same way, mental ability is required in order to learn, and learning increases mental ability. This mutual anteriority of two causes to one another is to be found wherever there is life, and indeed, wherever there is movement, as by running an engine it becomes less stiff, and by becoming less stiff it is helped to run. Here, then, at the point when the last practico-practical judgement is about to be made, the will applies the intellect to judge determinately what is to be done, and receives thereby from this determinate judgement, so instantaneously formed, the guidance and determination of the intellect in choosing that this is to be done. This may perhaps be compared to the action of the driver of a motor car, who switches on his headlights in order to see where to steer the car, and in doing so his motion receives formal determination from the light which he himself has caused. Thus the last judgement is not merely and wholly intellectual, but contains a large admixture of volition ; for if of the two partial goods proposed in the deliberation which thus ends, the will chooses one ; it only does so, and puts an end to the deliberation, when one or other of these goods sufficiently appeals to it, and suits its taste, for it to be satisfied with it. The goodness of the object is judged in relation to the appetite which it attracts. We thus avoid altogether the vicious circle in which we seemed to be involved, and with it the theory of liberty of equilibrium ; for we can and indeed must affirm, that just as an artist cannot work unless he first determines his action by the idea of the work to be executed, so the will cannot act unless it first be determined by the intellect, so that in all its actions it follows the lead of the intellect, and therefore the liberty of equilibrium is at once excluded. And, similarly, just as the artist's idea does not exercise its determining effect on his action, unless he actually, by acting, uses it as directive in his action, so the determination of the intellect is only effective in making the will dependent on it, if the will itself, by its own action, enters into this relation of dependence on the intellect. The same act of volition which thus follows the judgement, in a certain sense also precedes it, there being relative priority, from different points of view, of the acts of the intellect and will, with temporal simultaneity.

*The Answer to Psychological Determinism.    The Theory of Leibniz Excluded.*

It still seems, nevertheless, that if the will determines the judgement in this way, putting an end to the deliberation, it must do so because it is itself in a certain determinate state, and so could not choose otherwise : in such a way that a man placed twice in precisely the same circumstances, which include both exterior ones and interior dispositions, could not, in one case, decide to act, and in the other not to act. If he did so, it appears, his action would be without sufficient reason, unmotivated, irrational and so not human. We have only extricated ourselves from liberty of equilibrium to fall into the clutches of psychological determinism. In what has been said, in setting out the principles of intellectualism, the solution of this difficulty is already to be found, for though it is certain that the will must have a sufficient reason for determining the intellect, such sufficient reason cannot absolutely and infallibly determine it. This is clear from the very nature of the will which is completely satisfied by, and, of its nature, tends towards nothing less than the acquisition of total good. Consequently, no partial good can have an invincible attraction for it ; and no amount of interior or exterior impulses, so long as they are finite, can do so. They will incline it, perhaps with great force, to act or not to act, but can never necessitate it to do one or the other. The motive, then, which is finally accepted by the will, and which determines it, is relatively sufficient, i.e. in relation to the will itself at that particular moment, but it is not absolutely sufficient ; seeing that the range of the will is universal, as wide as being itself. When the choice is about to be made the will, of its own power, determines the judgement, which thereby determines the act of the will. The acceptance, or not, of any particular motive depends, then, on the gratuitous motion of the will, and this in turn on the state of the will at that moment. The motive in itself is powerless to force itself upon the will, and demand that it be accepted, and the intellect, which can judge in the abstract that such-and-such an action is advisable or not, is powerless to decide whether it is that one which is acceptable to the will in the concrete, and here and now. This applies in all free acts, acts which are rational, being determined by the reason, but free, since, unless the weight of the will's own power comes to supplement their force, they have not, of themselves, the power to attract it invincibly. This is clearly seen in relation to the act of faith, where the reasons for making it are cogent ; but it depends on the will itself, here and now, whether it will accept them, and make them its own reasons. ' *Qualis unusquisque est talis finis apparet ei,*' says Aristotle,[1] ' it is because we are persons of a certain kind that we put before ourselves such-and-such an end ' ; and, at any moment, we are persons of a certain kind by the self-determinations of the past, and by the non-necessitated acceptance of a self-determination here and now. It is not necessitated, since it does not satisfy our desires wholly, but partially only, so that it is in our power to accept it, or turn aside ; and thus, if we accept it, we determine ourselves, and are our own masters ; which is to be free. It is in this very continuous self-determination of the unified self that freedom essentially consists : the man, as a whole, ruling himself by reason and will, determines his own course of conduct, and is captain of his soul.[2] To be dragged from such dominion over himself by circumstances, passion, or error is, so far forth, to forfeit this dominion ; and for this reason, just as none would allow that vacillation and a wavering purpose is essential to liberty, so the Thomists have always maintained that freedom to sin is no integral part of freedom, but only a sign of it. Just as illness is a sign of life, or a limp possible only to one who can walk, so also a man could not sin unless he were free. A healthy animal, however, is more alive than a sick one, and a sinless man who masters himself, by a sane reason and a healthy will, is more free than one who does not ; but allows himself to be dominated by impulses not so controlled.

It follows also from our principles that a man who not only did not sin, but who was incapable of sinning, would be

[1] *Ethica Nicomachea*, Bk. III, Ch. V, 1114b23.
[2] Cf. Sorley, *Moral Values and the Idea of God*. Ch. XVII, esp. pp. 436 ff.

U

free in the highest degree ; for we have seen that the end
and object of the will is true good, while liberty is the power
to choose means which are in accordance with this end.   It
will, therefore, clearly be most perfect where there is no
power of choosing means which are discordant with the
attainment of true good, i.e. where there is no power of
sinning.   This, the theologians tell us, is the state of those
who have immediate knowledge of Good itself, which is God.
It belongs to the perfection of liberty, as S. Thomas points
out,[1] to be able to choose among different things which lead
to the desired end ; but to its imperfection to be able to
choose those which lead away from it.   Where, then, there is
no power of sinning there is none of choosing any means
which will lead away from the acquisition of true good, and
thus the imperfection of liberty is eliminated ; its perfection,
or the power of choosing among the means which will lead to
it, being maintained.   For just as when we wish to go from
place to place, we may suitably choose to travel by train, by
car, on foot, or by some other means, similarly, in seeking
goodness itself we should be wholly free in choosing among
the means of acquiring it, even if we were quite incapable of
choosing anything which diverted us from it.

For freedom of use does not imply freedom to misuse ; and
is indeed greater in proportion as the chance of misuse
diminishes.   So a barber who was incapable of making a slip
—if we can conceive such a marvel—would use his razor
much more freely than one who was not ; and, in fact, with
perfect freedom.

These considerations are sufficient to show us that the
power to sin is no necessary part of freedom ; its presence
in us is a sign, but still more, a defect of liberty.   Thus Von
Hugel, who so constantly and emphatically affirmed this
truth says : ' To be able to do, to be, evil is a defect, a restriction of liberty. . . . We should feel humbled, not only by
our actual sins, but already by the fact that we *can* commit
such things.'[2]

---

[1] *Summa Theologica*, I, Q. 62, a. 8, ad 3.
[2] Von Hugel, *Selected Letters*, p. 317.   Cf. *Essays and Addresses* (Second
Series), p. 203.

S. Augustine finely sets out this doctrine when, to the assertion of Julian that man could not be capable of his proper good, unless he were capable also of evil, he replies : ' Say rather that man's nature was first made capable of good and evil, not that it could not become capable of good only . . . so that if he had not sinned when he could sin, he would have come to that blessedness where he could not sin. For each is a great good, though one is less, the other greater. For it is less to be able not to sin, greater not to be able to sin.'[1]

Just as a man now is free, though unable to will anything except in so far as it appears to be good, so he would be wholly free if he could not will anything except in so far as it was in truth good. It is for this reason that S. Augustine also says : ' *Multo liberius erit arbitrium quod omnino non poterit servire peccato.*'[2]

There is one last point to which reference must be made before we close this consideration of liberty. We have said that the will in choosing has a sufficient motive, but one that does not infallibly determine it. But is not this to assert a contradiction, for how can the will be determined, and yet not infallibly determined ? It seems that this is both to be determined and not to be determined. Now we have already seen that in order to account for movement and multiplicity we were bound to assert the existence of a not-being, which, in a certain sense, is, viz. potency ;[3] so here, the fact of the relation between universal good and particular goods forces us to assert the existence of a determination which does not actually determine us, but is only able to do so. For it is precisely on these particular goods that the will bears, and since there is indetermination in its object, there must be also indetermination in the will. So S. Thomas' teaching on liberty joins up with the great central thesis of his philosophy, the division of finite being into potency and act. This division is demanded by the facts of multiplicity and of movement, and both the will of man, and its objects, must

[1] *Opus Imperfectum contra Julianum*, Liber V, LVIII. (*Opera Omnia*, ed. Cong. S. Mauri, Tom. X, 939 F.)
[2] *Enchiridion Fidei*, c. 105.
[3] Cf. *Cosmology*, ' Discussions on Motion and Individuality.'

share in this indetermination of finite being. This is a doctrine which has its roots deep down in the teaching of Plato and Aristotle ; and which is found at every stage of S. Thomas' presentation of the ' *philosophia perennis.*'

It will be useful to summarise the results arrived at in this chapter :

1. Man is free, since the judgement presented by the reason for his acceptance is never absolutely determined in itself, owing to the disproportion which exists between total good, the adequate object of desire, and the partial goods which are made known to us by the judgement.

2. Nevertheless, all the actions of his will are formally determined by the judgement, so that the theory of liberty of indifference, or equilibrium, is excluded : the judgement which determines the will owing its determination to the act of the will itself.

3. This strange fact is due to the unity of man's conscious life ; for that is desirable to a particular man which suits his particular state here and now. This can never be decided by the intellect, judging, as it were, in the abstract, but only by the concrete desire of the will.

4. This concrete self-determination of man is not a necessary consequent of his antecedent states, which, though affecting him, cannot infallibly determine him to choose one of two partial goods in preference to the other, since such goods are both equally incapable of satisfying his unlimited yearnings for absolute good. Thus psychological determinism is excluded by the domination of the will in action, over the intellect in judging. So man, by his will, is master of his judgement, and, under the guidance of judgement, so mastered, is master of himself.

Psychological determinism neglects the unity of the self, forgetting that a motive only becomes a motive for me here and now, if I desire it to be so, if I adopt and accept it. Indeterminism, on the other hand, makes the will an incalculable force which interferes with the guidance of reason, and turns it from its normal course without reason. Such irrational willing could not be freedom, but merely the emergence of some blind impulse, an impulse which is not under the man's control.  In neither of these ways can man be his own master, but only by the control of the will by the intellect, and of the intellect by the will, of the whole man by himself.

The more such freedom is developed the more will conflict and strain be eliminated ;  and, if its development were fully achieved, a man would be in possession of the un-fettered exercise of a good will, whereby, without deviation, he would uniformly desire only his true good :  to serve which is to rule.[1]

[1] For the whole of this subject the following may be consulted : Garigou-Lagrange, *Dieu, Son existence et sa nature*, 2ᵉ partie, Ch. IV. Sertillanges, *S. Thomas d'Aquin*, Tom. II, Livre VI, Ch. I–III.  Cf. also Sorley, op. cit., Sect. 17.  Ward, *The Realm of Ends*, Lectures 13 and 14.

# CHAPTER XIV

## THE NATURE OF THE INTELLECTUAL SOUL IN MAN

Its Substantiality—Its Spirituality—It is the Substantial Form—Simple—And One Only—Differing Specifically from that of Other Animals—Reasons for this View.

In the three preceding chapters we have seen something of the way in which the mind of man works ; and we now pass on to enquire what information we can gather, from our conclusions as to its working, with regard to its nature. What sort of thing is this mind, or intellectual soul ?

The phrase ' mind or intellectual soul ' by its very ambiguity at once suggests a question as to the nature of the intellectual principle in us, viz. is it merely a mental power, or is it something substantial ?—for mind may mean either mental powers, or a substantial principle of such powers. Our first question, then, is whether there is a substantial principle of our intellectual powers. The idea that there is not some principle which is capable of producing thoughts and retaining them, but which does not itself require to be produced or retained by any other principle—in a word, that there is not a substantial principle of intellectual operations—would hardly occur to common sense. Nevertheless, many philosophers have held that there is in us no substantial mind, but only a series of mental acts. Such a view must necessarily be taken by those who deny altogether the possibility of affirming the existence of any substance, as do the Phenomenalists, e.g. Hume and Taine. In accordance with this view, the Associationist Psychology was developed, to give some sort of account of our processes of thinking, and, if possible, some plausibility to the idea of thoughts without a thinker. Though Associationism finds little, if any, acceptance among modern psychologists, the phenomenalist point of view is still prevalent. The denial of the substantiality of the human mind is not confined to the Phenomenalists, for in Monist theories, such as those of Spinoza and Hegel, though the substantiality of mind is not, in a sense, denied, nevertheless, the mind which they recognise is either the Divine mind, in the case of Spinoza, or the Absolute, in the case of Hegel. Human minds are but an aspect or phase of these.[1] Consequently, such philosophies in no sense allow the substantiality of the individual mind of man.

The main stream of philosophic thought has, on the other hand, always considered that common sense is, on the whole, right ; and so has recognised that psychic phenomena, such as thoughts and volitions, need some substantial subject, which, owing to its capacity for supporting itself, is enabled to support them also. In the Platonic tradition this subject is called the soul.

This view of the matter is surely true, for how can we conceive of thoughts, volitions, etc., which have no subject to support them, since they are actions, and an action suspended in the void is quite inadmissible. Just as it is impossible to have motion without something which moves, so also it is impossible to have thought without a thinker, or willing without a subject who wills. Moreover, consciousness tells us, not only of the presence of thoughts and volitions, but also that it is I who think, feel, will, and so on. Hence this ' I ' remains permanent beneath the changing phenomena. If I, the man, am but a series of phenomena, with the passing of the phenomena, I should also pass away. But consciousness tells me that I endure. Thus, to say : ' I think, feel, will,' etc., is to testify that there is not merely a multitude of thoughts, volitions, etc., but that there is a single principle of them all. Further, such statements, expressing, as they do, a most clear conviction of consciousness, show that these phenomena cannot be attributed to any particular organ, or part of us, to the exclusion of the rest, but must be attributed to us as a whole, i.e. to some substantial principle in us.

[1] Cf. Stace, *The Philosophy of Hegel*, pp. 439 ff.

It might, perhaps, be suggested that the support which such phenomena necessarily require is merely the material organism. This, however, cannot be true, since the organism is not in itself a unity, but is composed of a multitude of diverse parts ; and, moreover, it is not fixed and permanent, but constantly changing, so that after a time it is entirely renewed. It follows, then, that the substantial principle must be something distinct from the body considered in isolation, or that the soul of man must be substantial, unifying the body.

We may add that if the soul were nothing but a succession of phenomena, memory, the conviction of the continuity of the Ego, and the feeling of responsibility become inexplicable. No reason could then be assigned why any thought, feeling, or desire, should be connected with any other.[1]

If, then, we recognise, with common sense, that there is in man a substantial principle of psychic acts, or a soul which is substantial ; we shall naturally wish to discover something concerning its nature. Such an enquiry can evidently be carried out only by philosophy ; it is one which is beyond the scope of experimental science, the inner nature of a substance not being amenable to experiment. Hence, experimental psychology rightly excludes such concepts as the simplicity or spirituality of the soul. Such exclusion should not, however, lead to denying these or other attributes to the conscious subject, in fact such a denial would be as much beyond the sphere of natural science as an affirmation of them would be.

If man is indeed in possession of intellect and will, as we have maintained, it follows at once that the substantial principle of these powers must also be intellectual, since they derive from it. Further, we have seen that this intellectual power in man is an immaterial one, though dependent on matter—i.e. on the body and the senses—in order to act ; in other words, it is one which is extrinsically dependent on matter, though not intrinsically, and subjectively in its own nature. The same, then, must also be true of the source of

---

[1] So Ward, *Psychological Principles*, pp. 34–41, and McDougall, *Outline of Psychology*, pp. 39 ff., affirm that we are obliged to recognise a ' conscious subject ' as ' an indispensable hypothesis.'

intellectual power, viz. the soul, which will, therefore, also be spiritual in this sense.

The principle of life in man, which we call the soul, must necessarily be of the nature of form, that which makes a thing what it is, since it is in virtue of the soul that man is a living intellectual being ; and since it is substantial, it will be his substantial form. Like all other substantial forms, it will not have quantitative parts of itself ; and we have seen reason to believe that the souls of the higher animals, among whom no doubt man must be reckoned, have no quantitative parts, even owing to their union with the body, and so are indivisible. We should conclude, then, that the human soul is quantitatively simple from our previous considerations, but we have now learned, in addition to these, the fact that it is spiritual, and so must be unextended ; extension being an attribute of the body, not of the spirit ; and consequently from this point of view also, we are led to affirm that the human soul is simple. But even if the intellectual soul be thus in itself spiritual and simple, it might be maintained, it seems, that there is more than one life-principle, or soul, in man. A little reflection will shew that this is impossible, for not only would this destroy the essential unity of the individual, since each life-principle must be a substantial form, so that any such principle, after the first, must form an accidental union with the already constituted compound ; but also it is clear that vegetative, sensitive and intellectual life mutually help or hinder one another, which could only be the case if they all proceed from one and the same principle. So sensitive and vegetative life are conditions *sine qua non* of intellectual life, and they, in turn, are guided and preserved by means of the intellect. We observe also that an intensity of action in any one of the three spheres results in diminution of activity in the others ; thus intense action of the senses, or vital organs, hinders mental operations. In the reverse order, intense mental activity leads to insensibility, generally partial, but in exceptional cases, complete ; as in the self-hypnotism practised by the fakirs.[1]

[1] An account of some instances of such self-hypnotism is given by Dr. William Brown in *Philosophy* (1931), pp. 215 ff.

So far we have considered the nature of the soul, in itself and intrinsically, and we have seen that it is substantial, spiritual, simple, and not accompanied by other life-principles in a single individual. We must now ask what is its relation to the life-principles in other animals. Is it of the same kind as these, or does it differ specifically from them, in such a way that we can assert that no animal, other than man, has an intellectual soul ? We shall be obliged to recognise a specific distinction if we find that in the life of man we have a positive addition of perfection, or actuality, and not merely a development, or increase, of powers which are possessed by animals lower in the scale than man. It is clear enough that the possession of intrinsic independence of matter, as contrasted with intrinsic dependence on it, will constitute a distinction of this kind, if it be established ; since here we should have a positive addition of immateri-ality, or of actuality ; for what is of itself dependent on matter cannot develop into something which it is not, i.e. something independent of matter ; so adding to itself a positive perfection or actuality, for which it has no capacity, and which is, indeed, excluded by its very nature.

We have already seen the evidences of such independence in man in his capacity for forming universal and so immaterial concepts, in his freedom, and in the unlimited range and scope of his intellect. To these we may add further signs, such as his capacity for progress, and his power of speech.

His freedom, as we saw, is rooted in his capacity for com-paring the particular goods proposed for his acceptance with universal good, and in the last resort in his spirituality, as is also the distinctive way in which his mind works in the formation of universal concepts. Capacity for progress, which man possesses, is but a consequence of this, for it is obtained by means of reflection, envisaging the end to be aimed at in general, and then comparing the various means which might be used to gain it. Consequently, it is a sign of the universality or immateriality of that mind which is the source of progress. The power of speech again is an indica-tion of the immateriality of the mind of the speaker ; for speech is articulated sound, composed of arbitrary symbols which are designed to express concepts. Speech, therefore, implies that the speaker has concepts to express, and indicates the existence of thought, even though it may sometimes, as has been suggested, serve to conceal thoughts.

Do we, in fact, find any evidence of the existence of these indications of intellectuality and immateriality in other animals than man ?

This, no doubt, is a disputable question ; and to answer it fully would require a minute observation and examination of the actions of all animals. Clearly, such an enquiry is far too extensive to be undertaken here, if indeed it can be undertaken at all. Nevertheless, if we look at the matter impartially, uninfluenced by any presupposition, either in favour of, or against, the evolutionary hypothesis, we shall see that there are a number of converging probabilities which all point to the conclusion that animals, other than man, have not that immateriality which we are obliged to ascribe to human beings.

In spite of the keen and wide observation of animal actions in recent years, no definite evidence of freedom has been discovered in them. Though it is true that when confronted with particular material obstacles to action they may modify their action to some extent, yet there is no indication that this arises from any abstract consideration of the problem, but can be wholly accounted for by a power of combining sense images.

It is not in dispute that, normally, each class of animal has its own determinate way of acting which never varies ; ' every swallow,' as S. Thomas says, ' building its nest in the same way.' Each species has its own definite mode of breeding, nesting, and feeding, from which it deviates little, if at all. There is thus : ' no evidence that it ever does, or makes anything according to a plan of its own.'[1] It shows none of the signs of freedom.

Similarly, no progress is observable among animals, such change as there is, not being initiated by themselves, but

[1] Cf. Ivy Mackenzie, *Aristotelian Society's Proceedings* (1927), pp. 275 f.

coming about from nature and circumstance, not of their own intention. No doubt they can learn, but only within very narrow limits, in so far as they associate particular sensations with particular acts. Nowadays, this fact is explained by the theory of conditioned reflexes ; but whatever explanation be accepted, the fact of their lack of initiative and progress is certain.

Do animals speak ? Certainly they communicate their emotions to one another by cries and sounds of various kinds, but there is no shred of evidence that they have any conventional system of articulate sounds ; in fact, since here, again, we find stereotyped sounds which differ in each species we are justified in concluding that their ' speech ' is fixed for them by nature, and not by themselves. Talking animals are a figment of the imagination of romantic story-tellers and are only to be found in fairy tales, not in nature. The absence of conventional speech has the advantage that they cannot lie, as man can.

From every point of view, then, we may conclude that it is as certain as such a thing can be that animals have not a mind and soul of the same immaterial kind as man has.

If this be so we once more find ourselves in the presence of two grades of life which are distinguished by an essential, a specific difference, and not merely a difference of degree. As living things differ from inanimate ones, as animals from plants, so also do men differ from the other animals. No evidence is forthcoming that animals are possessed of an abstractive universalising faculty such as the human intellect is ; but the progress of investigation shows them, even more clearly than common observation had done, as confined to particular objects of knowledge, and very limited in their modes of action even with regard to these. That the higher animals, at least, have a kind of intelligence, no one would deny ; but it does not appear to be of the kind which sees the meaning in things, but merely that which is able to observe that certain objects are desirable and useful to them here and now. Human beings, perceiving the meaning of objects, are not tied to the concrete, the particular, the material, and so in them there is a definite increment of immateriality, actuality or perfection over and above that found in the other animals.[1]

The intellectual soul of man is not, however, divorced from his material organism, but is evidently intimately connected with it ; which brings us to the question of the nature of this connection.

[1] Prof. Julian Huxley, though a decided opponent of the ideas here advocated, goes so far as to assert that ' there is no evidence at present that even the highest animals possess ideas, or even images.' (*Essays of a Biologist*, Essay II : ' Biology and Sociology,' p. 97, 1923 edition.) He quotes in support of this view Thorndike, *Animal Intelligence*, New York, 1911, and Washburn, *The Animal Mind*, New York, 1913.

# CHAPTER XV

## THE UNION OF SOUL AND BODY IN MAN

Views on the Question—Monism—Psycho-physical Parallelism—
Accidental and Essential Union—Reasons for the Thomist View
The Mode of the Union—How the Soul is Present to the Body.

THE question of the union of soul and body is, no doubt,
a very perplexing one, for if there is such union we must
assert that the material and the immaterial, the qualitative
and the quantitative, the necessary and the free are one.

In the few pages at our disposal we can give no adequate
account of all the theories on this subject which have been
advanced ; but it is necessary and possible to see what are
their general types.

In the first place, we may cut the knot by denying that
there is any union, inasmuch as there are not two entities or
entitative principles to unite but one only. This one may
be either the body alone, or the soul alone ; the first being
the solution of materialistic monism, which alleges that mind
is either a form of matter, or an appearance of matter, while
the second is the view of idealistic monism, according to
which matter, and body, is an illusion. In the materialistic
theory, mind or soul is something we construct owing to our
ignorance of the workings of material forces, and so is an
illusion like the dryads, river-gods, and other spiritual forces
which were supposed, by primitive peoples, to direct the
operations of nature, operations which we now know to be
the result of material forces only. Idealistic monism, on the
contrary, holds mind to be the only reality, and what we call
matter but a projection or shadow of mind.

In both these theories the problem disappears ; but
neither accords with common sense, since no one would
naturally suppose, either that thought and consciousness

are simply some kind of bodily secretion, nor yet that he had no body at all. If it be recognised, then, that there are, in fact, two realities in man, body and soul, it may still be denied that they are united, in which case they continue in company, side by side, but without affecting one another. How this unfailing concomitance is to be explained it is difficult to say, but it seems that it would have to be attributed to some kind of Pre-established Harmony.

These seem to exhaust all the possible ways of solving the problem of union by denying that body and soul are united. If, then, we allow that they are united, their union may be either essential, if they form one nature, or accidental, if they merely act on one another, while remaining in themselves distinct. This last type of view seems very natural to us, and has in fact been widely held, both by ordinary men and by philosophers, such as Plato. It is somewhat difficult to see how such diverse things as mind and matter could, in fact, act on one another ; but the chief objection to this theory is that it breaks up the essential unity of the self, so destroying human nature altogether. If consciousness tells us anything about ourselves, it is surely this, that we are unities ; not a soul which is imprisoned in, or hovering about, a body with which it is not connected by nature ; or, rather, to which it is by nature opposed. Neither body nor soul can be said to be the individual man, so that if they do not form one nature together, the man himself disappears. This difficulty is expressed in William de Morgan's epigrammatic lines :

> ' John has a soul.' Upon the whole
> The tombstone lies which says ' Hic jacet.'
> But if John really has a soul,
> What in the world is John who has it ?

It seems, then, that we are bound to assert that soul and body together form one nature ; that the union between them is an essential one. This is the view expressed by S. Thomas and constantly adhered to by the Thomists, in spite of the fact that the Platonic view, according to which the soul finds only a temporary home, or prison, in the body is clearly more easily reconcilable with the Christian doctrines of immortality and resurrection.

Scotus, who followed the Platonic and Augustinian tradition, thought that there are in man two substantial forms, that of the body, the form of corporeality, which makes it a specifically human body, and gives it existence as such ; and the soul-form, which is a substance in its own right ; while at the same time he maintained that the union of the soul and body is an essential one. If by substantial form we mean that act by which a thing is constituted in its specific nature and distinguished from others, it seems impossible to see how essential unity can, in this hypothesis, be maintained; for if the body is constituted as a body by the form of corporality, it cannot be given its nature by the soul since it already has it ; consequently, the soul cannot be its substantial form, but must be an accidental one, and the union will be accidental. If, on the other hand, we do not mean by substantial form that which gives specific substantial nature to a thing, then we must acknowledge either that the body never has such a nature, or that it receives it from something other than the form of corporeality, which consequently will be unable to do more than add something to a body already constituted as a substance ; in which case it is clearly an accidental form, and the union is once more an accidental one. We are, in fact, back again in our old dispute about the plurality of forms, about which enough has already been said.

It is not our business, however, to discuss the Scotist opinion, but to explain that which the Thomists hold. The latter, both on the grounds of observation and introspection, as well as on account of the logic of their system, feel obliged to assert that the body has no form of its own, but is immediately informed by the soul, which is, therefore, not a complete substance, but the actual element in the composite human substance. This position, it may be noticed, is not unaccompanied by difficulty ; since, according to the fundamental principles of Thomism, it is impossible to have numerical differentiation of any specific form except by the reception of this form in matter. Hence, it seems that when union with the body ceases at death, the soul will either not survive at all, or if it does, will be merged into a universal soul, losing its individuality.  S. Thomas was unable to accept either of these consequences, whether as a philosopher or theologian, and he points out that the relation of form and matter being a transcendental one,[1] which arises from the very nature of the related terms, so long as either of them remains in being, it will retain its relationship to the other.[2] If, then, the soul survives death, it will not cease to be individual, but will retain, as part of its very being, that essential relationship to the body which it had before its severance from it.

In order to establish the strictly essential character of the union of body and soul, the Thomists point, in the first place, to the observed actions of human beings ;  and they notice that some of them are, in their origin, common to both soul and body.  Such are anger, fear, and, in general, the emotions, as well as all sensation, since, as we have seen, this is organic, and so only possible as proceeding from body and soul in conjunction.  Now, though it is true that two principles of action might produce a single resultant action, as the motion of a wagon might be the single result of the pull of two or more horses, yet it is impossible that one and the same action should *issue* from more than one source of action, since the action of a thing is the consequence of its powers and so of its form ;  so the two essentially distinct principles of action, two forms, must produce actions which are also distinct, though they may combine in a common effect.  Hence a single common operation cannot proceed from two essentially distinct principles, and emotion and sensation, being such operations, their principle, the human being, must also be essentially one.

Further, similar considerations to those which led us to conclude that animals are essential unities will be applicable to the case of man.  For here, again, we find that all the operations of mind, and of the several organs of the body, tend to the preservation and well-being of the organism, or individual, as a whole ;  the parts of the body, under the

[1] Cf. S. Thomas, *Contra Gentiles*, II, c. 81.
[2] Cf. Vol. II, *General Metaphysics*.

x

influence of life, adjusting their actions in such a way that the normal functioning of the organism as a whole may not be impaired. If, then, both bodily and mental actions naturally tend to the well-being of the whole man, rather than to that of any particular part ; not to their own good, but to the good of the whole, we are justified in concluding that this is due to the fact that man himself, body and soul, is a single nature, an essential unity. For the natural tendencies of a thing are but the expression of its nature, so that the end to which a thing tends must correspond to the principle of its operations, which is its nature. If, therefore, various operations all tend constantly to a single end, this must be because it is their nature to do so, which nature must thus be common to them all, and so a single remote principle of them all.

We may here mention very briefly some further considerations which strengthen our conclusion. In the first place, we attribute all our actions, whether of mind or body, to one and the same self ; and say : 'I think, love, hear, see, feel, grow,' and so on. Consciousness, therefore, bears testimony to the fact that soul and body form a single nature.

Again, we fear death, the dissolution of the union of body and soul, a fact which finds no ready explanation if soul and body are joined only accidentally, or not joined at all, as Psycho-physical Parallelism suggests. According to these theories, it seems that we should 'dread the grave as little as our bed '; but we do not, and if our thesis is correct, ought not to do so.

The modern alternative to our theory is that of parallelism, which denies the causal influence of mind on body, and vice versa. Both these denials are faced by grave difficulties, for if body does not act on mind, how are we to account for sensation, which is certainly mental ? On the parallelist theory, it must arise from some mental cause, and no such cause is discoverable, either in my own previous mental states—for which among them can cause me to have sensation, e.g., of some sudden sound ?—nor in the action of any other mind. Again, if mind does not act on body, we must deny the influence of thought and volition on our bodily movements, such as walking, which seems fantastic ; and all handicrafts, and artificially constructed articles must be attributed simply to bodily motions without any intervention of thought or intention.[1]

It will be seen that though, from one point of view, the Thomist theory of the union of mind and body may be called an interaction theory, in so far as each exerts causal influence on the other ; nevertheless, since they are said to be united in a single nature, such causality is not to be understood as that of two complete beings, of different kinds, on one another ; as would be, for example, the action of a pure spirit on a material object. Soul and body are so interwoven that there is something of the body in the nature of the soul, and something of the soul in the organisation of the body. Human nature is something greater than either soul or body, and embraces them both. This idea is emphasised, and worked out, in the view which the Thomists hold as to the mode of their union, for they consider that the soul is, of its nature and without any intermediary, the substantial form of the body.

It is clear that it must be the body's substantial form, and not an accidental one, if the two are to form one nature, this being the very meaning of substantial, or essential, union as opposed to accidental. Moreover, it is by the soul that man is made a living, sentient and intellectual being ; and so, by it, he is constituted in his specific nature and distinguished from others, to do which is the office of substantial form. Again, it is the principle of being, which also is due to substantial form ; for in living things to live is to be, and since the soul is the principle of life, it is also that of being. It is also the principle of action, for human actions are vital ones, and the soul, as the life-principle, is, therefore, their source ; and so the substantial form in man.

Neither can there be, in addition to the soul, some substantial form which informs the body, as such ; and which is subsumed under the form which is the soul, for we have

[1] Space does not allow of a full discussion of these theories, but the reader may be referred to Broad, *The Mind and its Place in Nature*, pp. 13–117 ; McDougall, *Modern Materialism*, Ch. III ; Hobson, *The Domain of Natural Science*, pp. 67, 355 f. ; Driesch, *Mind and Body*.

seen that it is impossible to retain essential unity if there is more than one substantial form[1] since the first form would constitute the body as a substance, so that it could not be made so by the soul, which, therefore, could add to it no substantial, or essential, perfection, but only an accidental one ; and so would be joined to it accidentally. The same consideration also applies to the view, recently put forward, that the chemical elements in the body retain their own specific natures, and so their own substantial forms, even when they are parts of man's body. If this were so, a man would be a mere conglomeration of material elements, all essentially distinct, but, in some unexplained way, under the influence of the soul. There can be no question of there being such a thing as human nature in this case ; nor, since the chemical elements must, *a pari*, be also considered as essentially composite, of any specific chemical nature ; but all those differences in kind which we thought we found in the world of nature will be done away with. So true is it that unless we preserve essential unity we cannot have essential diversity : the many are impossible without the one. Again, we are at the very heart of the Thomistic view of the universe, which refuses to reject the many for the one, or the one for the many ; but, in the successive increments of actuality which it observes to be added to the potentiality of matter in the ascending scale of material things, clings firmly to variety in unity, specific variety in the unity of being, and individual variety in the unity of species. The only alternative to this view they consider to be some form of Monism ; all things being either some undifferentiated matter, or all some undifferentiated form or act. It is because they reject with all possible emphasis, on the basis both of experience and consciousness, such views as these, that they insist so untiringly on the unity of form in the individual.

If, then, we admit that the soul is the one substantial form of the body, giving their specific nature, as human, to all its parts, we see at once the mode of its presence to the body ; since it must be clearly be present to the whole body, making it human, and to each part of it. The whole of it must thus

---

[1] Cf. *Cosmology*, Ch. X, Q. 1, pp. 129 ff.

be present in the whole body, and in each and every one of its parts—in contradistinction to the way in which one extended thing is present in another, e.g. when a bottle is filled with beer, the whole of the beer is in the whole bottle, but not in each part of it. It does not follow that all the soul's powers are exercised in each part of the body. In fact it is obvious that this is not the case, for the soul cannot exercise the whole of its power in every part of the body, as the legs cannot be used for seeing, or the eyes for hearing ; while no part of the body, nor the whole of it, is fitted to be the instrument of intellectual operations, of thinking and willing.

Such essential presence is, evidently, not circumscriptive, a mode of location which belongs only to bodies ; nor yet definitive by means of operation, since the union of soul and body is essential, but definitive by means of information ;[1] so that the soul is tied, by its very nature, to the place which the body occupies, and cannot, at the same time, be also in another place.

[1] Cf. *Cosmology*, Ch. VI, Sect. I, esp. pp. 81 f.

# CHAPTER XVI

## THE ORIGIN AND DESTINY OF THE HUMAN SOUL

Origin—Not by Generation or Emanation, but by Creation—The
Transmigration of Souls—The Thomist View of the Succession
of Forms in the Individual—Immortality—Opinions—Reasons
for Thomist View—The Metaphysical Argument.

THE soul, then, is spiritual and simple, and yet, at the same
time, it has an essential relation to the body, forming one
nature with it. What light do these conclusions throw on
its origin and destiny ?

First, with regard to its origin, we observe that the soul is
a form, and a special kind of form, viz. a spiritual one :
which is independent of matter in its nature ; so that this
nature cannot have been derived from matter. In the case
of the forms of other animals, where this special consideration did not apply, we saw that it was not necessary to postulate any other cause of them than the vital powers of the
parents ; so that their generation belongs entirely to the
material order ; but, in the case of man, this cannot be so,
since that which is generated is a being which, as far as its
form is concerned, is a spiritual one. The cause, then, of a
human being must be at least as spiritual as this being
itself. Such a cause might be either the child's parents, or
God. As for the parents, they are doubtless, in any event,
the cause of the child's coming to be, for even if they do not
generate the soul, they do produce the body which is essentially related to it ; and since the term or result of any
generative process is neither matter nor form in disjunction
from one another, but the compound of the two, that agent
will properly be said to generate the compound which is
the cause of uniting a new form with matter. This is precisely what the parents do, since by forming a body which is

fitted to receive, and actually requires a human soul to inform it, they cause the union of matter and form to come about. It is not necessary, therefore, in order to maintain, as we certainly must, that parents generate their own child, to say that they produce its soul from their own substance. In fact, if we were to suppose that they did so, we should, if we grant that the soul is immaterial, find ourselves in an impossible position. It seems quite clear that it could not be produced by their purely physical or bodily powers, since it has a nature of a higher order than these. Nor yet could it be produced by their souls or spiritual powers, since the souls of the parents are indivisible. Since they have no parts, the souls of the children could not be parts of them, or divided off from them by emanation. Thus, the spirituality of the human soul debars us from saying that it is produced by the parents. It appears, then, that its production must be due to some other spiritual cause. We might conceive such a cause bringing the soul into being either by emanation from itself, or by way of creation; i.e. making it to be, without drawing it out of itself, or of any other pre-existing being. The emanationist hypothesis cannot be entertained for the reason just given, viz. that spiritual beings are indivisible, and so cannot separate anything from their own substance by way of emanation. It might be suggested that an infinite being of this kind could, without such separation or in other words, with the entirety of its being, be itself the spiritual principle of all men. This idea, apart from the fact that it is clearly pantheistic, is excluded by the other aspect of the human soul, the fact that it is the form of the individual man, and so limited and finite, as the correlative of a finite body. Consequently, it could not also be an infinite spirit. No other hypothesis, therefore, remains, with regard to the origin of the human soul, than the creationist one. We shall see later that such an act of creation, the absolute beginning and production of some being, cannot be effected by any finite cause; and, if this be true, we must conclude that human souls are created by an infinite spiritual being. Such an infinite being is commonly called God. The Scholastics are thus in general agreement in asserting that the human soul comes into existence by means of creation by God.

Even if this be accepted, we should wish to know when this ' infusion ' of the soul into the body, this coming into it ' from without,' of which Aristotle speaks,[1] takes place.

The doctrine that the soul is the form of the body, so having an essential relation to this individual body, and to this only ; excludes two notions as to the way in which it comes to be in it, viz. by metempsychosis, and by passing into it after a previous existence. The first view, the theory of the trans- migration of souls, has been, in the past, very widely accepted ; and even to-day is held by many, as by the Theosophists and the Hindus. Plato took over the idea from Pythagoras, who may himself have derived it from Orphism. It maintains that one soul may pass through many bodies, both of animals and men.[2] If, however, it be true that soul and body really form one nature, standing to one another in the relation of potentiality to act, it will be impossible for a soul, or act, which is thus essentially related to one body, to become essentially related to another, without parting with something essential to it, and so, at least breaking its actual continuity. In fact, it cannot so change essentially, being a simple nature or form, and must therefore continue to be related to one body, and one only. The doctrine of transmigration is, therefore, compatible with Platonism, where the union of the soul and body is looked on as accidental, but not with Aristoteleanism, in which the body derives its nature from the soul, giving to it, in turn, individuality. Such a relationship as this can, evidently, not be destroyed so long as the soul continues in existence. The supposition that the soul exists before the body is also seen to be gratuitous and bizarre, if their relationship is such as S. Thomas holds it to be ; for the soul's natural being is in the body, and if it existed before its

---

[1] *De Generatione Animalium*, II.3 ; 736ᵇ28. Δείπεται δὲ τὸν νοῦν μόνον θύραθεν ἐπεισιέναι καὶ θεῖον εἶναι μόνον.

[2] Cf. Taylor, *Plato : The Man and his Work*, p. 308 ; Stace, *Critical History of Greek Philosophy*, p. 217. See also the interesting account of the history of the doctrine, and of the light-hearted way in which it was treated by Plotinus, in Dean Inge's *Philosophy of Plotinus*, Vol. II, pp. 29– 36.

union with the body it would do so in a state of frustration, unable to fulfil its natural function ; and without any spiritual or intellectual activity, such as it would have if it continues to exist after separation from the body, since it would not naturally have acquired any knowledge in the pre-existing state. Under these conditions it seems almost impossible to attach any definite meaning to the question : did the soul exist before the body ?[1]

S. Thomas, as is fairly generally known, held a view of a contrary kind, viz. that what, by a process of evolution, becomes the human body existed, prior to its becoming so, in the two lower orders of life, the vegetative and the sensitive. Beginning its life with a vegetative form or soul, as organisation increases and advances far enough to make the foetus capable of sensitive activity, a corruption and a generation taking place, the body receives a sensitive, and with further development an intellectual, or human, soul.[2] He thus admits specific evolution, or development, within the individual, under the influence of a higher power, i.e. human life, or the souls of the parents ; these in turn, as he points out,[3] being, like all the activities and powers of nature, subordinated, as instruments, to the power of God. The principle which leads to this view is that matter must be proportionate to its form, and so, in this case, the body must be sufficiently organised to be a fitting correlative of the intellectual soul, before it is informed by it. Whatever may be thought of the truth of this view,[4] it no doubt harmonises well with the modern way of envisaging the development of life through the ages ; though embryology seems to show that sensitivity is present in the human foetus very early, if not from the start.

Whether we accept this view, or hold that the soul is infused at the moment of conception, our conclusion that

---

[1] Cf. S. Thomas, *Contra Gentiles*, Lib. II, Chaps. 83 and 84.
[2] *Summa Theol.*, I, Q. 118, a. 2, ad 2.
[3] *Contra Gentiles*, II, Ch. 89.
[4] For a discussion of it from a philosophical point of view cf. Hugon, *Cursus Philosophiæ Thomisticæ*, Vol. III, pp. 199 ff. Its theological aspect is dealt with in the *Dict. de Théologie Catholique, art.* "âme," Vol. I, Cols. 1306 ff., and Vol. VII, Col. 846. Cf. also Mercier, *Psychologie*, Vol. II, pp. 339–340.

the parents really generate their children, will not be affected, since the earlier life-principles will be but forms whose *raison d'être* is to lead up to, and prepare for the coming of, the human soul. Thus in either view the parents prepare the body, and make it proportionate to this soul.

We can, then, take it as proved that the human soul originates by means of creation, and is not produced by any kind of conception of it by the parents, whether spiritual or physical ; and, further, that it does not exist before union with the body ; though the supposition that it does so does not seem to be absolutely impossible. Moreover, it does not pass from body to body, since it is the form of this particular body. What, then, becomes of it when it is separated from the body at death ? Does it cease to exist altogether ? So we find ourselves brought naturally to the question of the immortality of the human soul, a question which, like that of liberty, and for a similar reason, has always been in the forefront in philosophical discussions : for it is vital to us, and not merely a matter of curiosity, to give an answer to it.

We shall, therefore, not attempt to give an account of the history of this question of survival, as this is impracticable in a short space ; but it is necessary to glance at some of the principal answers to the questions : can and will the soul survive death ?

First, there are, of course, those who deny the possibility of survival altogether, inasmuch as they think that life is essentially of the material order, and simply disappears when the organism ceases to function normally.[1] Few, perhaps, adopt an attitude quite so intransigent as this, but rather say that it is more probable that life altogether disappears at death. These profess to hold this only as an opinion, but actually they hold it so tenaciously that it is, for them, rather certain than probable.[2] If, on the other hand, it is allowed that there is some survival after death, we find no agreement

---

[1] So one of the materialists picturesquely asserted that it is as impossible for the soul to exist without the body as it would be for the flame of a candle to exist without the candle.

[2] Cf. E. S. P. Haynes, *The Belief in Personal Immortality.* In spite of his profession of open-mindedness, it seems clear the author regarded the belief as an illusion.

as to its nature ; and in particular there is a great difference of opinion on the question whether such survival is a personal or impersonal one. It may, perhaps, be said roughly that those who do not adhere to the Platonic and Christian tradition, as Spinoza, hold the latter view, while Christian philosophers adhere to the former. It is further supposed by some that those, who in life devote themselves to material and temporal interests, will cease to be when these interests cease, while those who live the higher life of the spirit will survive. ' We are what we love and care about.'[1]

The Thomistic doctrine is very definite, for it regards the soul of every human person as being of its nature indestructible, so that survival does not depend on its own activities during life ; and, moreover, since it is also by nature a finite form, it must survive as such ; and so, not as absorbed into the divinity, or in any collective fashion.

In support of their contention, modern Thomists use arguments of many different kinds ; which may perhaps be grouped under two heads, moral and metaphysical. Such is the general agreement of mankind as to the fact of survival, a belief which is found at all times and in all races ; the necessity for the rigorous enforcement of the moral law, or the supremacy of the good and the true over evil and irrationality.

This last argument must take the form that the purpose of the moral life is unattainable if death extinguishes life entirely. If, then, we recognise the absolute claim of morality, so that we feel certain that, whatever fails, right must endure and prevail, we shall be forced to recognise survival after death as the necessary condition for the fulfilment of this claim. No one who perceives at all clearly the fundamental notions of Thomism will be in any doubt as to the conclusions a Thomist must come to as to the permanence and absolute claim of moral good ; for, as we have seen all along, the intellect is, in their view, of its nature directed to nothing less than being as such, the entire range of reality ; and the will satisfied with nothing less than infinite good. Such good is permanent if anything is, and being

[1] Inge, *The Philosophy of Plotinus*, Vol. II, p. 25.

infinite, unattainable under the finite conditions of this life. Again, it is central in the philosophy of S. Thomas to judge of the nature of a thing from the end to which it tends, or, in S. Thomas' phrase, by its 'natural desires.' Such desires cannot be fruitless, incapable of satisfaction, for if they were the nature which, as a nature, tends towards their fulfilment, would clearly be tending to nothing and so not towards their fulfilment. It would therefore be and not be that nature. Desire, moreover, follows and is proportionate to knowledge, so that since man by his intellect grasps universal and perpetual being, and so, of his nature, desires it,[1] such perpetual existence must be attainable by him.[2] Such arguments as these, no doubt, need much fuller development than we are able to give them here if they are to strike the mind with their full force ; but even in this skeleton form it can be seen that they are not lightly to be dismissed.[3]

Let us now turn to the argument which is *par excellence* the metaphysical argument for the immortality of the soul.

We must first consider the ways in which anything can be corrupted or destroyed. This may come about owing either to some extrinsic or some intrinsic cause of corruption. It comes from intrinsic corruption when there are in the thing warring elements which seek to oust one another from it, or, at least, dissociable elements. Examples of the first are to be found in gasses which remain stable only under the influence of some external force, or pressure ; of the second in all chemical compounds. Another type of intrinsic corruption is that which occurs as a consequence of something on which there is dependence being corrupted ; as the sight fails when the eye is injured, or a picture is destroyed if the canvas rots. Now neither of these modes of corruption can affect the human soul ; for since it has no parts, whether quantitative, since it is not extended ; or essential, since it is form only and not a compound of form and matter, it is

---

[1] On this question of natural desire Fr. O'Mahoney's book, *The Desire of God in the Philosophy of St. Thomas Aquinas*, may be consulted with much profit.

[2] Cf. *Contra Gentiles*, L. II, Chaps. 55, 59 ; *Summa Theologica*, I.76,6.

[3] For a lucid and full exposition of the first argument cf. Taylor, *The Faith of a Moralist*, Series I, Lect. 7, pp. 281 ff.

obvious it cannot have any contrary or dissociable elements within it, and so is immune from the first kind of corruption. It is, in fact, impossible to suppose that the unifying principle should not be itself a unity. This indeed applies to all forms, which are all of them acts, and not a compound of act and potency, and yet we have seen that some of these are divisible with the division of the matter which they inform. This second kind of corruption and division cannot, however, affect the human soul, for as we saw again, it does not depend on the matter which it informs for its existence, but being in itself immaterial or spiritual, exists in its own right and independently. A material thing is corrupted when its form is separated from matter, but an immaterial thing cannot suffer this fate, since it is form, and form cannot be separated from itself. Thus, we see that neither in itself does the soul carry any seeds of death or corruption, being simple life ; nor yet can it be destroyed by the corruption of the body on which it never depends for existence.

But even if it is thus in itself intrinsically incorruptible, may it not be annihilated by the cause which gave it being ? The introduction of this question shows that no finally satisfactory solution of our problem can be arrived at without acknowledging the existence of such a cause of being, viz. God. Not only does it seem that immortality without God would not be desirable ; but also, that unless the soul is dependent for its being on a source which is altogether perfect and infinite, immortality could not be secure. The finite cause and power which brought it—if by an impossible supposition it could create—into being might fail to preserve it, whether through malice, caprice, or lack of power. To attribute to God, on the other hand, the purpose of annihilating the souls He had created, is an impossible supposition. Though it is true He has the power to annihilate, as to create; nevertheless, the exercise of this power is excluded by His essential perfection and wisdom ; since it is incredible that all-wise and all-knowing Being should deprive His creatures of the nature which He has given them. This is precisely what He would do if He were to annihilate intellectual natures, since they are essentially not subject to corruption, but have, in virtue of their nature, perpetual being. Such a suggestion must be particularly repugnant to those who are so attached to the inviolability of natural law that they are unwilling to allow that God can even suspend its operation. To deprive a soul of immortality after endowing it with an immortal nature would be an inconsistency even more flagrant than would be the endowment of material things with a nature which necessitates their coming together, in accordance with the law of gravitation, and then preventing them ever coming together in this way.

In the *Summa Contra Gentiles*,[1] S. Thomas gathered together a great array of arguments which all tend to prove the truth of personal immortality for man, and we may conclude this short indication of some of them, by reminding ourselves that what properly speaking perfects a man is itself incorruptible, viz. the knowledge of eternal truths, and the free but undeviating practice of virtue, which certainly is not material. The incorruptible cannot perfect the corruptible, or the immaterial what is essentially material ; but a perfection must be proportionate to that which it perfects, an act to the capacity for that act. We cannot, then, suppose that man belongs essentially to the temporal order with its change and corruption, but his nature finds its true perfection in a life eternal and incorruptible, where intellect and will find their full development, ever satisfied and never satiated.

[1] Lib. II, cc. 55, 79.

# CHAPTER XVII

## THE ORIGIN OF LIFE

The Origin of Life on Earth—Opinions—Spontaneous Generation—
Two Forms of the Theory—Their Possibility.

HAVING now investigated the three great divisions of animate
nature, we are in a position to survey it as a whole. We have
seen, in connection with each of them, that these three
species of living things are composed of individuals who, in
every case, act with an intrinsic tendency towards the
preservation and well-being of the living individual as a
whole, such actions originating with the life-principle
within them. Further, it has been established that through
the whole range the individual living thing is an essential
unity, and that, as between the three grades of living things,
there exist specific or essential differences. Thus we see
that the Aristotelean definition of the soul or life-principle
which we mentioned at the start—the soul is the first act of
a physical organic body—is fully justified.

If these results as to the world of animate nature be taken
as established, we still have left two questions which relate
to it considered as a whole : first, how did life originate ?
and, secondly, what are the relations between its different
manifestations ?

The first question, which is to be discussed in this chapter,
is concerned primarily with the origin of life on this planet ;
and though, from the point of view of biological science, life,
if it is allowed to be of a different nature to non-living matter,
may have to be accepted as an ultimate datum, as to the
origin of which no significant question can be asked ;[1] yet,

[1] As is asserted by Dr. Johnstone, *The Philosophy of Biology*, pp. 340 f.
He says : ' The problem of the origin of life, as it is usually stated, is only
a pseudo-problem ; we may as usefully discuss the origin of the second
law of thermodynamics ! If life is not only energy but also the direction

from the point of view of philosophy, this is not so, since it cannot be supposed that life, as we observe it, is ultimate in the order of being. In the same way, a physicist does not enquire how natural laws, such as that of entropy, i.e. the second law of thermodynamics, came into being, since these laws (indicating the natures of things which obey them) are taken as ultimate ; but the same is not true of the philosopher who must try to discover why nature is governed by such laws, in other words, to penetrate behind the laws to an understanding of the natures themselves which obey them ; so that he can properly ask what the origin of these laws is.

If, then, we ask how life originated on this earth, there are four possible answers : (1) that it did not begin, but was eternally present ; (2) that it came to this planet from some other part of the universe where it was eternally present ; (3) that it arose by spontaneous generation from inanimate matter ; (4) that it arose by creation.

As to the first view, this is clearly impossible since we know that the earth is itself not eternal, but had a beginning. Moreover—and this consideration disposes of the second view also—by asserting its eternity we do not answer the question as to its origin, for even if it were supposed to be eternal it would, since it is not self-sufficing and necessary, but dependent and contingent, still require a source from which it eternally proceeded, so that we are no nearer to a solution of the problem of its origin.

The second view encounters, moreover, another insuperable objection, inasmuch as the assertion that it came to earth from some other part of the universe does not solve the question of its origin, but only puts it one stage further back. It is interesting, however, to notice that this view has been held by many eminent men. It seems to have first been put forward by de Montlivault in 1821, and was developed thirty years later by Count Keyserling, who held that life, like the world, is eternal, but from time to time

and co-ordination of energies ; if it is a tendency of the same order, but of a different direction, from the tendency of inorganic processes, all that biology can usefully do is to inquire into the manner in which this tendency is manifested in material things and energy-transformations. But the tendency itself is something elemental.'

changes its habitat. He thought that it passes through the universe in the form of living germs. Some thought these germs were brought to us in cosmic dust or comets, while others, as Count de Salles-Guyon, Lord Kelvin, and Helmholtz supposed them to have come in meteorites. Since, however, the germs must come not only from the planets, but from the stars, they must be supposed to be incombustible, and even if it were conceded that this marvellous property might be possessed by some very minute germs, yet the minutest germs are destroyed by ultra-violet rays. The theory is therefore unacceptable from every point of view.[1]

Turning to the third hypothesis, we find that it had a longer and more honourable history. It was, in fact, the universal belief of men of science till the first part of the seventeenth century. Aristotle held that the more imperfect animals, such as parasites, were spontaneously generated by warmth, without the intervention of any living thing. This view was also held by S. Thomas.[2]

The first doubts seem to have been raised by Francesco Redi (1626–1697), who showed by experiment that no living organisms appeared in the flesh of a dead animal if it were carefully protected from the entry of living germs from without ; but he was not so successful in the case of parasites, whose origin was not established till the nineteenth century. The chief of the experimenters of this time was Louis Pasteur, who showed that all putrefaction and many kinds of fermentation are due to the presence of microscopic living organisms ; while Tyndall showed that absolute sterilisation of infusions could be attained by intermittent applications of heat. These discoveries led to the general acceptance of the law of biogenesis, which does not, as is sometimes supposed, assert that every living thing does, or still less must, originate from another living thing, but only that there is no known instance of living organisms arising from non-living matter. Whether under conditions widely different from

---

[1] Cf. Perrier, *The Earth before History*, pp. 61 ff.
[2] Cf. Aristotle, *Met.*, 1032ª 27 ; S. Thomas. *Comm. in Met.* (ed. Cathala), 1400, 1401 ; *Summa Theol.*, I, 105, 1, ad 1 ; I, 71, 1, ad 1 ; I, 72, ad 5.

those which come under our observation, this could happen,
must necessarily be, from the scientific point of view, a
matter of simple speculation, since the only scientific
method of deciding the question, that of observation and
experiment, is clearly not available. Consequently, any
dogmatic assertion that under such conditions life did, in
fact, arise from non-living matter must be considered to be
unscientific.[1] Many attempts, however, have been made to
find some positive justification of it ; of which the most
famous, or perhaps notorious, is that of Haeckel, who produced some of the ocean slime as the primordial living substance, to which Huxley, who at first accepted it as genuine
protoplasm, gave the name of Bathybius Haeckeli : i.e.
Haeckel's Low-life. Huxley later identified it as being only
a mineral precipitate of gelatinous appearance, which arises
when distilled alcohol is poured into sea-water containing
organic matter in suspension, and so essentially a non-living
substance.[2] Haeckel, however, persisted in his defence of it ;
and an attempt has been recently made to rehabilitate it.
Nevertheless, it is true to say that the production of the
living from the non-living, or abiogenesis, as at present
occurring, finds no definite positive support in modern
scientific investigation. This, of course, leaves the question
of the possibility of such an occurrence an open one ; and a
decision with regard to it can only come, if at all, from the
side of philosophy. Now, with regard to this possibility,
two hypotheses present themselves for discussion : first,
that life was originally produced by a fortuitous combination
and disposition of inorganic matter, or that such matter was
combined and arranged and life produced under the influence
of some cause of another order ; of what S. Thomas calls an
analogous cause, which is in itself superior to the effects
which it produces.

It may be stated at once that most modern scientists
incline to accept the first hypothesis as a result of their

[1] As, for example, that of Perrier : ' What we are unable to achieve
was done spontaneously in the beginning.' *The Earth before History*, p. 66
[2] Cf. Perrier, op. cit., p. 59.
[3] Cf. *Philosophy* (1932), art. by Prof. J. Johnstone, p. 293. Cf. also
Jeans, *Mysterious Universe*, pp. 6 ff.

general physical conceptions. Though they admit that the coming of life by such a chance combination of atoms is a highly improbable event, in the sense that the chances against its occurrence are enormous, yet they do not regard it as inconceivable.[1] In this belief they take for granted that life is not essentially different from inorganic matter ; as is shown by such assertions as that it is ' just as conceivable as would be the " spontaneous " segregation of, say, a litre volume of gas into two regions, one of which had a much greater density than the other one.'[2] Evidently, no new nature would appear in such a segregation, and if ' spontaneous generation ' is just as conceivable as this, it will be so only if no new nature appears in such generation, or if animate and inanimate matter are of the same kind. As, then, we are unable to accept this presupposition, neither can we accept the conclusion that spontaneous generation, due to a chance combination of atoms, is conceivable, though improbable. According to the view which we have been led by our consideration of living things to accept, these possess, in addition to the properties of inanimate ones, various perfections which the latter do not possess at all, such as the acts of nutrition, growth, and reproduction. It is here not a question of mere difference of properties, but of a positive addition to them, so that the living thing possesses the properties of non-living ones, and in addition, certain active characteristics which are entirely its own. If, then, life arose ' spontaneously ' in this sense, i.e. by chance and without any additional principle, from purely inorganic matter, such positive activities, such increases of perfection, would have to be held to have arisen from nothing ; since matter itself does not possess them, and no cause other than brute matter is, in this hypothesis, postulated.

An even more fundamental reason for disallowing the possibility of life originating solely from a random combination of inert bodies is to be found in a consideration of the finality of living things. These are essentially one, having one form only, which form tends to a single end, the good of the individual as a whole, and of the species. That the

---

[1] Cf. Johnstone, art. cit.      [2] *Ibid.*, loc. cit.

multiple tendencies, then, of a number of inanimate bodies should produce this single unified tendency of the living thing, in the absence of any directive power to unify and co-ordinate them, is strictly speaking inconceivable. The unconditioned union of things which are essentially different is impossible, for being by nature many they cannot also be by nature one, unless they are brought into this unity by some unifying and directive principle. Such a principle would not be present in the hypothesis we are considering, since it allows of no principle but the unco-ordinated and divergent forces of inanimate elements. This doctrine as to the impossibility of the unconditional union of the many is common to Platonism and Aristoteleanism, and, indeed, to the whole tradition of the ' *philosophia perennis.*' We shall have occasion to consider it again at a later stage.

It will be seen that the reasons we have just advanced do not militate against the possibility of life having arisen from inanimate matter under the direction and influence of some power higher than that of matter itself, by whose means life is brought from a state of potentiality to one of actuality. It was in this way that S. Thomas conceived of some forms of life being spontaneously generated from inanimate matter under the directive and unifying action of God ; and the same conception may perhaps be found in the theory of Emergent Evolution, which has had a certain vogue in recent times. Its exponents, however, do not seem to speak with any great consistency.[1]

As to the probability of such emergence of life being a fact, the evidence at present appears to be inadequate for the formation of any definite conclusion, but it does not seem that a Thomist is obliged to bang, bolt, and bar the door on its possibility.[2] If it is not thought probable we shall, of course, adopt the only remaining hypothesis to explain the origin of life, viz. that it was in the first instance created by God. Even if this be so, we may still be in doubt

[1] Cf. McDougall, *Modern Materialism and Emergent Evolution*, pp. 152 ff. ; Lloyd Morgan, *Emergent Evolution* ; Lloyd Morgan, Essay on Biology, pp. 111 ff. in *Evolution in the Light of Modern Knowledge.*

[2] With regard to its probability cf. McDougall, op. cit., Ch. V. Its possibility is discussed in *Revue Thomiste*, 1923, pp. 298 ff., 305 ff.

as to the origin of the different species of living things. Are we to attribute their existence to a series of creative acts, or is there reason to think that they have been developed, and progressively differentiated from one another, by a purely natural process ; so that all of them are to be thought of as being descended from some one primitive form of life ?

This is the question of evolution or transformism, the discussion of which in the next chapter will conclude our survey of the world of animate nature.

# CHAPTER XVIII

## TRANSFORMISM

Preliminary Remarks—Sketch of Evolutionary Theories—Lamarck—
Darwin—The Materialist Theory—Reasons which Exclude It—
Consideration of Evolutionary Theories in General.

PROBABLY no scientific theory has aroused such widespread
and heated controversy as that which is popularly known as
the theory of evolution.  This was due, not to its scientific
content, but to its philosophical and religious bearings, since
it seemed to imply an entire absence of purpose in nature ;
and, what appeared more objectionable both to the man in
the street and the upholders of orthodox religion, that man
was merely an intelligent kind of ape.  This suggestion was
not merely unflattering, but seemed to be clearly contrary
to the account of man's origin given in the Bible, on both of
which accounts it was at first vigorously repudiated.

The controversy has now died down to a great extent,
largely because prolonged investigation has shown what are
the true implications of the theory, as well as bringing to
light the serious, and perhaps insurmountable, difficulties
which attach to the suggested explanations of the method
by which evolution has proceeded.  Theological opposition,
in England at any rate, has practically ceased, owing to the
abandonment by the Protestant churches of belief in the
Biblical account of creation, and their acceptance in its
place of the infallible decisions of the biologists.  It is curious
to notice that both sides appeal to authority for the settle-
ment of this question.  In its early stages the theologians
attempted to silence the Darwinians by the authority of
Genesis, while at present the evolutionists try to silence the
doubter by the authority of scientific opinion.  This fact
suggests the reflection that the truth or falsity of this theory
may not indeed be very plain to reason, if our guides urge us

to accept or reject it on faith. These attempts at bullying failed, as they were bound to do, since those who were bludgeoned with the Bible were at least doubtful as to its infallibility, and those who are now threatened with ' scientific opinion ' and the views of ' every educated man ' are equally doubtful as to the infallibility of science. The method of authoritative imposition of beliefs, though invaluable if the competence of the authority be admitted, is, consequently, not one of universal application, being limited to the circle of ' true believers.' If we are, then, as philosophic method demands, to consider this question solely by the aid of natural reason, no fulminations of scientists accusing us of heresy, or of ignorance and stupidity, if we find ourselves unconvinced of the truth of their dogmas, can carry any weight with us ; unless on other grounds we have already admitted the infallibility of scientific opinion. In its proper sphere, and when it can be had, authoritative decision is an invaluable method of settling troublesome questions ; but this sphere is that of faith, not of reason. As S. Thomas says : ' *Locus ab auctoritate quæ fundatur super ratione humana est infirmissimus.*'[1]

We can therefore approach this question with an open mind, and see what reason can tell us as to the possibility of transformism. If it is found to be possible, the question of its probability is one which must be decided in the light of available evidence, a discussion of which belongs rather to natural science than to philosophy.

There is probably no one who has not at least a vague idea of what the word evolution, as applied to living things, means ; but in ordinary language it is confined to one particular transformation of a species, that which is naturally of most interest to ourselves, the transformation of some ape-like creature into man. This popular use of the word is, however, far from expressing the scientific idea ; and though fortunately we are not obliged to consider all its scientific applications, we must get some more precise notion of it than this narrow and inexact one.

The word ' evolution ' is itself not a strikingly happy one,

[1] *Summa Theol.*, I, Q. 1, a. 8, ad 2.

as applied to the transformation of living species, since many things unroll without being transformed, as carpets and snakes, while the transformation which is asserted in most modern evolutionary theories can hardly be called an unrolling. It has, however, been commonly adopted in England, and applied not only to the realm of living things, as in Biology and Psychology, but also to the development of the material universe in Cosmogony, and to its minutest constituents in Physics and Chemistry. Whether it is, in fact, applicable to any of these spheres except Biology, in a sense which is properly speaking analogical to that which it conveys in this science, is very doubtful, and has possibly led to confusion of ideas ; but this is a question which lies outside the boundaries of our present discussion.

The term Transformism, which is in general use on the continent of Europe, is much more exact, and indicates the transformation of living things into new species.

The idea of such transformism, or gradual development of living things from pre-existing forms, is not a modern one, but at least as old as the fifth century B.C. It occurred to the earliest Greek thinkers, and even the Darwinian method of evolution by survival of the fittest was suggested by Empedocles (495–435 B.C.). Aristotle, who was, of course, eminent among the Greeks for his biological observations, made the idea more precise ; but his theory of transformism consistently with his general fundamental principles was, in contrast with those of his predecessors, a decidedly teleological one. Rejecting the idea of the survival of the fittest, he maintains that nature successively adapts organs to their function, and this in the order of their necessity, those essential to life coming first, to be followed by those which are of service in the full functioning of the nature of particular species. Thus those animals which have eyes have them in order that they may exercise the powers of their nature. What determines the evolution of the animal is their nature, which strives to produce a certain result, so that ' the process of evolution is for the sake of the nature evolved, and not this nature for the sake of the process.'[1]

[1] Cf. Aristotle, *De partibus animalium*, 640ª18.

S. Augustine is generally thought to have been favourable
to a view of evolution in some form, and in spite of doubts
raised as to the precise meaning of his theory, it can hardly be
denied that he entertained the idea of new species arising
in virtue of the powers bestowed on matter at the creation.

It is not easy to determine S. Thomas' precise view on
this question, but he did not allow that material elements
have in themselves, or essentially, the power of producing
all animals, though they could do so under the influence of
an analogous cause.[1]

Though Cajetan supported a form of evolutionary theory,
in later times, and under the influence of Suarez, it was
generally abandoned among theologians, and the doctrine
of special creation was left without a rival. According to
this view, all existing species had been created at the beginning in their present forms ; so that as Linnæus says : ' *tot
nunc species sunt, quot ab initio creavit infinitum ens.*' In
order to square this view with the apparent appearance of
new species, some had recourse to a series of special creations,
thus dropping the ' *ab initio* ' ; or else maintained that the
so-called new species were not properly species at all, but
merely racial variations of already existing species. It was not
until the nineteenth century that evolutionary theories again
became prominent, and eventually were generally accepted.

The modern history of the problem really begins with
Lamarck, the most important forerunner of Darwin, whose
theory of evolution was first outlined in 1802, and fully
developed in his *Philosophie Zoologique* in 1809.

Four laws constitute the skeleton, so to speak, of his
system. These are : (1) the law of growth, (2) of functional
reaction, (3) of use and disuse, and (4) of use—inheritance.

The first asserts that the size of the living being is increased
by the activities of this body itself up to some limit imposed
by its own nature ; the second that new organs arise in
response to some new felt need ; the third that organs
develop proportionately to their use, and atrophy in so far as

---

[1] Cf. *Summa Theol.*, I, Q. 71 ; I.69,2 ; I.73, a.1, ad 3. The opinions of
S. Augustine and S. Thomas have recently been discussed by Dr. Messenger
in his *Evolution and Theology*, Part I, Chaps. VIII–X, and Ch. XIII.

they are not used ; while the fourth maintains that characteristics acquired by an individual organism in the course of
its life are transmitted to this individual's descendents.

The last two laws are particularly interesting, since the
third asserts that bodily structure depends on function, and
the last the heritability of acquired characters, a doctrine
which is still the subject of acute controversy. All four laws,
it should be noticed, embody a teleological conception of
evolution, and so, to this extent, are in line with the Aristotelean ideas on this subject.

In the period immediately preceding the publication of
Darwin's work the transmutation theory was shelved or
rejected, so that the appearance of *The Origin of Species* in
1859, followed by that of *The Descent of Man* in 1871, had a
startling and sensational effect. The reason of this was not
merely, and not chiefly, that transformism had fallen into
disrepute, so that Darwin's ideas had a certain freshness and
novelty, but essentially to the fact that he was the first to
give it such a basis as seemed to establish it firmly as a fact.
It was not his theory, but his facts which revolutionised
scientific opinion. The vast accumulation of facts which his
laborious researches, in the five years in which he was
travelling in the *Beagle*, and the twenty succeeding years,
had enabled him to collect, made a profound impression on
biologists ; and the sensation caused among the general
public by his theory, and especially by his account of man's
origin, is largely attributable to its antiteleological, and
apparently anti-religious, tendency, due to his attributing
transformism to Natural Selection, which works blindly and
automatically. Prof. Hobson asserts that ' after Darwin's
work it (i.e. the fact of organic evolution) was no longer a
speculative hypothesis, but a well-attested deduction from
observation. As regards the position of Natural Selection
as the chief factor in Evolution, it is not possible to speak so
positively : on this matter the opinions of Biologists have
been, and still are, much divided.'[1] This statement probably
represents the state of scientific opinion at the present day
fairly accurately.

[1] E. W. Hobson, *The Domain of Natural Science*, pp. 437 ff.

From what has been said the reader will have gathered that there are three main elements in Darwin's theory. The first the establishment by observation of the fact that new species have originated from older ones, the new being descended from some of the individuals of the older species. The second element is the attributing of this emergence of new species primarily and principally to Natural Selection, which works by causing those individuals, which happen to vary slightly from the norm of their species, to be more, or less, capable of surviving than normal members of the species would be, according as the possession of such variations puts them in an advantageous or disadvantageous position in the struggle for life. So, for example, we might suppose that those giraffes which have the longest necks would more easily be able to reach the higher branches of trees, and so could procure food more easily than the shorter-necked ones ; and thus, if food was scarce, only the long-necked ones would survive, the others dying of starvation. The same sort of process would occur in animals which possessed superior weapons of defence or offence. Thus nature herself would gradually eliminate the less fit, but blindly, and without any purpose. This brings us to the last element of the theory, which is perhaps the most important from the philosophical point of view, viz. its anti-teleological tendency ; since it accounts for what appears to be a purposive adaptation of the various species to their environment by a process which eliminates purpose altogether. Thus the peculiarities which appear to have been designed in order that the individual may survive owe their origin to chance, and their continuance to the less easy elimination of the individuals possessing them ; and not to any striving on the part of the individual itself. Since they have come about by chance they cannot be purposive, either in their inception or their continuance. As Huxley says : ' Darwin gave the death blow to teleology by showing that apparently purposive structures could arise by means of a non-purposive mechanism.'

In this way it was thought that Biology was brought into line with Physics, from which purpose had already been excluded. As Tennyson says in *In Memoriam*, alluding to the mechanistic view of Physics :

'The stars' she whispers 'blindly run';

and now it appeared that living things, animals and man also 'blindly run,' driven on by the whips of uncontrollable forces to an inexorable doom.

It has been necessary to give this account of the theories of Lamarck and Darwin in order to bring into prominence those characteristics of modern evolutionary theories which are of importance from a philosophical point of view. But it would not be to our purpose, even if it were possible, to trace the history of these theories to the present day ; since the modern theories, though showing many marked variations from those of Darwin and Lamarck, from which they are descended, have yet not changed their species, but remain true to the general principles which governed the parent theories. Thus interest has chiefly centred since Darwin's time on the discussion as to the relative importance of Natural Selection and the inheritance of acquired characters as the causes of mutations, the first being stressed by the neo-Darwinians, and the second by the neo-Lamarckians ; and, speaking generally, we have two theories or groups of theories, one of the Lamarckian and teleological, the other of the Darwinian or antiteleological type. The most important modification introduced into evolutionary theories of recent years is the assigning of the transformation of species by some scientists rather to sudden large mutations than to the slow accumulation of small ones, as was postulated by Darwin's original theory.[1] This modification was due to the investigations and discoveries of Mendel, de Vries, Bateson, and others, which threw doubt on the truth of the hypothesis that transformation of species was produced by an accumulation of small variations. This doubt was increased by the researches of Johannsen, Agar, and Jennings, which seemed to show that the small variations postulated by the Darwinian theory were not inheritable ; and thus

[1] Cf. E. W. Hobson, *The Domain of Natural Science*, pp. 449 ff. ; Dampier-Whetham, *A History of Science*, pp. 247 ff.

there arose a tendency altogether to discredit Natural Selection, as the instrument of evolution.[1]

Thus, while some biologists continue to maintain the sufficiency of Natural Selection as an explanation of transformism, many others incline to regard use and disuse and purposive striving as its chief causes, while others again are not prepared to commit themselves to any opinion as to its cause. So Bateson said : ' In dim outline evolution is evident enough. From the facts it is a conclusion which inevitably follows. But that particular and essential bit of the theory of evolution which is concerned with the origin and nature of *species* remains utterly mysterious.'[2]

From all this one thing is very plain, viz. that there is not that unanimity with regard to the theory of evolution which is often asserted, so that a controversialist who demands its acceptance because it is the opinion of all educated men is not only irrational, as we have seen, but also disingenuous. In fact, it is only the materialists or ' rationalists ' who adopt this unreasonable method of forcing their opinions down the throats of others ; and it will be convenient to examine this extreme form of evolutionism before passing on to see what light, if any, Thomistic principles can throw on the theory of transformism in general.

The professed Materialists, then, recognising no other reality than matter, assert that all species of living things have arisen from inorganic matter ; the first forms of life coming about by spontaneous generation, and later ones being differentiated from the primitive forms by a process of blind determined law ; without any internal teleological tendency, or any intervention of the first cause, which by hypothesis does not exist. The chief advantage of this theory, from the philosophical point of view, is that it gives a complete unity to all our knowledge of the world, everything being wholly and essentially material, though if thought and knowledge be, as the theory demands, but secretions of the brain, the advantage is more apparent than

---

[1] Cf. *Evolution in the Light of Modern Knowledge*, pp. 224 ff.
[2] *William Bateson, Naturalist*. Memoir by Beatrice Bateson, p. 395, quoted by Dampier-Whetham, op. cit., p. 353.

real. For this reason and because the theory, when thus plainly stated, seems self-condemned, we find that its adherents are not very anxious to set it down in black and white, but are inclined to hedge and to amuse themselves by ridiculing the 'Fundamentalists'; instead of establishing their own position. We should observe, however, that the slightest departure from this materialist scheme breaks the unity of the conception, and readmits those realities which the materialists are bent on excluding, viz. immaterial or spiritual ones.

The theory was put forward in an uncompromising form by Haeckel in the last century; and is adhered to, at the present day, by Biological Materialists, such as Sir Arthur Keith, and J. B. S. Haldane; while Bertrand Russell has, as it seems very reluctantly, made an act of infra-natural faith in the same view.

Since, from their own point of view, the opinions of such people are merely physical states induced by their own bodily conditions, no doubt they would be content to be dealt with rather by medical than philosophic methods. Nevertheless, as we do not concede their premises, it is worth while to see, for our own satisfaction, whether such an attitude as theirs is compatible with reason.

It is, of course, obvious that since this theory denies that there is any purpose, or teleology, in the evolutionary process, it denies also the principle of finality, according to which every agent acts for an end. Can this denial be rationally sustained? We can see the answer to this question by considering the consequences which follow from the denial of finality.

First of all, it is clear that any agent, when in act, is acting in a fixed way: it is performing this act and no other. Its act, therefore, has a definite direction and achieves a definite result. All this is allowed by the materialists who maintain, in fact, that biologically useful characters achieve by their use the survival of their owner. If they do this, they do it because they are a certain definite kind of character, e.g. a longer as compared with a shorter neck in a giraffe. Now, it is asserted that though the particular actions by whose

means the process is carried on have a definite direction and
tendency, yet the process as a whole has no purpose. It is
clear, however, that the evolutionary process is not something distinct from the actions of the evolving things, but is
merely the resultant of all these actions, and it is impossible
to see how if all its components have one definite tendency
the process itself should have none. But, it will be said, the
Materialists do not maintain that it has no tendency, and, in
fact, affirm that it causes the fittest to survive ; what they
do maintain is that it has no purpose, no conscious tendency,
no plan. Let us then consider what it is that makes an
inanimate thing act in a determined way and consequently,
without knowing it, tend to a definite end. Surely it is
because it has a definite and determined nature : just as the
eye sees and does not hear or smell, because of its particular
structure. It is easy to see, then, that any being which has a
determinate nature must act in a determinate way, such
direction of its action being due to the fact that its nature is
of a particular kind. Now, this theory of evolution has as its
object the explanation of the way in which all things come
by their determinate nature, and it cannot, therefore, assume
a determinate nature as a starting point. It must, therefore,
start with an indeterminate being, a thing with no definite
nature at all ; a thing, then, which is either simply nothing,
or at best a pure capacity or potentiality for everything. If
it is nothing we are left with the assertion that from nothing
everything comes ; which is simply unintelligible, and
obviously not an explanation. If it is a pure capacity for
everything, having no determination of its own, from what
does it derive the determination which starts the evolutionary
process ? Evidently not from itself ; and consequently from
something else, which has a determinate nature and action
of its own, i.e. from something which determines itself, and
so acts with purpose and intention. Such a being as this is,
however, absolutely excluded by the materialist hypothesis,
inasmuch as it denies finality of purpose altogether, and
moreover is, as we saw, obliged to start with the altogether
indeterminate. By denying finality, then, it is driven to
hold that the first being is not even a pure capacity for all

things, but strictly nothing ; and is essentially irrational and unintelligible.

The Scholastics, by means of their highly polished technical language, can express this argument very clearly and concisely. So they say that every agent must act for an end, at least in the order of execution, for otherwise it would not do one thing rather than another. This intention of the agent to gain a certain end, may be conscious, as in man, or unconscious, as in inanimate bodies. But even if unconscious it is still purposive since otherwise its tendency in a definite direction would be without reason of being. For this determinate direction must be in the agent, and if it is not present in it by conscious purpose, so that the agent actively directs itself to the end, it must be passively directed to it. Such passive direction, however, presupposes active direction which imparts it, and in the last resort, active self-determining, or conscious, direction. So there is conscious or unconscious purpose in the action of every agent, and the maxim : ' *potentia dicitur* ad *actum* ' is universally true. The whole *raison d'être* of any capacity, and so of any agent, is in its power of producing the effect, and so in its tendency towards that effect, that act or perfection.[1]

To deny such finality, therefore, as the materialist evolutionists do, is to deny the reason of being of the determinate direction of the agents, or to assert that something is which has no reason to be. This is obviously not to explain it ; and is, moreover, an assertion that something can and does come from nothing.[2]

The same conclusion is arrived at if we look at this process from the point of view of efficient causality, for few would be found to deny that life is a positive addition to matter without life, sentience to matter which is living but not sentient, intelligence or reason to being which is devoid of these. Now, according to this theory, matter destitute of life, of its own power produces it, living matter destitute of sentience, brings it forth, and sentient life having no intel-

[1] Cf. S. Thomas, *Summa Theol.*, IaIIae, Q. 1, a. 2.
[2] Cf. Garigou-Lagrange, *De Revelatione*, Vol. I, pp. 255 ff., 259 f., and the same author's *La Réalisme du Principe de Finalité*, Ch. II.

lect, evolves this from itself. In each case the greater being produced by the less, something is caused by nothing.

Further, no reason can be assigned in this theory why evolution, the first modification, and the perfection of the evolutionary process should be at all rather than not be ; while at the same time it is asserted that they are. Thus evolution can have no reason of being either in something other than itself, there being no cause apart from it, nor yet in itself, for it is a movement or transit from indetermination to determination, from potency to act, which cannot come about of itself, since indetermination neither is, nor contains in itself, determination. It has, and can have, therefore, no reason of being according to this view.

As Professor A. E. Taylor points out, evolution, if it is to be thinkable at all, must presuppose both environment and the environed interacting on one another : ' When there is change, there is reason for change . . . and the reason for a change can only be found in something not involved in that change. It follows that if there is such a thing as a process of change with a definite and discoverable law which embraces the whole of physical reality, the whole of physical reality must have a non physical environment.'[1]

Now, it is precisely this environment which is denied in the theory we are considering, which is thus strictly speaking unthinkable.

We are forced to the same conclusion when we consider the first modification which inaugurates the evolutionary process. It is ascribed in the theory to chance ; and this phrase might mean either that chance is the cause and reason of its appearance, or that we do not know what factor in nature actually was responsible for it. No doubt, it is the second sense which is intended, since chance cannot be conceived as a thing or reason which could of itself produce a positive effect. But the second sense does not avoid the difficulty, since the unknown element in the situation, whether internal to the being which produces the modification, or external to it, would in its turn have to be accounted

---

[1] A. E. Taylor, *Evolution in the Light of Modern Knowledge*, Ch. XII, pp. 449 ff. Cf. Lossky, art. ' The Limits of Evolution ' in the *Journal of Philosophical Studies*, October 1927.

z

for. Here again, it cannot be accounted for by ' chance,' using chance in the first of the senses given above, and so once more this must be accounted for by a further unknown factor in the physical situation. Now we cannot go on for ever finding the reason of one unknown factor in a preceding one, not because we should get tired of so doing, as has been suggested, but because each unknown factor essentially depends on another, so that all of them must in the last resort depend either on some determinate and knowable character in the physical situation and not on chance, or else depend on something outside the series altogether. For if the material world, which in the end produces the modified being, had no determinate nature at all it would be useless to look upon it as the source of the determinate modification ; and if it had a determinate nature, the fact that it had it could not be accounted for by means of something internal to itself, but must be sought outside it. By the theory, however, we are prohibited from going outside the physical world, since it maintains there is nothing else than that world. Hence, we must accept the origin of the first modification as being unaccountable, inexplicable, and unintelligible ; and as all the subsequent modifications depend on the first, the whole process becomes entirely unintelligible.

Lastly, the theory that evolution is a process of accumulation of modifications, offers no explanation of the fact of such accumulation in *the same direction*, and does not attempt to do so. It is not, however, only unexplained, but in fact inexplicable, on the theory, for what has to be accounted for is a series of modifications which all tend in the same specific and determinate direction. Now it is clear that the first modification cannot account for others in the same specific direction, since these are posterior to, and an addition to, itself ; and at the same time it is denied that there is any other determination present at the start, except this first modification. Consequently, there is nothing at all which can account for the accumulation of modifications of a definite kind, which remains therefore inexplicable and unintelligible.

In a word, to start with something altogether undifferentiated, indeterminate, and homogeneous, is to start with nothing: and from nothing, nothing comes. This is what a theory of materialistic evolution does and must do, since to start with a determinate and differentiated being would be to confess that evolution was unable to explain this being, and this determination, and was therefore bankrupt. Evolution is incapable of explaining the whole universe, as the materialists claim it can, but at best is only capable of explaining the development of parts of it.

In conclusion, then, we must shortly consider its ability to do this.

First, we must notice the distinction which is drawn between natural and systematic species. From a strictly metaphysical point of view, a natural species will be one which differs from other things by an essential difference, or a collection of individuals having the same essential properties, though differing as regards accidental ones. In accordance with this definition we shall say that man forms a natural species, inasmuch as he has a spiritual soul or form, whereby he is essentially differentiated, or made different in kind, from all other animals. We have further seen reason to conclude that the same holds good of the lower animals as distinct from plants. Further than this it seems impossible to go with any certainty from the metaphysical point of view.

If, however, looking at the world in this way, we may not be able to distinguish more than three natural species, yet it seems not unreasonable, regarding the matter in the concrete, to say that a natural species, in a general and wider sense, is a collection of living individuals which preserve the same powers and the same type, by means of generation one from another.

To natural species, taken in either of these senses, is opposed systematic species, which is a collection of individuals belonging to the same natural species, which have certain accidental characteristics in common, which characteristics are not found in the other members of the same natural species.

There is, clearly, no reason, from a philosophical point of

view, for refusing to admit the transformation of such systematic species, since there would be no change of nature, but merely one of accidental attributes. Whether it is to be admitted, or not, depends therefore on the weight of the observed evidence for, or against, its occurrence.

Considering, then, natural species in the strict sense, do our principles allow us to say that they could be transformed? There seems to be nothing in them to render it impossible for we should only have a striking example of substantial change. If we admit its possibility, however, we can only do so if it is allowed that the proper substantial form of the inferior living thing is drawn out of matter, when suitably disposed for the reception of such a form, while that of man, being spiritual, can only come from without. This last proviso evidently breaks the unity of the evolutionary scheme ; and so robs it of its chief æsthetic charm, viz. its unification of the whole material world as proceeding from one germ or source. But it is to be observed that it is already deprived of this attraction if we admit that an absolutely homogeneous and indeterminate entity—a polite name for nothing—cannot be the source of all that is. By this admission a dualism of the material world and its non-physical environment is introduced. Since reason absolutely demands that there should be a break in continuity here, the second break owing to the entrance of the spiritual soul, loses its importance. Neither of them is, however, acceptable to what is called ' the scientific mind ' ; and scientists have generally found the theory, according to which man's body is derived from other forms of life while his soul is not so derived, as objectionable as a downright denial of evolution as a whole.

Lastly, if natural species, in the strict sense of the expression, could be transformed, it follows, *a fortiori*, that natural species, in the wider sense, could be. In saying this, however, we do not affirm that they have been ; for indeed the scientific evidence of the transformation of such natural species, as of reptiles into birds, seems to be by no means conclusive. The question of fact in this regard is, therefore, one which belongs properly to physical science to decide.[1]

A conclusion of this indefinite kind has seemed unsatisfactory to many Scholastic philosophers, and consequently they have attempted to argue that species differ in nature, and that, therefore, there can be no transit from one to another. Both these propositions, however. are open to objection, since there seems to be no test by which we can determine the difference of essence as between, say, two animals ; and, further, the impossibility of transit from one essence to another is not proved. As Guibert says : ' To say that living species have not a common origin because they differ in their essence, would be to argue from the unknown. It would be better to say, if the species have a common origin, perhaps the differences between them are not essential. However difficult the problem of the origin of species may be, it is without doubt more accessible than that of distinction of essences.'[2]

What philosophy can tell us, then, about evolution is first, that purely materialistic evolution of the type put forward by Haeckel is impossible ; and, secondly, that any theory of evolution which sets out to give an account of the way in which the animate world has come to be in its present state, and aims at making such an account satisfactory from the philosophical point of view, i.e. as giving an ultimate explanation of the whole matter, must take account both of teleology and purpose, and of the action of the first cause. On the other hand, an evolutionary theory might be regarded as a purely scientific one, a working scheme which covers the facts known at a particular time ; and from this point of view, if it did not find teleology and the action of the first cause useful for such a scheme, it might, and indeed ought, to omit them. In doing so, however, it could not exclude them from reality, but only from the picture it makes of the world for its own practical purposes. Few Darwinians have,

[1] The evidence for and against the transformation of natural species is summarised by Monaco, *Prælectiones Metaphysicæ Specialis*, Pars II, *De Viventibus seu Psychologia*, pp. 215–239.

[2] J. Guibert, *Les Origines*, translated by G. S. Whitmarsh as *In the Beginning*, p. 152.

in fact, been content with this modest programme, but finding, or at least considering that they had found, that these concepts were unnecessary in the construction of a simple all-inclusive and homogeneous scheme of the action and development of living organisms, they have jumped to the conclusion that they had no place in life as lived, instead of concluding that they had no place in life as conceived in a particular scientific picture. The world of life, as lived, is fuller and more solid than the picture which biological science is able to paint of it ; for the reason that biology, of its very nature, can take account only of its proximate causes, and not of its ultimate nature and ground. When these are also considered we see that it must be set against a background of life underived and self-sufficing, a background which is unchanging and eternal.

## Conclusion.

This reflection leads us on to consider what ultimate truths reason can extract from the material provided by observation of the physical world, a subject which is discussed in Metaphysics ; the last great branch or genus of the philosophical sciences ; and it is to this science of metaphysics that we are now to direct our attention.

Before doing so, it may be convenient to glance down the ladder of being which we have been ascending, and notice its principal steps ; which are all concerned, in different ways, with the problem of multiplicity and unity, of the many and the one, of potency and act.

Thus, we saw that the endeavours made both by mechanism and dynamism to reduce the material world to a simple unity were unsuccessful ; and that we must recognise in it a double multiplicity, that of nature, and that of the individual. We saw that the material world is composed of a large number of bodies which differ essentially ; the element which thus specifically differentiates them from others being the same as that which causes them to be essential unities in themselves, viz. their form or act. Many of them, however, are not simple unities, but combine, with unity of

nature, great heterogeneity of accident or quality ; and thus
have a certain organisation ; and may be called organic.
The individual, on the other hand, considered merely as an
individual, is a simple unity, but a negative one, inasmuch as
its unity consists in its distinction from all other individuals ;
which distinction is due to the material element in it. Here,
then, matter is the source of unity, though a unity of a
negative kind.

With reference to the next step in the ladder, that of
quantitative being, we found that the abstract continuum is
composed of parts which are not actual in it, but potential
only, though the physical continuum is actually multiple.
These considerations found an application in the two special
forms of the continuum which we call space and time.
Passing to the next step we found again a multiplicity in
unity. The more complicated forms of inanimate things
having already exhibited a certain material organisation, as
soon as we enter the world of living things we observe a
formal organisation whereby living things move themselves,
one part moving another. These things, then, are, in a
fuller sense, organisms. This organisation does not, however, interfere with their natural or essential unity. At the
same time, there is not unity of nature, of form or act, all
through the animate world ; but we saw reason to distinguish at least three natures among living things, those of
plants, of animals, and of man. As we rise thus in the scale
of being, we find unity becoming more prominent, and
multiplicity of nature less so. There is more of act and less
of potency, and, moreover, the forms of the two higher
grades of life, the animal and human, possess in their unity
the perfections of the lower ; man thus, by means of his
spiritual soul, being a sort of epitome of the whole material
creation. A further unification is introduced into the world
of living things by means of knowledge, the knower and the
known being joined in the closest of all unions, so that the
soul is ' in a certain way ' all things. The soul of man,
moreover, being spiritual, introduces us into a world which
is immaterial ; and as, in a sense, the more complex material
substances lead us up to the organisms found in the world of

life, so man, being formally spiritual, leads us up to that of immaterial being.  He is thus a denizen of two worlds, the material and the immaterial ;  the second of which is considered in the science which deals with being as such, viz. Metaphysics, the explanation of which is to form the subject of our second volume.

END OF  VOLUME  I